Children Reading Pictures

This book describes the fascinating results of a two-year study of children's responses to contemporary picturebooks. Children of primary school age, from a range of backgrounds, read and discussed books by the award-winning artists Anthony Browne and Satoshi Kitamura. They then made their own drawings in response to the books.

The authors found that children are sophisticated readers of visual texts, and are able to make sense of complex images on literal, visual and metaphorical levels. They are able to understand different viewpoints, analyse moods, messages and emotions, and articulate personal responses to picturebooks – even when they struggle with the written word.

With colour illustrations, and interviews with the two authors whose books were included in the study, this book demonstrates how important visual literacy is to children's understanding and development. Primary and early years teachers, literacy co-ordinators and all those interested in children's literature will find this a captivating read.

Evelyn Arizpe is a freelance researcher attached to the Faculty of Education, University of Cambridge. **Morag Styles** is a Senior Lecturer at the University of Cambridge and Reader in Children's Literature at Homerton College, Cambridge.

Children Reading Pictures

Interpreting visual texts

Evelyn Arizpe
and Morag Styles

With contributions from
Helen Bromley, Kathy Coulthard
and Kate Rabey

RoutledgeFalmer
Taylor & Francis Group

LONDON AND NEW YORK

This book is dedicated to our children – Flora and Isabel Leask and Ross Styles

First published 2003
by RoutledgeFalmer
2 Park Square, Milton Park, Abingdon, Oxon OX14 4RN

Simultaneously published in the USA and Canada
by RoutledgeFalmer
270 Madison Avenue, New York, NY 10016

RoutledgeFalmer is an imprint of the Taylor & Francis Group

© 2003 Morag Styles and Evelyn Arizpe, apart from Chapter 6, Kate Rabey; Chapter 7, Helen Bromley; Chapter 8, Kathy Coulthard

Reprinted 2004

Typeset in Goudy by Taylor & Francis Books Ltd
Printed and bound in Great Britain by TJ International Ltd, Padstow, Cornwall

British Library Cataloguing in Publication Data
A catalogue record for this book is available from the British Library

Library of Congress Cataloging in Publication Data
Styles, Morag.
Children reading pictures: interpreting visual texts / Morag Styles and Evelyn Arizpe; with contributions from Helen Bromley, Kathy Coulthard and Kate Rabey.
Includes bibliographical references and index.
1. Visual learning. 2. Pictures in education. 3. Children–Books and reading. I. Arizpe, Evelyn. II. Title.

LB1067.5 .S79   2002
371.33'5–dc21   2002026983

ISBN 0–415–27576–8 (hbk)
ISBN 0–415–27577–6 (pbk)

Contents

N.B. All the chapters in this book have been written by Evelyn
   Arizpe and Morag Styles unless otherwise indicated

Illustrations

Notes on contributors

Helen Bromley has taught in primary schools for 16 years, latterly as Deputy Headteacher, before becoming an advisory teacher, then tutor for the Centre for Language in Primary Education. She is currently a freelance consultant running courses in literacy, oracy and media texts throughout the UK. She is working on the links between play, popular culture and writing for her Ph.D. Publications include *Book Based Reading Games* (2001). She writes for journals such as *Reading* and *Cambridge Journal of Education*, as well as contributing chapters to *Talking Pictures* (Watson and Styles 1997), *Small Screens* (Buckingham 2002) and *Pikachu's Global Adventure: Making Sense of the Rise and Fall of Pokemon* (Tobin 2002)

Kathy Coulthard is currently an advisor for ethnic minority achievement in the London borough of Enfield, having previously been a primary teacher and advisor for English and Assessment. She is author of *Scaffolding Learning in the Multilingual Classroom* (1998) and contributes to journals such as *English in Education* and *Language Matters*. She is in demand as a speaker on teaching and learning in multilingual classrooms.

Kate Robey took a first class degree from Cambridge in Art and Early Years Education in 1998, then spent three years as a classroom teacher. During that period, she also worked on projects in art education for the Fitzwilliam Museum and Kettle's Yard, Cambridge. She was one of the organisers of the exhibition, Picture This!: Picturebook Art at the Millennium at the Fitzwilliam Museum (2000) and co-author of the catalogue which accompanied it. She is now working towards a Ph.D. on visual literacy and as a researcher for the Young Cultural Creators Project, based at the Tate Gallery, London. She has contributed to *The Cambridge Guide to Children's Books in English* (Watson 2002) and *Teaching Through Texts* (Anderson and Styles 2001).

Preface – a personal preamble

Morag Styles

Art's most satisfying function is that it allows us to exercise our minds.
(Yenawine 1991: 25)

Learning to look

The first time I read Jan Ormerod's delightful *Chicken Licken*, I was so busy analysing the different levels at which the text was operating that I completely failed to spot the baby (whose antics form one of the key narratives in this multi-layered picturebook) until the end of the story. I have yet to encounter a child who doesn't notice the baby from the opening page. For years I have been learning about picturebooks from children. In most other parts of the curriculum, I felt there was probably more I could teach children than they could teach me, but every time I read a visual text with a child (and usually the younger, the better), they saw things I didn't. Although I was actively looking for meaning in every image, the 5-year-old by my side would invariably point excitedly to a detail I had missed, sometimes engendering a new reading of a familiar text. Where picturebooks are concerned, in some significant respects young children are more ahead of the game than experienced readers.

My belief in children as sophisticated readers of visual texts was heightened some years ago when I went into my local school to do some field work for research into picturebooks.[1] When I laid out piles of delectable picturebooks[2] in the library which was at the centre of the school where children passed between lessons, I noticed how many of the older pupils looked longingly at the books, or begged me to work with them, or made the sort of 'Ahhh' and 'Mmm' appreciative noises that are more suggestive of the sounds children usually make when encountering delicious food! The picturebooks had an instant aesthetic appeal, but was there more to it than that? If I had often been disappointed in the past at the dismissive and relatively superficial response of 8–11-year-olds to picturebooks (compared to younger readers), would this still be true of children at the turn of the millennium who had grown up in a much more visual world and who had read many picturebooks in their early years of schooling? Or do schools still place such high value on reading print that illustrated books are cast aside as early as possible? Was it still likely to be the case that younger children were more observant of pictures and their meaning than older pupils? When did the interplay between word and image, a strong feature of many picturebooks, become more significant? Are young children capable of sophisticated multi-modal reading? Do cultural factors make a difference?

The project team

These were some of the questions I was grappling with in 1999 when I was already busily involved in a project on visual literacy, which included organising a large international symposium on the subject and mounting an ambitious exhibition of picturebook artists at the Fitzwilliam Museum, Cambridge. I am not sure what madness prompted me to take on a third strand of the Reading Pictures Project by asking the Arts and Humanities Research Board for a study leave to investigate how children read images in picturebooks, but that is what I did. It is due to the generosity of AHRB and Homerton College that this investigation became a reality.

I did, however, have the sense to realise I couldn't do all of this myself and was lucky enough to tempt Evelyn Arizpe to be joint convenor. We have collaborated closely throughout the research, though Evelyn has had to hold the threads together at various times when I was burdened with other parts of the project. During the course of our work, Evelyn keenly observed her eldest daughter, Isabel's, response to visual texts. When Evelyn became pregnant with her second child, Flora, who at the time of writing this book is 2 years old, she developed these observations into a literacy journal of her daughters. These two girls were present at some of our meetings (mercifully asleep!) and seemed part of the project from the outset, so we have taken advantage of Evelyn's occasional notes on very young children as readers of image.

In the fullness of time, we recruited some talented teacher/ researchers to work with us. Kate Rabey had recently gained a first class degree at the University of Cambridge in Fine Art and Education and had distinguished herself in the final year children's literature course, particularly for her work on picturebooks. Kate was teaching 4- and 5-year-olds in a local Cambridge school that was perfect for inclusion in our study. She brought a knowledge of art and an understanding of young children and their drawings to the project that was to prove invaluable.

Kathy Coulthard and I had been friends since we had taken a course on reading together in the early 1980s and we had always wanted an excuse to work together. Now that she was working as an advisor for ethnic minority achievement in a north London borough, it made her the perfect choice to join the project with her colleague, Janet Campbell, choosing schools well known to them in Enfield. Kathy and Janet brought their immense experience of working with teachers and pupils in multi-ethnic settings to our study. Their insightful comments and commitment were all the more remarkable given their incredibly busy schedules at the time.

The final member of the group was Helen Bromley, who had distinguished herself on our Advanced Diploma in Language and Literature some years before and had since been in great demand as a speaker with a particular interest in reading, media texts and oracy. Helen had also been working at the Centre for Language in Primary Education and, although battling with a debilitating illness at the time, her refreshing enthusiasm for the project and the quality of her contribution made her a valued member of the team. Helen's research took place in a school in Essex.

Lessons for teachers?

We are living in a golden age of picturebooks today. The sheer talent of so many picturebook artists, the quality, variety and sophistication of output is quite extraordinary and, I think, too much taken for granted. Most teachers enjoy reading these texts to children and story-time is now an established part of the early years curriculum in Britain and, I suspect, in many classrooms all over the world where there is the funding and the access to fine picturebooks. Furthermore, we live in an increasingly visual world where it is widely held to be the case that image is superseding the word as the dominant means of communication. Most contemporary children who are lucky enough to have access to videos, computers and electronic games are masters of their range and repertoire, amazing their ham-fisted elders with their skill and poise. This combination of (1) the availability of a wide range of excellent picturebooks; (2) their popularity with teachers and pupils as part of essential classroom practices, now well established; and (3) the dominance of image in all our lives today, suggested to us that children might be very sophisticated readers of image.

Sadly, this skill of visual literacy is not widely understood or exploited in our educational system. In England and Wales, where we have had a National Curriculum for nearly 15 years, although picturebooks are seen as the main literary texts for children before the age of 6 or 7, pictorial cues are not included as one of the key skills for learning to read. In fact, visual literacy is not mentioned in the National Curriculum for Reading. And although there are many picturebooks which challenge older readers, they are not considered by most teachers or pupils to be a suitable genre for reading above the age of 7. Furthermore, in the National Literacy Strategy introduced in the UK in 1998, the hundreds of pages devoted to the skills that children need to acquire in order to be literate, plus ideas for how to use these skills in the classroom, barely mention visual texts. Clearly the results of our research were likely to have implications for the primary curriculum and its teaching methods.

Conclusion

In some ways, a metaphor for our research could be that of a simply equipped, small boat setting out on turbulent seas, often rowing against the current and finding ourselves on unexpected foreign shores. The journey was exhilarating and we had a terrific crew; if we did it again, we might use a finer vessel or steer a different course. Even so, we are very glad we took this trip in the splendid company of children, teachers, artists and scholars. We hope our adventures into visual literacy will prove just as rewarding for the reader.

Notes

1   See chapter 2, Watson and Styles (1996).
2   The picturebooks were by the Ahlbergs, Sendak, Smith and Scieszka, Burningham, McKee, McNaughton, Kitamura, Browne, Hughes *et al.*

Acknowledgements

The authors would like to thank the team (Helen Bromley, Janet Campbell, Kathy Coulthard and Kate Rabey) for their passionate commitment to the project. Working with such a gifted group of people was often exhilarating, always enjoyable.

We should also like to thank the seven head teachers and 21 teachers with whom we worked and to express our appreciation for the warm welcome we received from the schools in the project. As for the children, their reactions made all our efforts worthwhile.

Anthony Browne and Satoshi Kitamura were helpful and supportive throughout the project and we are very grateful for their collaboration.

This project would not have been possible without the study leave granted by the Arts and Humanities Research Board; it was also helped by a small grant from the British Academy. Homerton College was a generous employer in many ways, allowing time and resources for research and writing. Morag Styles would also like to thank her colleagues at Homerton College and Cambridge Faculty of Education for their support.

The authors are grateful to the following for permission to reproduce material: illustrations from *Zoo* by Anthony Browne, published by Julia MacRae, reprinted by permission of The Random House Group; illustrations and text from *Lily Takes a Walk* by Satoshi Kitamura, reprinted by permission of The Penguin Group; illustrations from *The Tunnel* copyright 1989 Anthony Browne. Reproduced by permission of Walker Books and Random House Inc.

On a personal note:

Evelyn Arizpe: warm thanks are due to my husband, Nigel Leask, for his encouragement and all the support he has given me during the project.

Morag Styles: some special friends have been very important to me while I was working on this project. You know who you are. Thank you for everything.

Introduction

Contexts and methodologies

> What we see is not simply given, but is the product of past experi-
> ence and future expectations.
>
> (Gombrich 1982: 28–9)

Research design and methodology

There have been surprisingly few systematic attempts to ask children
about their reading/viewing of pictorial text in terms of their understanding of visual art, and appreciation of artistic techniques and their
implications for the teaching and learning of visual literacy.[1] Most
research is limited to particular psychological, linguistic or artistic
development issues, where subjects are tested in a context that may
not have much in common with the setting in which they relate to
pictures. Within the studies that do look at response to pictures in
books, few have focussed on the same picturebook and asked the same
set of questions to children of different ages and in different schools.
Also, few have taken account of the way the child perceives the relationship between images and words.

The principal aim of our research was to investigate how visual texts
are read by children using the work of well-known picturebook artists.
We wanted to explore the potential of visual literacy and the skills children need to deal with visual texts. A subsidiary aim was to identify the
perspectives of the artists, particularly in terms of their perceptions of
how young readers might respond to their work, and to set this alongside
information gathered through the research about the responses of the
young readers themselves. Some of the questions we set ourselves to
explore have not been asked before of readers of different ages. When
confronted with complex picturebooks, how do they understand narrative through pictures? What are the specific skills that young readers

bring to interpreting visual texts? How do they perceive the relationship between word and image? How can they best articulate their response? What is the relationship between thinking and seeing? What is the role of written text in making sense of image? How does the reading background of the children affect their viewing? What part do visual texts and media play in their ability to analyse pictures? Do gender and ethnicity have an influence on the understanding of image? What do children's own drawings reveal about their viewing skills? What do complex picturebooks teach them about looking? How does talking about a book in depth, with their peers and with adults, change their responses?

The research design was based on the conclusions of a pilot study during which various research instruments were refined. The basic structure was as follows: we worked in seven primary schools serving varied catchment areas, interviewing two boys and two girls per class from three different classes per school, one of which was early years, one lower primary and one upper primary. This meant we worked closely with twelve children of varying ages in each school, usually requiring three whole-day visits as well as preliminary conferences with teachers. We revisited one-third of the sample several months after the initial interviews.

The schools

Seven primary schools participated in the research, ranging from multi-ethnic and economically deprived settings in north London to suburban schools in Essex. The schools were chosen to include those with differing intakes in terms of social class, though we did not systematically control for these variables, confining ourselves to collecting data on the proportion of pupils having free school meals.

All of the schools were to some extent multi-ethnic and multilingual, with the exception of School D in the south east of England, where the pupils were predominantly white, monolingual speakers of English. This was in contrast to the London schools, where a whole spread of ethnic groups could be found, including a large percentage of refugees from the African and Asian subcontinents. In the schools in Cambridge, around 20 per cent of the pupils had a second language.

The interviews

In-depth semi-structured interviews were conducted with 84 children (matched for gender), 21 of whom were followed up in a second inter-

School	Population	Socio-economic information	Free school meals (%)
A	363	City council estate, mainly working class	22
B	466	Suburban, mixed housing, working/middle class	7
C	400	City, mixed housing, working/middle class	12
D	300	Suburban, middle class	9
E	518	Outer London borough, working class (32% ethnic minority pupils)	33
F	550	Outer London borough, working class (70% ethnic minority pupils)	30
G	898	Outer London borough, mixed housing (40% ethnic minority pupils)	52

view. An interview schedule was closely followed, normally 45 minutes long, with about ten questions common to all interviews and a further ten which were book specific (these questions can be found in the Appendix). We began by asking about the appeal of the cover and how it showed what the picturebook might be about (later in the interviews we asked if, in retrospect, the covers were right for the books). We asked children to tell us about each illustration in turn, using specific and open-ended questions. We invited them to show us their favourite pictures, to tell us how they read pictures and to talk about the relationship between words and pictures. We questioned them about the actions, expressions and feelings of the characters; the intratextual and intertextual elements; what the artist needed to know in order to draw, and the ways in which he used colour, body language and perspective etc. In addition, we took research notes which included reference to children's own body language (pointing, gazing, tone of voice, use of hand, facial expressions) while reading the books.

Group discussions

After the individual interviews, the children participated in a group discussion with other members of their class who had been interviewed, plus two extra children who had been identified by the teacher in case of the absence of the interviewees. In total, 126 pupils were involved in these discussions, which lasted up to an hour and were normally conducted later in the same day. During these discussions, the researchers were free to review interesting issues that had come up in the interviews, open up new areas for debate and give the children who had not been interviewed a chance to grapple with the text.

Drawing in response to pictures

We invited the children to draw a picture in response to the text which had been the focus of the interview. The purpose of the drawing was to access some of their knowledge which may not have been verbally articulated during the interviews.[2] The researchers provided materials when necessary and the pupils were allowed time to draw, either while others were being interviewed, or later in the day. During the follow-up interviews, the children were asked to do a second drawing. The drawings are analysed by Kate Rabey in chapter 6.

Revisiting

Preliminary findings indicated that repeated readings of a picturebook could be an important element in pupils constructing meaning, so we were interested to find out whether significant changes in interpretation had occurred some time after the initial research. Accordingly we decided to carry out follow-up interviews three to six months later with one fifth of our original sample, i.e. one child from each class. The children were chosen to represent a range of responses to the first interviews – from children who had been outstandingly interesting the first time round, to those who had barely been willing to participate, from children with specific learning difficulties to those who were described by their teachers as more or less average readers. In the revisiting, the emphasis of the questions changed from detailed examination of individual pages to a consideration of the book as a whole.[3]

Procedures

Five different researchers carried out the interviews in schools. Their role was to follow the interview schedules as closely as possible, while allowing for flexibility in following children's leads and pursuing further questioning when they thought it appropriate to do so. Analysis of the transcripts showed that each researcher had their own interviewing style which influenced the results in intriguing ways (see chapter 12). In some cases, particularly when working with young or bilingual children, the pupil's willingness and ability to talk determined the way in which the interview was conducted. Each of the researchers used their own criteria in deciding which questions or pictures seemed to elicit the most interesting responses from the interviewees and were free to choose when and where to probe further.

The questionnaire

In order to provide a context against which to set our results, we used a short questionnaire to find out about the reading habits of the pupils in the seven schools that participated in the study.[4] It invited information on their favourite picturebooks, television programmes, videos and computer games. It was also a way of finding out whether they were familiar with the picturebooks used in our research. A total of 486 children from Reception to Year 6 (ages 4 to 11) answered the questionnaire, which provided us with a glimpse of the reading backgrounds of pupils as well as of their interests by age and gender.[5]

Data analysis

The amount of data resulting from the interviews and discussions was considerable and required many careful readings.[6] The transcripts from the initial and the follow-up interviews were analysed qualitatively, partially employing a grounded theory approach (Glaser and Strauss 1967 and Strauss 1987), but also using codes derived from previous studies on response to text (for example Thomson 1987). We also took into account the data analysis carried out by two of the most systematic studies on response to picturebooks – Kiefer (1993) and Madura (1998).[7] Kiefer developed categories and subcategories of response according to four of Halliday's functions of language: informative, heuristic, imaginative and personal. Madura takes Kiefer's framework into account but grouped responses to the particular books she used into three main categories: descriptive, interpretive and the identification of thematic trends.[8]

Although we found these categories useful, both as analytical tools and as a means of corroborating our findings, we developed codes from our own data which were successively modified through further analysis. In order to facilitate this analysis, oral response was divided into two groups – although it is clear that these groups are closely linked.

We identified one group as 'categories of perception' because the responses were based on codes derived from what the children took from the picturebook, such as, for example, the noticing of significant details, intra- and intertextual references or the relationship between the text and the image. Responses in the second group, 'levels of interpretation', corresponded to the way in which the children made sense of these picturebook codes, for example, giving the interviewer literal, implausible or plausible explanations, interrogating or evaluating the text and/or images (the complete list of categories can be found in the Appendix). This initial categorisation served as framework for organising the data. Once this was achieved, researchers took the analysis further in different directions, for example, looking more closely at response to visual features, ethical and moral issues, the interaction between written text and image (depending on the picturebook in question) or concentrating on the linguistic and cultural context of readers. The results of these diverse analytical approaches are discussed in chapters 3–9.

The picturebooks

We spent some time trialling a range of picturebooks by contemporary artists to find examples of multi-layered texts which would appeal equally to children aged 4–11; this proved no easy task. In Anthony Browne and Satoshi Kitamura we had two of the most popular, successful and challenging exponents of picturebook art. We decided to concentrate on only three books which we believed would appeal to a wide age range and allow for comparisons and in-depth discussion: *The Tunnel* and *Zoo* by Browne and *Lily Takes a Walk* by Kitamura (which we will refer to as *Lily* elsewhere in the book). *The Tunnel* was read in three of the seven schools; *Lily* and *Zoo* were each read in two schools. Both artists were interviewed at length and were enthusiastic and supportive of the project.

By means of the questionnaire, pupils from all the schools participating in the project were asked whether they had previously read any books by either Browne or Kitamura (depending on which book was to be read in their school). Of the schools who used *Lily*, only 8 pupils in School C (out of 64) and 4 in School D (out of 80) had read any books by Kitamura. Browne was more familiar: around half of the pupils in Schools B, E and G knew one or more of his books, yet in Schools A and G only a very small number of the children had heard of him. (It seems that children are quite sketchy at remembering authors and titles of books they have read.) We did not notice any significant difference in response by children who knew the authors' work well before the exercise began and those who didn't. What made a huge difference to the level of response was children's previous exposure to a wide range of texts. Having said that, it was also exciting to note the number of children without much experience of books who showed great facility in reading pictorial texts.

The children

The interview sample was constructed in order to produce equal representation of boys and girls and to include children from diverse class and ethnic backgrounds. In addition, the class teacher's estimate of the reading ability of each child was obtained, providing a useful point of comparison when assessing children's ability to read pictures. Researchers had no knowledge of these reading abilities until *after* the interviews took place, though we had asked teachers to select two experienced and two relatively inexperienced readers. In the event, teachers took a fair bit of licence with our requests, including children who were fairly average readers and often selecting 'interesting' children whom they thought the experience would be good for. Overall, we had a sample of children from 4 to 11 years old with a wide range of abilities responding to the same questions based on the picturebook used in their school.

Approximately 35 per cent of the interviewed children were bilingual with varying linguistic backgrounds, from two pupils who had recently arrived in the UK with little knowledge of English to third-generation bilinguals.[9] Where necessary, interviews were conducted with a translator. A few children had slight learning difficulties associated with moderate dyslexia, autism and hyperactivity, but these were not found to interfere with their responses. Despite some shyness at the beginning of the interviews, and once they were assured this was not a test, most children were eager to participate, to answer the interviewer's questions, to draw, and by the time of the group discussion, were almost always completely involved in the picturebook. When roughly one-third of the sample were reinterviewed a few months later, they remembered the initial interviews and could recall many details of the books even though most had not seen them for a few months. N.B. We have changed the names of all the children in the study. The pseudonyms take account of ethnicity.

The pupils' reading backgrounds

The data from the questionnaire revealed fewer differences between schools in terms of children's reading habits and preferences than we had expected to find. However, it was clear that the pupils in the three London schools (Schools E, F and G) had less exposure to books (at least in English) than pupils in the other schools. The economically deprived catchment area of these schools was probably a reason for this as well as the fact that English was not the first language in many of their homes. They also had less access to videos and computer games, but, like their counterparts in the other schools, their preference for these was far greater than for books. Other reading material, such as magazines and comics, was also popular among pupils in the London schools, while non-fiction and poetry were hardly mentioned.

The crucial role of the school for facilitating access to books at Key Stage 1 (ages 4–7), became evident through the questionnaires. Results revealed that approximately 60 per cent of pupils from Schools F, G and A read mostly in school, while nearly 90 per cent of those in Schools B and D (more 'middle-class' schools) read mostly at home.[10] These figures changed at Key Stage 2 (ages 7–11), with students in all schools reading mainly at home. At this stage there was a slight increase in the preference for books, although videos and computer games were still more popular, and the reading of magazines and comics increased noticeably. These differences were linked to the responses to the question about reading books on their own and talking about them with friends and family. In School A, 40 per cent of the pupils said they did not read books on their own or talk about them out of school, whereas in School B, 70 per cent enjoyed reading on their own and also talking about books at home.

At the end of the questionnaire, the children were asked to list their favourite videos, television programmes, computer games and picturebooks. The lists for the first three categories were longer by far than for picturebooks. Out of 486 pupils, 39 left the question about favourite picturebooks blank, and 25 boys and 11 girls wrote 'none' or 'don't read picturebooks'. The longest lists came from pupils between 7 and 8 years old. The pupils in the London schools listed fewer books than those in the other schools.[11]

All told, the list of picturebooks is quite limited and some of their choices were illustrated books rather than picturebooks. The same books tended to come up again and again, with picturebooks by Browne at the top of the list, followed by various books by Dahl. Other books that were frequently mentioned were: *Pokemon* (36 mentions),

Elmer (27), *Where's Wally?* (25), *Winnie the Pooh* (16), *The Snowman* (14), *Rainbow Fish* (9) and several books by the Ahlbergs (*Each Peach Pear Plum, Peepo, The Jolly Postman*). Many of the books mentioned were clearly those being read at school as the whole class listed them. One boy mentioned 'Turkish' books, but that was the only reference to books in other languages.

The age of 7 seems to be the peak age of reading picturebooks, with more girls than boys enjoying them. It is also when other reading, from non-fiction to magazines and comics begins to increase, presumably because children become more independent readers. It was not surprising that up to this age the majority of pupils (more girls than boys) said they liked to read picturebooks. After 7, the reading of picturebooks begins to decrease and this coincides with the older pupils' belief (also confirmed by the interviews) that picturebooks are best for young children.

Taking into account that children may have had difficulty remembering the names of the picturebooks or with spelling them, their range of books still seems limited considering the number of picturebooks available. The data from the questionnaire suggests that most of the children's contact with image has occurred through media texts rather than through books. How this contact influences their perception of pictures in books was one of the questions in the back of our minds throughout our study; however, much more research would be required to reach an answer.

Questions, questions, questions ...

Although we set out to understand and measure what the children could do with visual texts, it seems that the way we asked and responded to the questions actually taught some of the children how to look closely and analyse image. We examine further how the scaffolding and apprenticeship model of learning was conducted (albeit sometimes unconsciously by the researchers) in chapter 12.

To summarise the research process: the participants would first listen and look at the picturebook with their teacher and classmates (about twenty minutes), followed by an individual interview (about 45 minutes) which accompanied a second reading. Although this gave the children an hour's exposure to a single text and a chance to 'dig' into it, many things were missed on this initial reading. Later the children had a chance to think about the book and what it had to say and how it conveyed meaning by drawing a picture (about thirty minutes) of their own choice in response. Finally, the book was examined again in a group discussion situation (about 1 hour) where new insights were often gained. Inadvertently (we didn't consciously plan this) our methodology enabled the children to engage deeply with texts in the way we set up the schedule of activities. Rather than finding out what they already knew about picturebooks, were we actively teaching them how to look?

The crucial role of good questions in eliciting quality responses from the children was highlighted again and again in our discussions. Even so, children often needed a few simple questions, to which they gave straightforward answers, before getting into their stride. Consequently, at the beginning of interviews we asked a few general questions about their reading of picturebooks and whether they were familiar with the artist's work. Here is Kathy Coulthard's account of working on *The Tunnel* with 6-year-olds:

> They were insecure with more open questions at first, possibly because they were uncertain about the required response. They sense the interviewer has a 'right' answer in her head. For example, to the question 'Does the cover make you want to read the book?', they all answered 'yes', but found difficulty in interrogating their own reasons why. By contrast, it seems they are on much more familiar territory when questioned about particular illustrations or are asked to name specific features they found strange. 'What' seems to be comfortable, but 'why' elicited fewer responses at first. There are implications for the need for children to experience more book sharing with discussion.[12]

Most of our questions required children to probe the visual text analytically. Unlike the National Curriculum tests for reading print, which have a high percentage of information retrieval questions (24 per cent in 1998, 32 per cent in 1999, 44 per cent in 2000) according to Mary Hilton (2001), few of our questions came in that category. Instead, we concentrated on questions which required children to use inference and deduction.

We always began with easy questions which asked children to make a simple personal response to the pictures, such as these using *Zoo* as an exemplar:

- What do you notice about the people in the queue?
- Tell me about the elephant and the people visiting the zoo.

Some of our personal response questions were more demanding:

- Did the cover make you want to read *Zoo*? (Why or why not?)
- What do you find interesting about the gorilla picture?
- Would you describe *Zoo* as funny or serious? (Why?)

Here is a typical example of a question requiring inference:

- Why do you think Anthony Browne showed a hamster on the title page before the story begins, when it's a book about going to the zoo?

Other questions could be categorised as 'explaining textual evidence'. For example:

- Did you notice anything special about the way Anthony Browne used colour / body language / perspective in *Zoo*?
- Why do you think we are not shown the orang-utan's face?

Although the younger readers found our questions taxing,[13] the overall response to all three texts was very positive and the children appeared to find them interesting and the questions inviting. They also seemed to respond well to the fact that, when they volunteered information, we would often encourage them to probe more deeply. The rigour of the analysis and the amount of time devoted to considering a single picture-book appeared to surprise the children, but they also seemed to enjoy rising to the challenge. By the time they had the group discussion at the end of the day, instead of understandable reactions such as boredom or 'we've done this already', on most occasions children were eager to contribute, especially when we made it clear we didn't want repetitions of what they had said in the earlier interviews. Like Kiefer's respondents in *The Potential of Picture Books* (1995: 24) we found that 'children in all settings displayed an enthusiastic willingness to immerse themselves in the contents of their picture books, and verbal language seemed to give them the tools to understand these complex art objects'.

In the interviews, all the researchers asked the same prescribed questions, though we took a fair amount of licence in asking supplementary questions when replies opened up interesting channels of discussion. In what follows, the first interview question was scripted; after that further questions were devised by interviewers on the spot, if it seemed worthwhile to pursue a line of inquiry. The following examples are typical of how we responded to the children to help them keep probing the meaning. Sometimes all that was required was a simple 'Why?' or 'Is there anything else you would like to say?'

I: Do you think Anthony Browne is a good artist?
CHLOE (8): Yes, yes.
I: Why?
CHLOE: Because he like thinks about the animals, then he like puts all the detail in them. And like because he's all serious, he puts horns up there [picture of Dad where the clouds behind him look like horns, a visual metaphor for the devilish way he is behaving]. It's clouds, and like he gets all the detail in the floors [a reference to Browne's hyper-real style and famous attention to detail in wooden floors, brick walls etc.].

I: What do you think Anthony Browne wants us to imagine in that picture?
SIMONE (10): Erm ... to imagine that you're there so you can see everything.
I: Now is it just about seeing everything or? ...
SIMONE: He makes us feel like you're in her shoes to make you feel how she's scared or you're in his shoes [the brother's] making her scared.

Other times the researchers asked thoughtful questions which meshed with what children appeared to be trying to express. Sometimes the questions had no effect and, despite our hunches that children were on the point of breakthrough, they remained clammed up. At other times, the questions seemed to release previously unarticulated ideas. Without the supplementary questions, much of the children's knowledge and understanding would have remained unknown to us.

I: Why does Anthony Browne show us a picture of a hamster in a cage?
ERIN (7): Well a hamster is an animal and at the zoo you see animals.
I: Is there any other reason for choosing the hamster?
ERIN: They're also in zoos and got funny cages. [The first comment is incorrect, of course.]
I: So why might he have chosen to put a hamster in a cage?
ERIN: I don't know.

In this extract the interviewer wants to know whether Erin understands that Browne is suggesting that pets are often kept in captivity as well as exotic animals in a zoo. He's opening a debate about captivity and freedom and the relationship between human beings and animals. She suspects that Erin understands this connection, as she has noticed many other subtle things about the book. But on this occasion, her questions do not elicit any further understanding from Erin, though the interviewer is probably right in her hunch.

In the extract that follows, the interviewer finds out by further questioning, not only that Paul feels empathy for the orang-utan's unhappiness, but that he also associates it with being caged and reads the animal's body language correctly (see figure 2 in plate section).

I: Why do you think we are not shown the orang-utan's face?
PAUL (5): Because he's sad?
I: Why do you think he's sad?
PAUL: Because he's trapped in a cage.
I: How does Anthony Browne show us that he's sad?
PAUL: Because he's trapped.
I: How do you know that?
PAUL: Because there's a cage there [pointing].
I: Is there any other way that Anthony Browne shows us that he's sad?
PAUL: Because he's sitting against the wall and won't show his face.

The children were invited to comment on anything they found interesting as we looked at the picturebooks. We wanted to be open to possibilities we hadn't thought of and to follow any train of thought the children wanted to take, even if they had not been anticipated.[14] In discussions the researchers deliberately opted for freedom to go in any direction that seemed productive and to move on the children's thinking whenever possible, without forcing. At that point some of the researchers moved into teacher mode, as is clear from the transcripts. Sometimes when children saw things the researcher had not noticed, the level of discussion improved dramatically. As Kathy Coulthard put it, 'We've given up the monopoly of power and knowledge and … when the right questions are asked, the children can get there … some questions we ask cause children to see in a different way.'

Looking ahead

We began with a descriptive, personal narrative account of our research in the preface, in addition to providing background information and identifying some of the issues that are taken up more fully elsewhere. Chapters 1 and 2 review the literature and some of the theory on which our work is based including a review of models of response to image – busy readers may want to peruse them later. Part II examines the empirical evidence, with the children's responses to each of the picturebooks, followed by Kate Rabey's analysis of the children's drawings in response to the texts. In this part we have also included vignettes of four children whose responses to the picturebooks illustrate our arguments in more depth. In Part III, Helen Bromley deals with children learning through talking, while Kathy Coulthard discusses how bilingual learners made breakthroughs in their reading of visual texts, despite struggling to express themselves in a language which was not their mother tongue (this chapter is slightly longer than the others as Kathy's findings turned out to be highly significant). Metacognitive approaches at work, as children told us how they constructed meaning from pictures, were also considered in this third part. In the final part, we conclude with what the artists had to say about their intentions in producing these picturebooks. In chapters 11 and 12, our overall findings are explored more fully and the role of visual literacy considered within the current educational climate.

Notes

1 Sinatra (1986) notes the lack of data in what he calls picture comprehension and that, while some research has studied the effects of visual presentation on viewers, the processes through which meaning is made have not been looked at.
2 Because of the difficulties involved in articulating verbal response to a work of art, Gardner suggests that 'nonverbal means, preferably involving the medium itself, would seem preferable for determining the full range of the child's competence' (1973: 180).
3 Some of the children had their birthdays in the interim, hence the difference in their ages when quoted.
4 Because this was mainly a qualitative study, the questionnaires were meant to provide descriptive examples, comparisons and contrasts rather than results of statistical value. The questionnaire format was adapted from Davies and Brember (1993).
5 Due to differences in pupil numbers for each school and because no data was available for some year groups (for reasons out of our control), the statistical analysis was based on two groups: Key Stage 1 (ages between 4 and 7) and Key Stage 2 (ages between 8 and 11). A random sample of questionnaires from each stage was selected for analysis. The results correspond to five schools for KS1 (with a total of 100 pupils) and six schools for KS2 (with a total of 300 pupils).
6 All the interviews were transcribed. In the examples used throughout this book, the use of (…) indicates a gap in the transcription.

7 As far as we are aware, no previous study has analysed children drawing in response to picturebooks. The data analysis in this instance (chapter 6) was based mainly on aesthetic interpretations of children's drawings.

8 Day (1996) uses Doonan's categories of denotation and exemplification to begin to understand the schemata children bring to the act of reading picturebooks. She also uses three other categories: references to artistic techniques, allusions to other literature and the creation of dialogue for the characters in the books.

9 Nationalities included Greek, Italian, Turkish Cypriot, Turkish mainland, Kurdish, Tanzanian, Nigerian, Afghani, Chinese, Colombian, Kosovo-Albanian and Sri-Lankan among others.

10 School A was an interesting example because a strong emphasis was being put on literacy at the time the questionnaire was applied. This may explain not only why these children had such a high preference for poetry compared to children in the other schools, but also why the interviewed children seemed more comfortable talking about books (and perhaps why a greater number of them – in comparison to other schools – came up with such insightful comments about the picturebook used in the interviews). The government inspection report for this school (carried out the year before our study) repeatedly refers to the fact that children enter this school achieving less than the national average but are either at the same level or above it by the time they leave the school. It praises the 'good quality' of the teaching and stresses that children enjoy reading and make good progress in reading and other language skills.

11 More girls were able both to identify their favourite picturebooks and to write longer lists. One of the interesting findings in relation to gender preferences was that more boys than girls marked 'stories' as a commonly read genre. Although there was a decrease in reading stories for both sexes after the ages of 9 or 10, stories were still four times more likely to be marked by boys. In general, however, results indicated that more girls than boys read and talk about books. Girls were more likely to say they did 'not mind' books, even when they preferred media texts, whereas boys were more likely to express an active dislike of books and reading (a finding confirmed by Millard 1997). See chapter 11 for more on results pertaining to gender.

12 Kathy Coulthard's closing comment is a reference to the Literacy Hour in England which has led to literature being used in a mechanistic way in many classrooms in order to teach a specific point about punctuation, grammar, spelling or some aspect of story. What has been lost is the time that used to be spent on reading books to children and talking about them in an unstructured way.

13 Despite every sign of their interest in *Zoo*, including their body language, one class of 4- and 5-year-old children said unanimously at the end of the discussion that they hadn't liked the book. The fact that they went on to do such outstanding work from this text (see chapters 4 and 6) belies this response. We feel fairly certain that what the children meant was that it was very hard work and they were tired. On the transcript children asked for drinks and volunteered comments about tiredness.

14 As the younger children were less forthcoming in interviews, it was the older children who tended to be asked supplementary questions.

Part I

Definitions, processes and models

Chapter 1

The nature of picturebooks

Theories about visual texts and readers

Picturebooks successfully combining the imaginary and the symbolic, the iconic and the conventional, have achieved something that no other literary form has mastered.

(Nikolajeva and Scott 2000: 262)

Pictures form a point of peculiar friction and discomfort across a broad range of intellectual inquiry.

(Mitchell 1994: 13)

Defining picturebooks

In the opening to *American Picture Books*, Bader (1976) offers a succinct definition:[1]

> A picture book is text, illustrations, total design; an item of manufacture and a commercial product; a social, cultural, historical document; and foremost an experience for a child. As an art form it hinges on the interdependence of pictures and words, on the simultaneous display of two facing pages, and on the drama of the turning page.

In this book we will be concerned with most of the notions mentioned by Bader: sophisticated picturebooks which require sophisticated readings; picturebooks which are simultaneously art objects and the primary literature of childhood; the importance of design and the interconnections between word and image; picturebooks as compelling narrative texts which, indeed, work on the basis of 'the drama of the turning page' (1996: 1). The fact that texts carry cultural, social and historical messages and that they are constructed as items of merchandise will not feature prominently in our discussion, but will be part of the implicit theoretical background to our study.

Nodelman takes the definition a little further when he argues that 'picture books are a significant means by which we integrate young children into the ideology of our culture. Like most narratives, picture book stories most forcefully guide readers into culturally acceptable ideas about who they are through the privileging of the point of view from which they report on the events they describe ... (in other words) to see and understand events and people as the narrator invites us to see them' (Nodelman in Hunt 1996: 116–18). Similarly, in *Language and Ideology in Children's Fiction* (1992), Stephens discusses the social-ising and educative intentions of picturebooks and considers how the reader is positioned according to style, perspective and word–picture interaction, stressing that picturebooks can never be said to exist 'without a specific orientation towards the reality constructed by the society that produces them' (Stephens 1992: 158).

Although this book is about what children say about picturebooks and not about the picturebook itself, scholarly work on the subject has obviously informed our research. We shall therefore give a brief account of the theories that have furthered the study of the picture-book as an aesthetic object and, in some cases, of children's understanding of this object.

How picturebooks work

Our understanding of the reading process owes a great debt to Iser[2] and Rosenblatt. At the heart of the reading experience is the gap in the text which has to be filled by the reader, particularly pronounced, of course, in picturebooks. Iser draws on Laing's belief, forcefully argued in *The Politics of Experience*, about human beings 'continually filling in a central gap in our experience ... ' and goes on to say, 'it is the gaps, the fundamental asymmetry between text and reader, that give rise to communication in the reading process' (1980: 165–7). Rosenblatt took up a similar theme when she argued that: 'The literary work exists in a live circuit set up between reader and text; the reader infuses intellectual and emotional meanings into the pattern of verbal symbols and these symbols channel his thoughts and feelings. Out of this process emerges a more or less organised imaginative experience' (1978: 25).

Whereas Iser and Rosenblatt focus on literary texts, Nikolajeva and Scott examine picturebooks which, they argue, lend themselves to hermeneutic analysis; the reader starts with the whole, looks at details, then goes back to the whole picture, as the process begins anew.

> Whichever we start with, the verbal or the visual, it creates expectations for the other, which in turn provides new experiences and new expectations. The reader turns from verbal to visual and back again, in an ever-expanding concentration of understanding. ... Presumably, children know this by intuition when they demand that the same book be read aloud to them over and over again. Actually, they do not read the same book; they go more and more deeply into its meaning. Too often adults have lost the ability to read picturebooks in this way, because they ignore the whole and regard the illustrations as merely decorative. This most probably has to do with the dominant position of verbal, especially written, communication in our society, although this is on the wane in generations raised on television and now computers.
>
> (2000: 2)

This description of the hermeneutic circle may seem self-evident, but our study showed how complex such a process could be with regard to sophisticated picturebooks.

If anyone still doubts that picturebooks are anything more than vehicles of childish entertainment, a glance at a number of recent critical texts devoted to understanding the nature of this apparently simple genre should suffice to convince them. Such critics draw on the latest literary theories – from poststructuralism to postcolonialism, from psychoanalysis to gender theory – to analyse these books and still they cannot encompass the multi-modal dynamic between image and text (which has no equivalent in adult literature as it goes well beyond that of even the graphic novel).

To the parent or teacher who may chiefly come across picturebooks at children's bedtime or during the Literacy Hour, at the very least picturebooks can provide some escape from routine and reality. But to adults who approach them with some awareness of how they work, the reading of a picturebook can be much more significant as intellectual excitement converges with aesthetic pleasure, sometimes with emotional resonance and often with some humour thrown in. As Nikolajeva points out, most adults may need even more help than children in appreciating a picturebook beyond the plot level. In fact, conventional criteria about what constitutes culture, art, literature (including children's 'classics' and memories of childhood reading) can get in the way, as can certain kinds of 'fixed' moral and religious beliefs. Fortunately children, especially very young children, do not approach picturebooks with these preconceptions and prejudices and their openness and curiosity can teach many of us adults lessons about looking.

The relationship between words and pictures

It must be emphasised that we are talking here about picturebooks – not books with illustrations, but books in which the story depends on the interaction between written text and image and where both have been created with a conscious aesthetic intention (not just for pedagogic and commercial purposes). We are talking about picturebooks composed of pictures and words whose intimate interaction creates layers of meaning, open to different interpretations and which have the potential to arouse their readers to reflect on the act of reading itself. With some notable exceptions, we are referring to picturebooks published within the last twenty years or so where a quiet revolution has been taking place within children's literature. These picturebooks (along with other branches of children's literature) diverge from any concept of children's books as 'simple', if by simple we are referring to such aspects as clear-cut narrative structures, a chronological order of events, an unambiguous narrative voice and, not least, clearly delineated and fixed borders between fantasy and reality. We can observe a shift in artistic representation from the mimetic toward the symbolic. This shift in approach may be correlated with the postmodern interrogation of the arts' ability to reflect reality by means of language, or indeed by visual means. (See, for example, Nikolajeva and Scott 2000: 260–1.)

The relationship between word and image in a picturebook is particularly interesting. Mitchell (1994) talks about a complex relationship of mutual translation and interpretation, while Kress and van Leeuwen focus on the visual component of a text as an 'independently organised and structured message connected with the verbal text. … The two sets of meanings are therefore neither fully conflated, nor entirely opposed' (1996: 16–17). Kümmerling-Meibauer suggests that the relationship between word and image is always dialogical and that, in learning from text and pictures, the cognitive functions they perform are the most significant: 'the tension between the text and the pictures is the central subject of these picture books. Visual discovery, isolation of things, and disruption of traditional context lead to transformation and demand higher cognitive awareness on behalf of the viewer ... the pictures change the meaning of the words' (1999: 163–76). In an article exploring the possibility of a semiotically framed theory of text–picture relationships, Sipe shows us how sophisticated picturebooks demand recursive reading: 'There is thus a tension between our impulse to gaze at the pictures ... and not to interrupt the temporal narrative flow. The verbal text drives us to read in a linear way, where the illustrations seduce us into stopping to look' (1998: 101).

Sipe (1998) and Lewis (2001)[3] both review recent attempts to theorise the relationships between written text and pictures and to find appropriate metaphorical language to describe this complex and varied interaction. Between them they cite Moebius's attempts at a geological comparison with 'plate tectonics' and 'polysystemy'; Schwarcz's use of 'congruency' for harmonious relationships between word and image; Nodelman's use of irony to describe the dynamic way 'the words change the pictures' and vice versa; Meek's 'interanimation', Mitchell's 'mutual translation', Sipe's 'transmediation' and Lewis's own ecological analogy, which he develops at length in *Reading Contemporary Picturebooks*; and various musical metaphors such as author, Ahlberg's, 'antiphonal fugue effect' and illustrator, Sendak's, conceptualisation of his craft as 'almost like a composer thinking music when reading poetry' or 'counterpoint' used differently by Pullman (1989), Schwarcz (1982) and Nikolajeva and Scott (2001).

Art, educational and literary criticism

Since the 1960s there has been a growing body of writing about illustration in children's literature in general, including picturebooks. The work of Hurlimann (1968), Alderson (1973), MacCann and Richard (1973) and Bader (1976) among others has pioneered the study of illustration. According to Nikolajeva and Scott, the first book to consider the picturebook as a whole, as a sequence of 'symbolic communication' rather than individual pictures, was Schwarcz (1982). He not only tried to understand how pictures carry meaning but also how they relate to the verbal text and he explored specific elements such as motifs, metaphors, patterns and contexts in order to raise awareness of how the illustrator worked. Others, such as Roxburgh (1983), Moebius (1986), Bradford (1993) and Sipe (1998) have tackled the issue of text–picture dynamics from different theoretical angles.

One of the most influential studies which raised the tone of the discussion around picturebooks and gave it greater academic status, is that of Nodelman. In *Words About Pictures* he examines visual features in depth (as well as style, symbols and movement) to show how communication is achieved. He was one of the first critics to consider the relationship between words and pictures for the text's meaning as a whole, believing that: 'placing them into relationship with each other inevitably changes the meaning of both, so that good picture books as a whole are a richer experience than just the simple sum of their parts'. He goes on to say that the most successful picturebooks seem to be those in which 'unity on a higher level' emerges from pictures and written texts which are noticeably fragmentary and whose differences from each other are a significant part of the effect and meaning of the whole (1988: 199–200).

It is the differences between words and pictures that make us rein-terpret each in the light of the other; this led Nodelman to theorise that their relationship is mainly ironical. However, as Kümmerling-Meibauer points out in her detailed exploration of irony in picturebooks, the picture–text relationship is not always ironical, it only applies to some instances of the genre. Whether or not a picture-book is ironical, she concludes:

> what should be abundantly clear is that most of the key elements of sophisticated narratives are present in a simpler form in picture books. These statements suggest that the modern picture book as an art form is now ready to claim its own territory, both artistically and as a field of research.
>
> (1999: 177)

Another fruitful approach was taken by Graham (1990) in *Pictures on the Page*, as she discussed how artists convey emotions through themes, character, settings and story. Graham also shows how this teaches the reader about narrative conventions and develops their literary competence, arguing that children react to these emotions and have the ability to interpret complex 'post-modern' books such as those by Browne, Sendak or Burningham which take the implied reader seriously.

Doonan is a most perceptive and original critic; in *Looking at Pictures in Picture Books* (and various articles in international journals), she uses her extensive knowledge of art and individual artists to show us how to become 'beholders'.[4] Doonan (1993) examines picturebooks as aesthetic objects and increases readers' understanding of how visual features work, pointing out that abstract elements of picture making –

colour, line, shape, composition – together with chosen materials and style, 'allude to complex psychological states through images which function as the visual equivalent of simile, metaphor and intertextuality'. Doonan explains that readers must 'tolerate ambiguity' and 'remain genuinely open-minded and prepared to give the whole process plenty of time' (1993: 9–11). She is outstanding in her analysis of Browne and Kitamura's work; her influence on the present authors is evident as her wise commentaries are studded throughout this book.

In *How Picturebooks Work*, Nikolajeva and Scott argue that, although the work of Schwarcz, Moebius, Nodelman and Doonan provide help in decoding pictures, it does not go far enough in 'decoding the specific text of picturebooks, the text created by the interaction of verbal and visual information' (2000: 4). By building on the work of other international scholars,[5] Nikolajeva and Scott attempt to arrive at a system of categories which describe this interaction. A thorough examination of picturebooks where the words and the pictures provide 'mutually dependent narratives' (a category of picturebook they label 'counterpointing') allows them to arrive at a terminology which, as their title says, helpfully describes how these books work.

Although Nikolajeva and Scott are interested in how the reader's imagination is involved in the reading, they do not discuss children's responses. While admitting that they avoid the problem of audience, they believe picturebooks provide a special occasion for a collaborative relationship between children and adults, for picturebooks empower children and adults much more equally. 'Those less bound to the accepted conventions of decoding text are freer to respond to the less traditional work, so children's very naïveté serves them well in this arena, making them truer partners in the reading experience. Children's ability, therefore, to perceive and sift visual detail often outdistances that of the adult' (2000: 261). We would argue that it is not only children's 'ability to perceive and sift' that empowers them, but that, although they may be 'naïve' with respect to literary conventions, they are equally if not more sophisticated than adults in other respects.

Unlike the scholars above, Lewis does actually report children's responses to some of the picturebooks he discusses. In his article on Burningham's *Where's Julius?* (1992), Lewis compares his own reading of this picturebook with that of his two children. He describes the book in detail and the way in which his understanding of it changed through hearing the children's difficulties with retelling this story. He then discusses the way in which the conventional relationship between image and text is subverted and how a game is played by the readers in order to make sense of a metafictive and open-ended picturebook such as this one. He argues that this type of book forces the child (and adult) reader to involve critical skills that teach us about the actual nature of reading pictures.[6]

In a later article Lewis says:

> I can see at least two routes to finding ways forward in the study and criticism of the picture book, neither of them new, and both involving a focus upon individual texts in an attempt to accommodate diversity and difference. One route involves careful and patient listening to what children say as they read, the other an equally patient, careful description of individual books.
>
> (1996: 113)

In Lewis's recent study he decided to take the latter route because, although he does occasionally draw on his conversations with primary school children about some of the books, and in various places emphasises the importance of taking into account both children's and adults' responses, *Reading Contemporary Picturebooks* (2001) is more about understanding the nature of the picturebook than about children's understanding of them. Lewis begins by discussing formal features of picturebooks and reviewing taxonomies (including those of Nikolajeva and Scott) of the interaction between words and pictures. He goes on to explore the multiform and constantly developing nature of this genre through the concepts of ecology, play, postmodernism[7] and Wittgenstein's later philosophical work on language games etc. He also experiments with applying Kress and Van Leeuwen's grammar of visual design to the images in picturebooks. Lewis alerts us to the many forms that picturebooks take and will continue to take in the future. It is because of this constant change that he claims 'the picturebook is thus ideally suited to the task of absorbing, reinterpreting and re-presenting the world to an audience for whom negotiating newness is a daily task' (2001: 137). Once again he reminds us of the importance of looking closely at the reading event itself.

Discordant voices

Unfortunately, we live increasingly in an official educational culture which 'underestimates the power of the picturebook to give rise to a variety of intellectual and emotional responses' as Kiefer tells us in *The*

Potential of Picture Books. She goes on to document how educational systems have:

> neglected the potential of picture books to develop visual literacy, just as reading and writing researchers have overlooked the opportunities for language and literacy learning provided by picture books. Children live in a highly complex visual world and are bombarded with visual stimuli more intensely than most preceding generations. Yet few teachers spend time helping children sort out, recognise, and understand the many forms of visual information they encounter, certainly not in the same way teachers deal with print literacy.
>
> (1995: 10)

Goldsmith, author of *Research into Illustration*, admits as much: 'although a number of researchers had investigated the place of illustration in the teaching of reading, not only were the findings apparently contradictory, but few ... paid proper attention to the nature of the illustration itself' (1984: 2).

We believe that these attributes should be valued in schools, but in Britain and America, and probably most educational systems across the world, the skills of visual literacy are under-rated or, in extreme cases, despised. Take the work of Protheroe; in a book whose title says it all – *Vexed Texts: How Children's Picture Books Promote Illiteracy* – she asserts that at school

> [children] are being exposed to what is called 'contextualised' or 'context-embedded' language ... (they) do not have to imagine anything. ... How can they [create meaning for themselves] if 'meaning' is always provided in the form of objects or pictures? They can't. ... My contention [is] that illustrated books are harmful to developing reading skills ... and may permanently stunt their intellectual growth. ... Right from the beginning [children] need stories without pictures.
>
> (1992: 8 –10, 158)

Not only do we think that Protheroe is misguided, but the whole of *Children Reading Pictures* provides evidence in support of the opposite argument. Our research shows that picturebooks encourage intellectual growth in children and we believe that they should be used more widely with older pupils as well as with younger children who are learning the rudiments of reading.

There is, however, some evidence to suggest that pictures are not always beneficial to young readers. Although Goldsmith asserts that 'in communicating in print with people who cannot read, pictures are essential', she goes on to quote Hale and Piper (1973) who found that under research conditions 'children younger than thirteen have difficulty in ignoring irrelevant material. This means that a picture, if not a positive help, could become a hindrance.' She also notes that Donlan (1977) found that children were more imaginative in their drawing and use of colours in response to a story if they had not previously seen the illustrations (1986: 111). Goldsmith also suggests that, 'once the ability to produce internal structures exists (around 8/9 years) for tasks of a given level of difficulty, pictures hinder rather than help learning … [and] can have a leveling effect, helping slower learners and retarding the others'. But Goldsmith's understanding of the possibilities made available by complex picturebooks seems rather limited, as she also suggests that text and picture 'should convey as nearly as possible the same message to the viewer' (1984: 78–9, 354–95). From *Rosie's Walk* to *The Stinky Cheese Man*, and most pointedly in *Zoo* and *Lily*, picturebook artists have successfully demonstrated how the opposite can be true; indeed, most ironic picturebooks (see chapter 4) work precisely on the principle that the words and pictures tell contrasting stories which challenge readers to make their own interpretations.

Readers and teachers

All of the scholars discussed above have furthered our understanding of the picturebook, particularly in its most recent and complex forms, and all of them are aware of the importance of audience. However, there is another body of recent work which has attempted to bring children's voices into the picture and suggested how pedagogy may help extend children's knowledge and enjoyment of picturebooks.

One of the main influences has been Meek's seminal *How Texts Teach What Readers Learn* (1988) which describes how children's books can initiate readers into understanding how different kinds of narratives work. These reading 'games' can only be properly learned by immersion in a wide range of texts which gradually reveal their secrets. These ideas probably influenced Hollindale (1997), who argues for a 'childist criticism' of children's literature, a critical approach which values the child's opinions and preferences and also reflects on the context in which the act of reading takes place. It is an approach often linked to reader-response theory which focusses on the active role of the reader in the reading process, a process Rosenblatt calls 'transactional' because reader and text 'shape' each other. According to Watson, the result of this interaction is not only that the text is multi-layered but that so is the act of reading: readers bring their 'potential for engaged responsiveness' to the texts which at the same time invite the reader to increase their engagement and realise the potential of those texts. A good teacher will recognise this and build on both of these potentials (Watson in Styles and Drummond 1993).

Michaels and Walsh (1990) discuss different types of picturebooks and reader response to the visual text, and how they can be used in primary and secondary classrooms to teach aspects such as narrative, gender and register. Baddeley and Eddershaw (1994) follow a similar line in *Not So Simple Picture Books*, where they analyse children's responses to show how picturebooks demand sophisticated visual and intellectual skills from the reader and how children are able to rise to the challenge. Consequently, they criticise the National Curriculum in Britain for not taking advantage of the teaching picturebooks can offer to both younger and older readers. They show, in a variety of ways, how this can be achieved with teacher guidance. Anstey and Bull's *Reading the Visual* (2000) provides a comprehensive introduction to the genre and discusses the place of the picturebook in the curriculum within the Australian context. *Talking Pictures* (Watson and Styles 1996), particularly the chapters by Bromley, Rosen, Styles and Watson, puts children in the spotlight, often analysing shared readings which demonstrate how very young readers can engage intellectually with picturebooks. The importance of young readers' response is also emphasised in another collection of articles, *What's in the Picture?* (Evans 1998).

At the heart of the work by both art specialists and educationalists is the desire to understand how picturebooks work and to use this understanding to further both adults' and children's knowledge and appreciation of this art form. Nodelman's study, for example, intended to:

> bring such invisible knowledge to the surface so that we may better appreciate the amazing learning capabilities of children and so that we can allow children themselves to appreciate it also. My own experience with children confirms that many of them can learn to develop a rich and subtle consciousness of the special characteristics of picturebook narrative and can immensely enjoy doing so. But such knowledge cannot be learned if it is not taught.
> (1988: 37)

In what follows, we explore some of the ways in which this learning develops in children and how it can be more fruitfully taught.

Cognitive psychology and visual literacy

Much of the literature on how children read pictures comes from developmental psychology. The main focus of research in this field examines, usually under test conditions, how children respond to particular, often isolated images, or pictures in text books. Because of its close focus on the cognitive, such research mostly fails to take account of the outstanding art work in many picturebooks which provokes affective as well as cognitive reactions in young readers, and also ignores the dynamic relationship between viewer and text which is so evident to those of us studying children's overall reactions to picturebooks.

Although neither Piaget nor Vygotsky refer specifically to the ways in which children look at artistic images of the kind we are concerned with, their theories (and later, Bruner's) on cognitive development underlie our understanding of how children learn to think. In observing how children from 4 to 11 make sense of pictures, it was inevitable that we returned to their seminal ideas, though we do not pretend to be conversant with all the debates surrounding their work or the huge scholarship in this field.

One of Piaget's major theories linked thinking with experience; children act upon the world through their senses and develop hypotheses based on the consequences of their actions. Vygotsky takes a different tack: while he goes along with Piaget's view that action is crucial to learning, for Vygotsky it is language that plays an indispensable role in mediating internal thought processes such as the ability to reason and to reflect. Like Dewey, Vygotsky goes on to argue that language is a way of sorting out thoughts, a primary vehicle for cognition and socialisation, emphasising the social, collaborative and cultural aspects of learning. Vygotsky did attempt to link psychology with art, literature, emotion and other aspects of culture; had he lived longer he might well have extended his thinking to children learning specifically through image.

Piaget showed how babies discovered predictable patterns and learned to anticipate. He believed that perception was subordinated to action so that children could only make sense of the world within their developmental stage. Piaget's influence on educators has been enormous, including those interested in visual texts such as Sipe discussing what he calls the 'transmediation' of word and image in picturebooks:

> Each new page opening presents us with a new set of words and new illustrations to factor into our construction of meaning. Reviewing and rereading will produce ever-new insights as we construct new connections and make modifications of our previous interpretations, in a Piagetian process of assimilation and accommodation. In other words, we assimilate new information and in the process we change our cognitive structures, accommodating them to the new information.
>
> (1998: 106)

It follows from Piaget's theory that young children are not capable of seeing the world as older children or as adults do because they lack the mental operations to make sense of what they see. Wood,[8] however, argues that perhaps it 'is not young children's inability to perform logical operations but their general lack of expertise which leads them to perceive situations in different ways from the adult' (1998: 36). This is in tune with Vygotsky's notion that children's development interacts with their cultural experience, and that perception, action and speech are inseparable and necessary for the acquisition of knowledge.

As Bruner has pointed out (1983), in Piaget's theory the child is very much alone in sorting out actions and thoughts, receiving little help from others. Bruner also stresses the importance of problem-solving in learning but he is more interested in the social processes it implies. According to Bruner,[9] building on Vygotsky's insights, the development of knowledge and the formation of concepts can be accelerated by 'scaffolding', particularly through the use of mediated language as the more experienced inducts the less experienced learner into understanding. Like Vygotsky, he believes that language has a crucial role to play in developing knowledge and thinking, so these processes are developed in the child through social interaction rather than tackled by the child on her own. This is where Vygotsky's influential concept of the 'zone of proximal development' also comes into play. He defined this as 'the distance between the actual developmental level as determined by independent problem solving and the level of potential development as determined through problem-solving under adult guidance or in collaboration with more capable peers' (1978: 86).

In our research, the results of co-operatively achieved learning were evident particularly in the group discussions and follow-up interviews. Questions were not only working as tools for inquiry, but also as the 'planks' and 'poles' of scaffolding which allowed children to move further into their zones of proximal development. Researchers became facilitators, especially in terms of providing a language through which the children could talk about pictures, modelling concepts and using prompts and leading questions. More experienced peers (those who had had greater access to the culture which produced the picturebook) unconsciously helped their schoolmates in their understanding as they talked about what they saw and how they made sense of it. This leads us to concur with the idea that communal expertise played a more crucial role than individual logical mental operations in determining how far children could make sense of visual texts. We also noted the central role of language in developing thought, but found that, with the younger children what could not be communicated verbally, could sometimes be shown in their drawings.

Perhaps the following example (an observation of Flora aged 17 months as she read *Peepo!* taken from Evelyn Arizpe's informal literacy journal of her children) can show how cognitive theories can be applied to reading pictures.

I have always had misgivings about reading the Ahlbergs' *Peepo!* with a toddler. Although Flora enjoyed the story with its rollicking verse and repetitions and, of course, the peep-hole, I felt there was too much detail in the pictures for her to distinguish any of it clearly, except for the baby which constantly appears on the left-hand page. But my older daughter loved the book, so Flora must have seen it about a dozen times before the particular reading I will now describe. For some reason, it struck me that this time Flora was enjoying the book more fully and this was because she had made the connection between the baby on the left, the peep-hole, and the picture on the other side. Although it is hard to explain this intuition in words (especially as Flora could not talk at this stage), the evidence for thinking she had made a leap in understanding was her keen and prolonged scrutiny of the pictures after the reading. On the page where the baby is in a high chair, Flora pointed to the foot without a shoe. 'Where's the shoe?' I asked her, then turned the page with the peep-hole and showed her the missing shoe under the table. Flora's finger then went from the shoe under the table, back to the shoe-less foot and on to her own feet. She began pointing to the things she was familiar with on other pages, such as the bowl of porridge, cake and toy duck. I thought it was interesting that this awareness had occurred after Flora had spent two weeks in another house which was chaotic and full of objects and extended family, not unlike those in the book. It was as if this experience had helped Flora to distinguish individual objects amongst all the rest and connect them to the baby and herself.

This shows how Piaget's 'pre-operational child' is dealing with the environment at a perceptual level and acting upon it, using both eyes and hands (literally grasping, turning pages, putting fingers through the holes and pointing). Flora has learnt to predict and anticipate there will be a baby, a peep-hole and a larger picture on every page. Flora's behaviour also gives an illustration of Nikolajeva and Scott's hermeneutic circle in action, and relates to Clark's first phase of understanding a visual work of art (see chapter 2) in which the viewer engages with a text by getting a general impression of the whole and then goes on to the second stage, which is careful looking – something that needs to take time. Through my asking questions (about things which I know she has experience of) and providing cues and prompts, we have now reached Flora's zone of proximal development and she is moving towards a new level of understanding.

In Clark's third phase, the viewer connects to her own experience (sitting on a high chair watching lots of family members going in and out of a cluttered room) and knowledge (shoes often get lost). This leads to a re-examination of the images, where Flora registers what she knows and is on the alert for other objects that she might recognise; in this case, in the next reading she suddenly saw the little objects at the corner of the frame around the baby. It is difficult to say in what way

Flora's everyday world has been altered by looking at the pictures (Clark's final stage), but it is certain that the accumulation of knowledge from looking at this and many other picturebooks will have an impact on how she views the world.

The intelligent eye

> To read the artist's picture is to mobilise our memories and our experience of the visible world and to test his image through tentative projections. ... It is not the 'innocent eye', however, that can achieve this match but only the inquiring mind that knows how to probe the ambiguities of vision.
>
> (Gombrich 1962: 264)

As Barthes and others have shown us, far from coming to texts with an innocent eye, the reader is 'a socialised being', a collection of 'subjectivities' responding to the visual world with a body and mind shaped by the realities in which he or she grew up' (Raney 1998: 39).

In his book, *Visual Thinking*, Arnheim is concerned with visual perception as a cognitive activity. He argues that artistic activity is a form of reasoning, in which perceiving and thinking are indivisibly intertwined: 'My contention is that the cognitive operations called thinking are not the privilege of mental processes above and beyond perception but the essential ingredients of perception itself.' Arnheim takes us back to Plato's belief in 'the wisdom of direct vision' and his equation of Socrates' blindness with 'losing the eye of the mind'. Arguing that the Greek philosophers first conceived the dichotomy of perceiving and reasoning, Arnheim reminds us that they never forgot that 'direct vision is the first and final source of wisdom' (1970: 7–13).

In a later work, Arnheim describes the process by which children gain their first 'intellectual concepts' through intelligent observation:

> Perceptual intuition is the mind's primary way of exploring and understanding the world. Before the young mind defines its notion of what is, say, a house, it grasps intuitively something of a large object that keeps presenting itself in daily experience. All those buildings look different from one another, but they have something in common, and this common character is what is apprehended intuitively by the observant mind. I call it a 'percep-

tual concept'. ... The young mind now acquires its first 'intellectual concepts'.

(1989: 28)

Langer had already discussed the power of the image and how it
works on the human psyche back in the 1940s in her important
work, *Philosophy in a New Key*. In a later book she elaborates: 'The
exhilaration of a direct aesthetic experience indicates the depth of
human mentality to which that experience goes. What it does to us
is to formulate our conceptions of feeling and our conceptions of
visual, factual and audible reality together. It gives us forms of imagination and forms of intuition itself. That is why it has the force of a
revelation, and inspires a feeling of deep intellectual satisfaction'
(1953: 397).

Few educationalists, other than those concerned in arts education
and some psychologists, seem aware of what hard discipline is required
in looking attentively at pictures. In *Iconology: Image, Text, Ideology*,
Mitchell asserts: 'More clearly than any other use of the eyes, the
wrestling with a work of visual art reveals how active a task of shape-
building is involved in what goes by the simple names of 'seeing' or
'looking' (1986: 36). In a similar vein, writing in the foreword to
Arnheim's *Thoughts on Art Education*, Eisner points out:

> The eye, as Arnheim tells us, is a part of the mind. For the mind
> to flourish, it needs context to reflect upon. The senses, as part of
> an inseparable cognitive whole, provide that context ... The
> optimal development of mind requires attention not only to intel-
> lectual processes but to intuitive ones as well. Children and
> adolescents should be encouraged to see the whole, not only the
> parts. Art can teach this ... The gist of Arnheim's message is that
> vision itself is a function of intelligence, that perception is a
> cognitive event, that interpretation and meaning are an indivis-
> ible aspect of seeing, and that educational processes can thwart or
> foster such human abilities.
>
> (Eisner in Arnheim 1989: 4–7)

Visual literacy and the arts

The work of Gardner and his Project Zero Team based at Harvard
University has produced much evidence and ground-breaking theories
on arts education, including work on multiple intelligences and visual

analysis. In his attempt to link human development and the artistic process, Gardner studies the moment in which children begin to understand and use symbolic systems. He describes this moment as a 'revolution' because the child is no longer limited to making, perceiving and feeling in relation to material objects and events, but can now invent imaginary objects and events and use them to mediate feelings, experiences, ideas and desires. He also thinks it probable that, by the ages of 3 or 4, children can experience 'discrete emotions', including those in response to a work of art, though they will not be able to articulate those emotions. In opposition to cognitive theorists, Gardner believes this transition – from operating with direct actions on the world to operating on a plane of symbols – happens in the early period between the ages of 2 and 7 even though the child might lack the words to express this new knowledge.[10] Both means of operating are present when making or responding to art:

> I contend that, as the child develops, he may continue to make, feel and respond to objects and experiences, both in the direct way characteristic of the sensorimotor period, and on a superimposed plane of symbolic experience. Making a painting involves acting upon objects and performing motor skills, as well as dealing with a symbolic system of great delicacy; similarly viewing a painting involves consideration of its status as a 'thing' in the world, as an attractive object, and as a comment on aspects of the world couched in a symbolic medium. The power and fascination of the arts rests precisely on the fact that individuals become involved with them on both the sensorimotor and the symbolic planes.
>
> (1973: 132)

However, Gardner also quotes Piaget to warn us depressingly that this artistic aptitude can regress 'without an appropriate arts education which will succeed in cultivating these means of expression and in encouraging these first manifestations of aesthetic creation. The actions of adults and the restraints of school and family life have the effect in most cases of checking or thwarting such tendencies instead of enriching them' (1973: 19).

Perkins was also part of the Project Zero research team; his illuminating observations about how looking at art engenders thinking set us off on a fruitful line of inquiry. In *The Intelligent Eye: Learning to Think by Looking at Art*, Perkins shows how this works:

looking at art has an instrumental value. It provides an excellent setting for the development of better thinking, for the cultivation of what might be called the art of intelligence ... [and] a context especially well suited for cultivating thinking dispositions ... as [works of art] demand thoughtful attention to discover what they have to show and say. Also, works of art connect to social, personal and other dimensions of life with strong affective overtures.

(1994: 3–4)

Perkins goes on to identify six categories which help foster a thinking disposition:

- *sensory anchoring* – it is helpful to have a physical object to focus on;
- *instant access* – art is open to everyone who can see and by its nature encourages looking closer or offers a fresh angle on the familiar;
- *personal engagement* – art is made to hold the attention and helps to sustain prolonged reflection;
- *dispositional atmosphere* – art cultivates thinking dispositions and brings an atmosphere of heightened affect;
- *multi-connectedness* – art encourages connection-making through social and moral issues, philosophical allusions, historical themes, formal structures, relevance to personal experience ...
- *wide-spectrum cognition* – looking at art recruits different kinds of cognition such as visual processing, analytical thinking, posing questions, testing hypotheses, verbal reasoning.

(1994: 4–5)

Perkins goes on to develop the idea of what he calls 'experiential and reflective intelligence' which he describes as 'the deployment of one's intellectual resources to intelligent behaviour ... By cultivating awareness of our own thinking, asking ourselves good questions, guiding ourselves with strategies, we steer our experiential intelligence in fruitful directions' (1994: 11). His conclusions perfectly mirror our findings, which is why we have quoted them at length in this chapter.

Kress and van Leeuwen point out that, although the image is now at least as powerful as the word, this recognition has not been understood by decision-makers, particularly those involved in education: 'the dominant visual language is now controlled by the global cultural technological empires of the mass media [and we now see] the incursion of the visual into many domains of public communication where formerly language was the sole and dominant mode'. Kress and van Leeuwen go on to bemoan 'the staggering inability on all our parts to talk and think in any way seriously about what is actually communicated by means of images and visual design' (1996: 4, 13–16). The rest of this book is an attempt to show the serious thinking children do to make sense of image. Chapters 3–9 provide the empirical evidence and our analysis of it; chapter 2 deals with the many models, taxonomies and frameworks which attempt to explain different phases or stages in the process of appreciating pictures or simply learning how to look.

Notes

1 Like Lewis (2001) and Nikolajeva and Scott (2000), and unlike Bader (1976), we spell 'picturebooks' as a compound word, indicating that its nature is dependent on both words and pictures. (Some of our quotations spell picture books as two separate words.)

2 Iser gave us concepts like the 'implied reader' and taught us about the co-construction of meaning between the reader and the writer: 'the text represents a potential effect that is realised in the reading process ... the poles of text and reader, together with the interaction that occurs between them, form the ground-plan on which a theory of literary communication may be built ... [aesthetic response in reading is] a dialectic relationship between text, reader, and their interaction' (1980: ix–x).

3 For a fuller discussion see Lewis's *Reading Contemporary Picturebooks* (2001), chapters 2 and 3.

4 Doonan uses this term to describe someone with formal understanding of visual images that are not free-standing works of art, or one-off decorations, but sequences of scenes, comic-book frames or illustrations in books.

5 We have not included them here as their work has not been translated into English.

6 Although Lewis refers to the image of parent and child sharing a book, it is important to remember that this may not be the case for many children whose 'reading events' are more likely to take place in school.

7 Anstey and Bull point to the postmodern picturebook as aiding readers to become more active in their interaction with the text precisely because of the multiple narratives, ambiguity and contradictions the text offers.

8 Wood (1998) provides one of the most influential of many critiques of Piaget's work.

9 Bruner coined the term 'scaffolding' with Wood and other colleagues but, as this tends to mean one-to-one tutoring, the more inclusive term, 'guided participation' (Rogoff 1990) is also useful.

10 We certainly saw evidence of this among the youngest children in our study. Further discussion of Gardner's developmental theories can be found in chapter 5.

Chapter 2

Visual literacy – processes, frameworks and models

Towards a developmental theory of response to visual texts

> I have only scratched the surface with the worn-out instrument of words. For quite apart from shortcomings of perception, there is the difference of turning visible experiences into language.
>
> (Clark 1960: 17, cited in Benson 1986)

Several theorists have attempted to construct models outlining a developmental response to visual texts. (We are using text in the loosest sense – it could be a painting, a photograph, a video, a picture in a book, an art object … .) Others have tried to identify the phases viewers go through in their deepening responses to works of art. In this chapter we have provided a survey of some of the key works in this field, which takes in a wide range of disciplines, from art history to psychology, aesthetics to cultural studies, information technology to education. Some scholars take a special interest in children; others are more concerned with adult responses to art. Whereas Parsons spent years collecting data to develop his model of aesthetic response, others, such as Clark, include some discussion of the process of responding to works of art within a huge and varied body of work. We will begin by looking at definitions for the slippery concept of visual literacy, then move on to examine some of the processes, frameworks and developmental models of response to visual texts.

Definitions and debates of visual literacy

The term visual literacy was probably first coined by Debes (1968: 28) in the late 1960s. His focus was on what a visually literate person could do: 'discriminate and interpret the visible actions, objects, symbols, natural or man-made, that he encounters in his environment', as well as the 'creative' application of these competencies for communication with others and appreciation of visual texts. The concept quickly gained currency in media studies, information technology, cultural studies and visual arts education.

Visual literacy also has its roots in structuralism (Saussure, Lévi-Strauss, Barthes *et al.*) and fits comfortably within notions of literacies (as opposed to the narrow view of literacy singular as reading and writing) as social practices (which brings in cultural and ideological considerations), pioneered by scholars such as Street (1984) in the UK and Brice Heath (1983) in the USA who herself straddles the disciplines of social anthropology, linguistics, English and education. Heath's most recent work links developments in neurobiology to explain 'recursive interactions between peripheral images and higher cortical centres that process symbolic representation. Collaborative work through art enables verbal explication and explanation about details, abstractions and process that lead to theory building dependent on propositional, procedural and dispositional knowledge' (2000: 121). How the brain functions in processing symbolic representation is a fascinating, relatively new field of study which goes beyond the scope of this book.

Other commentators, such as Allen (1994), believe that any definition of visual literacy should be extended to take account of research into English in education, which has been engaged with the concept and pedagogy of literacy for at least twenty years. Citing writers such as Hoggart, Street and Burgess, and drawing on Boughton's conceptions of visual literacy (1986), Allen argues for a broad approach to the topic which includes critical, philosophical and art historical discussion.

As will be evident by now, visual literacy is a contentious term, the site of many debates, which often gets squeezed into the particular shape required by different disciplines. Suhor and Little (1988: 470), for example, see visual literacy as an 'aggregate concept' and no longer 'a coherent area of study but, at best, an ingenious orchestration of ideas'. Some writers favour simple, 'common sense' definitions, such as Hortin (1997: 281), an educational technologist, who describes it as: 'the ability to understand and use images to think and learn in terms of images i.e. to think visually'. Sinatra (1986: 5) considers the three essential components of visual literacy to be viewing, sensorimotor exploration and non-verbal representation. He believes that visual literacy is indispensable to thinking and defines it persuasively as 'the active reconstruction of past experiences with incoming visual information to obtain meaning'. Others, such as Dondis (1973) define visual literacy as visual syntax comparable to linguistic grammar, using terms such as line, colour, shape, tone, dimensions, texture etc. instead of verb, clause and sentence etc.

Raney, however, warns us of the dangers of going too far down that road, as it might 'replicate the assumption of an autonomous model of literacy – that there is a fixed or "single code" to be learnt, that looking at things is a science, or that classifying and dissecting images will uncover their meanings'. Raney goes on to suggest that notions like reading competence or decoding should be replaced with considering:

> our relationship to the visual world in terms of empowerment, choice, habit, passion or delight. ... The driving force is prior expectations of meaning [which are] set up by the social fields in which an object is encountered ... whether it is the frame of 'art', inclinations of gender, class identity or generation, or personal experience and associations.
>
> (1998: 39)

In fact, it is Raney herself who provides one of the most all-encompassing and, for us, convincing definitions of visual literacy: 'it is the history of thinking about what images and objects mean, how they are put together, how we respond to or interpret them, how they might function as modes of thought, and how they are seated within the societies which gave rise to them' (1998: 38).

Raney's research from the perspective of media education, art and English[1] has led her to construct a framework of different kinds of visual literacy, identifying five separate dimensions. *Perceptual sensitivity* is basic visual reception available to all sighted people, but the level of sensitivity is variable, shaped by cultural factors that can be deepened by education. *Cultural habit* alludes to the variations which can be accounted for by different cultural practices and historical periods. *Critical knowledge* refers to understandings about how visual representation is shaped and mediated historically, culturally and artistically and how the viewer is placed in relation to it. *Aesthetic openness* describes 'our capacity for visual delight'. Here, Raney is concerned with emotional and sensual responses to visual experience which offer 'immediate access to meaning ... it is the experience that colours our ideas'. Raney's final dimension is *visual eloquence* 'in which all of the above are integrated in the act of making things to be looked at ... calling for a complex mixture of perceptual sensitivity, cultural habit, critical knowledge and aesthetic openness' (1998: 41). In most cases, the pupils in our study showed a high level of perceptual sensitivity and a powerful aesthetic openness; their drawings testify to great visual eloquence and charm, especially those of the youngest children.

Turning visual experience into language

There are many debates about whether spoken and written language can ever adequately take account of visual experience. (The same argument applies to music and dance, of course.) In her work on media education, Raney wonders if, 'Adopting a language metaphor may be part of the long-standing efforts of visual historians, artists and designers to plead for the dignity and complexity of visual images and objects, which are commonly considered to be mute and simple in contrast to the eloquent word' (1998: 37).

Kress has led the challenge against the dominance of verbal language over visual texts in his many publications and is probably the most influential educational scholar in this field, with seminal texts to his credit, such as *Reading Images: the Grammar of Visual Design*. Like Dondis, he is keen to develop 'an established theoretical framework within which visual forms of representation can be discussed' (Kress and van Leeuwen 1996: 20) and his work has reclaimed the language of syntax and applied it to visual texts. He argues persuasively that images can be the central medium of communication in any text and reminds us that ideology is always present. Kress points out that 'visual communication is always coded – it seems transparent only because we know the code already' (Kress and van Leeuwen 1996: 32). He shows us how we can read images by analysing visual grammar. His semiotic code of pictures uses the vocabulary of design – with terms like vectors representing action verbs, actors and reactors as nouns, colour and focus acting as locative prepositions, and contrasting, for example, rectangular forms as representational of the mechanical, logical, man-made [*sic*] constructions, with the more organic, natural disposition in curves and circles. The viewer, in turn, responds to the visual address produced by the image, but has some choice about how to respond. As we will see in our data, even one of the most powerful 'demand gaze/s' in contemporary picturebooks, the gorilla image in *Zoo*, can be resisted, subverted or misinterpreted by the reader.

In a fascinating article on art and language in middle childhood, Benson poses fundamental questions about whether spoken and written language are suitable ways of appreciating art. 'There are very complex questions which should prompt educational theorists to take a closer look at the pedagogical process of talking about pictures as a translational problem. ... A primary feature of looking and seeing is silence. The look and the gaze are essentially non-verbal.' Benson goes on to suggest that the arts would not exist if all meanings could be adequately expressed by words. 'There are values and meanings that can be expressed only by immediate visible and audible qualities and to ask what they mean in the sense of something that can be put in words is to deny their distinctive existence.' After analysing the metapictorial beliefs of young children, Benson wonders whether the 'ambiguity and multiple references' produced by art objects can result in 'the sort of intellectual tension that leads to a growth in under-standing' (1986: 134–8).

Phases of response to visual texts

The well-known art historian, Kenneth Clark, argued that there were four phases involved in appreciating visual works of art (1960: 69). First, he talks about a work of art having an *impact* on a viewer who gets a general impression of the picture as a whole, including subject matter, colour, shape, composition etc. If there is no impact, nothing will happen, so an engagement between the see-er and the seen is an essential starting point. If understanding is to follow, the next stage is *scrutiny* – careful looking. Clark describes this as the purely aesthetic stage of response where the critical faculties come into operation and reminds us of the importance of patience and persistence: 'Looking at pictures requires active participation, and, in the early stages, a certain amount of discipline.' As viewers look at the image, the third stage of *recollection* may follow where they make connections with their own experience, asking questions of the painting. Clearly this stage of the process involves thinking and leads on to the final stage which is *renewal*. The original image is re-examined more deeply, features previously overlooked come into focus, perhaps fitting into pre-existing knowledge. This could be described as looking, developing into *seeing*, through memory, imagination and thought.[2]

Clark's simple schema provides an illuminating framework in which to consider how the children in our study responded to picturebooks. The question of prior knowledge, understanding and exposure to visual texts comes into play. Some children drew on sophisticated repertoires of multi-modal reading and were familiar with literacy practices which centred on drawing meaning from texts; other inexperienced readers used what resources they had, making naive, instinctive responses to the books. This wide variety of experience of visual literacy, ranged at one extreme from a 5-year-old child recently arrived from another culture who did not yet speak English and who had little exposure to books, to confident, fluent readers of 11 with wide book knowledge who were already familiar with the artist's picturebooks.

Returning to Clark's schema, it was rare for the picturebooks to fail to make an impact on the children in our study, but in the odd individual (in one case a hyperactive child with a short attention span), little or no engagement occurred between viewer and text and so the activity was fairly worthless. (As teachers, of course, we would be concerned about those children and would want to develop strategies to aid concentration and help them find ways to take pleasure in books.) But for the vast majority of children in our sample, the impact of an appealing and challenging text encouraged them to move into the second phase of scrutiny.

Now scrutiny is obviously crucial; if real understanding is to follow, the child has to look carefully in a sustained way for some time. Looking is not easy. Think about your last visit to an art gallery. How long did you spend on individual paintings, sculptures or installations? (As we were writing this chapter, a friend rang to tell us that she and her partner, who are regular visitors at museums and galleries, had visited the Vermeer exhibition at the National Gallery and the Ingres to Matisse exhibition at the Royal Academy, between arriving in London before 11: 00 a.m. and getting the train back to Cambridge about 2: 00 p.m. – and that included lunch! Even with two smallish exhibitions of 50 paintings apiece, that allows for just over one minute per painting.) Most visitors do little more than glance at a work of art. It takes serious concentration to keep looking at the work as a whole, at individual parts of it, close up, further away, concentrating on a detail, thinking about light or colour or tone or genre, other work by the artist or other work of the same period, or back to taking in the sweep of the whole painting, and so on. Yet that serious, sustained looking is what most of the children aged 4 to 11 willingly agreed to do with our chosen picturebooks. The evidence for the value of that looking is in the rest of this book.

As you look, you have to think or, as Clark puts it, 'recollect'. This is also hard work, as the brain integrates the new knowledge with what we already know. But at the same time, other processes are likely to be going on which are more involuntary: memories of personal experience crowd in as the painting intersects with our lives in a text-to-life moment; ideas begin to bubble up and hints of deeper understandings begin to suggest themselves. This is the creative process at work which is a

mixture of imagination, fantasy, recollection and wonder – the unconscious in collaboration with cognitive activity. This is the moment
when a child says something insightful they didn't know they knew or
had never thought about before. It's when, for example, Lara (10),
suddenly realises the horror of captivity for animals after reading *Zoo*:

LARA: If you think about it, if you had to be put in a cage, that is
    where you would stay. You would stay there and I can't imagine
    living in that sort of conditions.
I: Did you think of that before you read the book?
LARA: No, I just thought about it a moment ago.

Finally, renewal; over and over again we found the children going back
to the books, looking at them almost with new eyes. In Clark's final
phase of response, the viewer may be 'looking at his own everyday
world in a way that was altered by looking at that picture' (Benson
quoting Clark 1986: 138). And the pupils in our sample made extraordinary progress in understanding *over the course of several hours*. What
couldn't they do if visual texts and art appreciation were given time
and status and became a serious part of the curriculum?

Multiple intelligences and visual literacy

Perkins is more interested in how exposure to works of art encourages
children to think analytically. Rather then produce a model of
aesthetic appreciation, he cites the characteristics offered to viewers by
works of art and relates them to young learners. (Some of these ideas
have already been discussed in chapter 1, so we just mention a few
further points for consideration here.) First, he talks about the *instant
access* offered by a work of art which 'can be physically present as you
think and talk, providing an anchor for attention over a prolonged
period of exploration. ... The image is here and now' (1994: 85).
Instant access is followed by *personal engagement*: 'Works of art invite
and welcome sustained involvement ... by their very nature [they are]
likely to stimulate one kind of spasm (sympathy, revulsion ...) or
another ... thinking is a passionate enterprise [calling for] concern and
commitment, spirit and persistence' (1994: 13). Many of the theorists
in this chapter recognise the importance of personal engagement in
looking at visual texts, but only Perkins alludes to the powerful reactions this can provoke, such as genuine passion in the eye of the
beholder, something we observed in many of the children in our study.

Perkins goes on to talk about works of art addressing a range of symbol systems through *wide-spectrum cognition*, which generates the involvement of multiple sensory modalities (e.g. spatial, pictorial, verbal). Finally, Perkins argues that art is *multiconnected*, linking social issues, aesthetic concerns, trends of the times, personal convictions, different cultures, 'creating opportunities to bridge thinking dispositions across to diverse other contexts explored in tandem with the work of art' (1994: 85). He is particularly excited by 'the challenge of transfer' where learning in one context impacts on another.

This 'model' is prefaced on Perkins' concept of *experiential intelligence*, 'the contribution of applied prior experience to intellectual functioning' and *reflective intelligence*, which refers to the knowledge, skills and attitudes that contribute to mental self-management. 'We can prompt our experiential intelligence, cajole it, aim it, redirect it, to arrive at more varied and deeper readings of the work before our eyes. … By cultivating awareness of our own thinking, asking ourselves good questions, guiding ourselves with strategies, we steer our experiential intelligence in fruitful directions' (1994: 82–5). Perkins' two kinds of intelligence saw many echoes in our study with the second, richer vein of thoughtful interpretation, emerging after some time had elapsed from first looking at the visual text.

Gardner first coined the notion of 'multiple intelligences' about twenty years ago, and has been writing and developing these ideas ever since. He believes human beings have at least eight different intelligences to varying degrees, including linguistic, logical-mathematical, musical, spatial, bodily-kinaesthetic, personal, naturalist and existential. The one that usually comes to mind in relation to works of art is spatial intelligence, but Perkins points to the interconnectedness of thinking involved in appreciating art, which inevitably draws on other intelligences. We certainly saw examples of many children using personal intelligence in our study (see chapter 7) and some also drew on linguistic, naturalist and existential intelligence.

Children responding to picturebooks

Madura (1998) of the University of Nevada makes reference to the work of Gardner, Perkins and other theorists considered in this chapter in her article on how children responded to the work of two American picturebook artists. Madura closely followed the progress of four 6-year-old learners as a teacher/researcher, documenting the reading and writing of these children in their natural setting, as well as working in one-to-one, paired and small-group sessions to explore their responses to visual texts. (It should be noted that Madura approached her teaching with a commitment to integrated literature/literacy approaches and consciously taught children about art and aesthetics. She was also keen to promote talking and learning, all practices which the authors of this book would thoroughly endorse.)

Madura's findings were as follows: *descriptive responses* to picturebooks involved retellings and plot summaries, though Madura does puzzlingly include within this category 'comments on illustrations and how they were created'. (It does seem to us that while the former were the most simple responses to be expected from young children, the latter were not necessarily so.) *Interpretive responses* included comments about the story, text-to-life and personal experiences; *thematic trends* showed the children appreciative of the artist/authors' themes, styles and techniques.

Madura then outlines a simple mode of instruction which begins by asking pupils 'to *describe* the book as a verbal and visual unit, to tell or *interpret* what they thought about it ... and then to find links (*thematic trends*) with past reading, writing and art production experiences' (1998: 374). Here Madura's emphasis on links with other knowledge and experiences strongly connects with Perkins' notion of 'multiconnectedness'. While Madura's model is less developed and precise than those already outlined, she provides an interesting account of her young learners' responses to multi-modal texts which has many parallels with our research.

Madura draws on Kiefer's work in one of the only studies where the researcher actually used picturebooks to investigate children's visual literacy. Kiefer constructed a developmental model of children's oral responses to picturebooks which she describes as 'useful for helping to understand how children *learn to mean* in the world of the picture book' (1993: 271). Drawing on Halliday's seminal work on functions of spoken language, Kiefer focuses on four categories employed by the children in verbal responses to picturebooks: *informative*, where comments focus on the content of illustrations, the story line, text-to-life observations and make comparisons with other books; *heuristic*, where problem-solving is involved, inferences are made and hypothetical language is commonly used; *imaginative*, where children enter into the life of the book, often using figurative language; and *personal*, where children express feelings and opinions, relate to characters and evaluate the illustrations.

Kiefer goes on to note developmental differences in the way children approach picturebooks. Noticing details seems to come first and, so strong is that urge, that children often see features that adults miss and, Kiefer suggests, sharing 'secrets with the illustrator may in turn help children become more sensitive to the artistic qualities in picture books. ... I found that they developed more critical thinking not only about cognitive factors but also about aesthetic factors and that this awareness was different depending on the age of the child' (1993: 278). She also mentions that awareness of the artists and their intentions seemed to develop in parallel with age, though 'all children seemed to be familiar with elements like lines, shapes, and colours, although they didn't always have the correct nomenclature.' Finally, Kiefer noted 'how children seemed to grow in understanding the meaning-making power of visual art' (1993: 278–9).

In general terms, we concur with these observations, but we would wish to point out that some younger children could reach remarkably sophisticated interpretations, if the conditions were right. (We also noted that Kiefer did not take any account of word–image relationships.) However, we would totally endorse some of Kiefer's closing comments: 'Books that engendered such deep emotions rather than those the children liked were the ones around which the longest-lasting response grew and deepened.' And her pupils, almost echoing the words of our pupils across the Atlantic, argued that 'an important criteria for a picture book was not to make it "easy for you to find things: but to make us think more"' (1993: 280). Her work further reflects our findings in emphasising the importance of giving children time to look and time to talk about pictures within a classroom community of readers in an atmosphere of 'mutual exploration' between pupils and teachers.

Parsons' developmental model for response to art

The most substantial developmental theory about the way people come to understand art is by Parsons (1987). He contends that children respond naturally from a young age to the aesthetic qualities of art. On the evidence of about ten years of somewhat eclectic research with a wide variety of adults and children, Parsons has come up with a set of stages of aesthetic response to art. The first stage he calls *favouritism* as 'an intuitive delight in most paintings, a strong attraction to colour, and a freewheeling associative response to subject matter. ... Most young children understand paintings at this level' (1987: 22). This stage is characterised by simple responses such as liking the subject matter or the colour of the picture. The second stage is characterised by *beauty and realism*, where the viewer recognises other people's viewpoints as well as her own. At this stage, realism tends to be favoured above other styles of painting. The third stage Parsons describes as *expressive*, when the feelings provoked by the work of art begin to become more significant and the viewer becomes more interested in the artist's intentions. The fourth stage focuses on *medium, style and form*: 'The new insight here is that the significance of a painting is a social rather than an individual achievement. It exists within a tradition, which is composed by a number of people looking over time at a number of works and talking about them' (1987: 24). In Parsons' final stage, *autonomy, judgement and dialogue* are the keystones: 'The result is an alert awareness of the character of one's own experience, a questioning of the influences upon it, a wondering whether one really sees what one thinks one sees' (1987: 25). This Parsons links with dialogue and reflection.

If Parsons' model is applied to our study, some of the children reach level 5 on aesthetic appreciation. This is clearly not what Parsons intended as he only expects a small number of adults well educated in visual literacy to reach this accomplished position. While we would agree with Parsons that most children's initial responses to art fall within categories 1 and 2, using his own criteria we can provide several examples of children fulfilling stages 3–5 in many regards. Accepting that all children reach level 1 as of right, let us take one of the key criteria in each stage and examine it in the light of our evidence.

Stage 2: realism

It is true that most children like realism in pictures. We have many examples of children making comments to that effect. One of the three picturebooks in our study was mainly realist in style (*The Tunnel*), while in *Zoo* Browne depicts the animals with almost photographic realism, contrasted with a mixture of realism and surrealism, as people turn into animals. However, the non-realistic aspects of *Zoo* were as appealing to the children as the realistic; while they loved the pictures of the animals, they were often as fascinated, by the strangely metamorphosing humans growing webbed feet, stripey bodies and tails. Kitamura's *Lily* does not use realism at all, drawing instead on a highly stylised style of painting, with many characteristics in common with the cartoon world into which most children have been saturated by exposure to television. None of the children seemed to find *Lily* less interesting or enjoyable because it deviated from realism. Our findings suggest that, although children do favour realism as a style of painting, they can find other styles of art equally absorbing and understandable. Many other best-selling picturebook authors, like Burningham, McKee, Carle and Sendak, do not use realism in their work. It seems more likely that children favour styles of art that amuse, delight and challenge them and that the range of styles which they take pleasure in and understand is much wider than Parsons suggests. Of course, the fact that his study only included paintings by famous artists, rather than narrative texts geared to children, may make a significant difference.

Stage 3: expressiveness

Children from 4 to 11 showed strong emotional reactions to the picturebooks. *The Tunnel*, a tale of conflict and reconciliation between siblings in a part modern/part fairy tale setting, provoked fear, sympathy and joy in equal measure; empathy and revulsion were the strongest feelings expressed about *Zoo*, which unleashed a debate about captivity and freedom; whereas the children who read *Lily* were aware of the menace in the text, but could distance themselves from it through the humour and the contrasting viewpoints of the two central characters. In response to all three books, the children not only talked about their feelings or related the subject matter intelligently to their own experience, but often considered the artist's intentions most thoughtfully when invited to do so by the interviewer. (See chapters 3–9) Our evidence suggests, therefore, that many of the children in our study reached level 3 of Parsons' hierarchy in the interview and discussion situation. How much this was brought about because of the nature of our questions and how much the children would have spontaneously achieved by themselves is a question we return to in the conclusion.

Stage 4: medium, style and form

In this category, Parsons is concerned with understanding the social and artistic context of a work of art and the sense of the artist working within a tradition. This is a sophisticated position which Parsons assumes only a minority of viewers will achieve. However, we should like to emphasise the number of times pupils made references to other books by the same artist, comparing and contrasting what they were doing in the book in question with his other work. For example, 4-year-old Amy is devoted to examining *Zoo* for the 'changes' she knows Browne makes in other books, including *Changes*. Before she was 3 years old, Evelyn's daughter, Isabel, on entering an exhibition of picturebook artists, shouted 'Lily' on seeing examples of Kitamura's work on the walls. These particular pictures were not taken from *Lily* which she was familiar with; Isabel had simply recognised Kitamura's style of painting. Many of the children in our study were very interested in how the artists had painted the pictures, what medium they were working in and why they used a particular style, voicing their opinions with confidence ('He's a good artist because..'). We would suggest that many of the children in our study fulfilled significant elements of stage 4.

Stage 5: autonomy, judgement and dialogue

We want to emphasise the serious, careful way most children examined the texts in our study. The interviews gave children the opportunity to take their time to think about the books in the supportive context of a one-to-one conversation with an interviewer. The discussions gave them the chance to listen to what others had to say, to exchange views with their peers and generally to collaborate in their learning. In so doing, their judgement was being extended by the research situation. We believe our evidence shows that children can be very good critics of works of art, if the conditions are right, giving them the sort of undivided attention which is usually only lavished on pictures by a small number of professionals. Schiller's (1995) work in a pre-school classroom in Ohio to test children's understanding of art conveyed through conversations tallied with Parsons' framework and endorsed our findings (1995).

All of the frameworks, models, schemas and theories we have briefly outlined in this chapter have something useful to offer in terms of understanding how children read image and most have contributed to the analysis of our data. The following two sections provide some of the empirical evidence for our assertion that time, careful looking and constructive dialogue enabled some children (including some of those who are very young or who do not speak English fluently or do not read print well) to make worthwhile judgements about pictures which were often profound, complex and richly interconnected with other ideas or symbolic systems, leading them to produce autonomous responses worthy of Parsons' elite stage 5.

Notes

1   Raney conducted a research project into visual literacy for the Arts Council and Middlesex University.

2   Clark's phases are similar to those used by others also attempting to describe the process of image decoding. Avgerinou and Ericson summarise several studies to arrive at four phases: 'a] description of the graphic elements composing the image, b] analysis of the ways those elements have been arranged, c] interpretation of the messages being communicated, and, d] aesthetic appreciation of the image' (1997: 286). The second two phases are usually considered to involve aspects such as the appreciation of the symbolic, the creation of personal associations and the critical evaluation of the image.

Part II

Looking and seeing

Children responding to picturebooks

Chapter 3

On a walk with Lily and Satoshi Kitamura

How children link words and pictures along the way

> I think you need the words really, to take the story along.
>
> (Lauren 11)

Lily is a cheery little girl who likes going for walks with her dog, Nicky. She watches the sunset, buys groceries and flowers, looks at the stars, says goodnight to the ducks, arrives back in time for supper and finally goes happily to bed. This is Lily's story and it is the story told by the words. But to understand why next to the smiling Lily there is always an anxious-looking Nicky, we need to 'read' the story told by the pictures. As Lily and Nicky take a walk, the pictures show us that the dog encounters (or he imagines), among other things, a snake, a tree with a wicked grin, a fierce-looking post-box, lamp posts with eyes, a vampire-like man emerging from a poster on the wall and various monsters. When they get home, Nicky seems to be trying to tell Lily and her parents what he saw, but they are not paying attention. Exhausted, he finally lies down, only to be plagued by a group of mice trying to get into his basket with a ladder!

Seeing things in a different perspective

Like the hen in *Rosie's Walk* (Hutchins 1970) who apparently never notices the fox that is following her, Lily goes out and returns home seemingly unaware of the creatures that frighten her dog. The text tells us that 'even if it is dark, Lily is not afraid because Nicky is with her'. Is she so confident with Nicky that she is oblivious to danger? Or is Nicky so neurotic that he will see monsters wherever he looks? Is it irony? Or perhaps, as one of the young readers we spoke to speculated (and not without reason), Lily is not afraid because she and her family are also ghostly monsters, a point which we will take up later.

Lily is a postmodern picturebook in the sense that it leaves the reader to deal with the questions mentioned above, fill in the gaps and resolve the ambiguities of the pictorial text (Styles 1996). These aspects belie the apparently simple narrative and lead the reader into a world of alternative meanings where fears can be dealt with through humour and irony. This picturebook is also illustrating one of the defining aspects of its genre: the relationship between image and written text. Lewis writes that 'the picture book always has a double aspect, an ability to look in two directions at once and to play off the two perspectives against each other ... the picture book is thus not just a form of text, it is also a *process*, a way of making things happen to words and to pictures' (1996: 109–10).

In *Lily* we have two characters, each literally looking in a different direction, and as their perspectives play off against each other, readers find themselves participating in the process of making a story happen. They perceive at least two contrasting versions of the same events at the same time and perhaps understand that reality is never quite simple. If this seems too complicated a concept for young readers, it is worth quoting Kathy (7) even if she is struggling to express her reply to why Lily and Nicky might always be looking in different directions: 'Because they might have different like ... say if Lily heard a joke and Lily laughed but Nicky couldn't laugh because he didn't get it ... so they might have different possibilities.'

Nikolajeva and Scott (2000) call this particular dynamic 'perspectival counterpoint';[1] it stimulates the reader's imagination because of the different possibilities of interpretation.[2] In the case of *Lily*, Nikolajeva and Scott argue that this dynamic is 'highly developed' and that '[t]he counterpoint between the two perspectives and the ambiguity of the actual events shape the book's impact and the reader's involvement in decoding it' (2000: 234–5). Certainly we found that, when the readers became aware of the counterpoint pattern, they began to anticipate it and to show they appreciated the humour of 'the jokes in-between the pages' (Lauren 11).

As in many of his other books, Kitamura's 'jokes' are part of a serious game he plays with the relationship between the illustrations and the written texts. In this particular picture he invites his audience to join Lily and Nicky as they walk along, encouraging readers to become aware of the complexities in postmodern narrative. As Meek (1988) tells us, it is the text that teaches what readers need to learn. It may be that some inexperienced readers will require more help in this understanding, and this is where the teacher should come in, as the more experienced reader who listens to the children's responses and asks the questions that will lead them to develop critical awareness of the text and of their role as readers.

But how do young readers learn how picturebooks work? How do they join the artist's game, if in fact they do? How do they make sense of the discourse of the pictures? How do they relate it to the words? And how do they deal with the incoherent and the incomplete? We now explore some of these queries as interviewers and children follow Lily and Nicky's footsteps through the picturebook.[3]

Walking with Lily and Nicky

The children became interested the moment they saw the cover and became keener as they turned the pages. The cover sets the tone for the rest of the book: the seemingly innocuous title which is Lily's story, together with the threatening background of blank, dark windows, empty streets and frightening monsters (see plate 7). It shows a smiling Lily carrying her groceries towards the left side of the page while Nicky stands facing the opposite way with a frightened look on his face, his eyes are wide open, his nose, ears and tail are pointing upwards and his mouth crumpled into a worried grimace. From Nicky's expression, the children – from the youngest to the oldest – gathered that there would be something menacing to come. This lured them to find out what he was scared of and to read the rest of the book. As Keith (10) said, '[You think] what's the dog scared of? So you like turn the page and then look and then just carry on reading and there's some more monsters and you just want to see the rest of it.'[4]

Despite the sinister atmosphere, the children expected a 'scary' but, at the same time, 'funny' book, because they were reassured by the cartoonish style of the drawing. Colin (8), for example, predicted it might be 'a bit like a comedy'. Readers become involved when they can form analogies between the text and their own experience. For example, Judy (6) was immediately interested because of a building which looks like a church she goes to; others spoke of their own or other people's dogs. Interestingly, for many readers (myself included), it was not until the first reading was over and the cover was scrutinised again, that they discovered what it was that Nicky was looking at: a frightening face made by trees with fierce-looking nostrils, bent lamp posts as eyes, and a mouth full of tree trunks with iron railings for teeth. At this point there was unanimous agreement that the cover was a good one for the book because, as Janet (4) put it: 'it looked like what was going to happen in the story'.

The title page belies the cover in that the dog is actually looking quite happy to be going for a walk. Perhaps this is because they are just starting out or because Lily is actually looking at him for once. Several children noticed the house in the background and wondered whether it was Lily's home. On the next page, back on the pavement, both characters are looking at the reader; Lily is smiling but Nicky is already looking anxious and seems to be inviting us to share in his apprehension.

Empathy also encourages involvement, and it was not surprising that most readers were more concerned about the feelings of the over-imaginative dog than with the child, while at the same time laughing – not unkindly – at him. This also allows quite young readers to enjoy the experience of feeling a little more grown up or mature than the characters in the book. Some of the children reasoned that the dog was worried because he was hungry or tired, but most of them realised it was because of what he might see on the walk. Several children commented on this direct gaze. Flavia (10) said it was as if someone was taking a picture of him from outside the book, while Selma (11) noted that they were looking at 'us, the reader'. Nikolajeva and Scott (2000) equate Lily's lack of observation or imagination to that of an insensitive parent (although they also question the dog's reliability), though this does not correspond to the representation of Lily as a child who enjoys the sunset and the stars and who likes animals (even bats!).

Next we have a double-page spread (like all the remaining pictures in the book), which shows them once again in the country or a park. Lily has her back to us as she admires the sunset, but Nicky is startled to see a snake as he lifts his leg against a bush. Several children said this was their favourite spread because of the rich colours, especially the blues and greens, and they also commented on the way the grass and the trees were drawn. Carol (10) liked the 'texture' and the way the trees looked 'scribbled' but were actually 'very carefully done'. As Lily walks along towards the right-hand corner of the page, Nicky's imagination really starts working. He looks behind him to see a tree giving him a wicked grin. Then, when Lily stops at the grocer's stall, his eyes widen in terror when he sees a post-box leaning over, with its open top full of pointed teeth and letters dropping from its 'mouth'. Some of the children mentioned the empty can and other litter in these two spreads, and, as we will see, they followed this trail and later reached the conclusion that Kitamura was saying something about pollution.[5]

As it gets darker, we find ourselves in one of the more frightening places on the walk: while Lily looks up at the stars, Nicky sees a face in the tunnel, a wide gaping mouth with lamp posts for eyes and traffic cones for teeth (see figure 3.1). The alley is dark and deserted like the rest of the streets, except for a skip full of rubbish. Most of the readers commented on the menacing atmosphere, the older ones being more specific about which details made it frightening:

> It's kind of scary, but it's funny because … street lights with just a tunnel wouldn't scare you at all, but it's just because it's together it makes it look real, like it's actually alive. … All the detail, like even the skip with the rubbish falling out, and another reason why it's frightening is because not only that the dog's not looking at her, but because the dog's on the other side of the wall looking at something and she's just kind of talking to herself.
>
> (Keith 10)

A younger child, Judy (6), was probably making an association with her own fears: 'Scary, there might be baddies' houses and as it is dark I thought there might be a baddie in [the skip].'

The evening has become purple and on the right side of the page, the moon appears and becomes one of the eyes, together with the clock on the tower, of an owlish-looking face with tree trunks for teeth and a lamp post nose. Nicky stares at it in horror while, on the other side of the page, Lily seems to be looking directly at us, although the written text says that she is waving to a Mrs Hall. Mrs Hall is not depicted; she would have to be facing Lily, where we, the readers are. This gap, the 'missing' Mrs Hall, was only a problem for the younger readers, some of whom said that she must be in one of the windows *behind* Lily. The older ones said rightly that she must be off the page: 'It's like you're Mrs Hall because she's looking at you, because you can't actually see the window … so she's waving to you' (Keith 10).

As she continues her walk, now almost in the dark, Lily points out to Nicky how clever the bats are, but he is shaking at the sight of a strange-looking man who is tipping his top hat with one hand and holding a glass of blood-coloured juice in the other. He seems to be coming out of a poster advertising tomato juice, bending a lamp post in the process and spilling tomatoes on to the pavement. Keith observed that the dog was not 'round' but 'fuzzy', which meant he's 'even more scared'. When asked what sort of man he was, the children used the picture's clues to define him as a witch, 'because it's got a witchy hat and coat' (Janet 4) or a vampire, 'because it's got very pale white skin and it's got a blood stain there [on the cuff]' (Hugh 9). Anne (9) even gave him a part in the narrative: 'He has that sort of spiky collar and

Figure 3.1 From *Lily Takes a Walk* by Satoshi Kitamura

Bats flitter and swoop in the evening sky.
'Aren't they clever, Nicky?' says Lily. 'Not far, now.'

Figure 3.2 From *Lily Takes a Walk* by Satoshi Kitamura

maybe he's pretending that's blood, blood juice and also there is a bat swooping around and going "Oh do not get near this poster or the evil bloodsucking vampire will have you for dinner!"' (see figure 3.2).

The next spread shows Lily saying goodnight to the ducks and gulls on one side of the bridge, while on the other a dinosaur or Loch Ness monster-like creature stares down at Nicky, who is rooted to the spot despite his fast-moving legs. All the children were able to explain why Nicky seems to have eight legs in this picture and some exemplified it by moving their own legs very quickly. In this spread, it is Janet (4) who gives a voice to the monster: ' "Aaaggg!". He's getting burnt [as he leans over the lamp post]'. There are still a few more monsters to terrify Nicky, popping out at him from rubbish bins before he and Lily get home. According to Keith (10) they looked '3D' and Carol (10) described how Kitamura's lines make them look scary: 'he's made them all like all different angles and all different triangle shapes and all sticking out and stuff and this one's just all straight, then zig-zagged'.

Once at home, over dinner, Lily tells her parents about her walk. We can see the father smiling but we can't see the mother's face. On the opposite page, Nicky has his mouth open, surrounded by little bubbles with the pictures of the monsters he has seen. Many of the children again showed their familiarity with the cartoonish style by saying these were the dog's 'speech' bubbles (one compared them to those in *Asterix* and *Tin Tin*): 'Well you can see the mother asking Lily and she's just like saying some nice things and he's just thinking of the things he's seen' Martin (7) (see figure 3.3).

As the text says, it's time for bed and Lily sleeps happily underneath the duvet with her name written all over it (only the older pupils noticed this). Nicky has also settled into his basket and is just about to relax when, as the flap over the last page opens, a group of mice give him a last shock by trying to climb into his basket with a ladder.[6] When asked how they felt about this picture before and after opening the flap, some of the readers remarked on the cosiness and messiness of her bedroom (and immediately compared it with their own) and at the same time remarked upon details which reminded them of the uncanny atmosphere, such as the fact that three of the stuffed animals look rather worried and sad, that the tiger in what is presumably Lily's drawing looks scared and that dark, blank windows are looking into her room. As Anne (9) rightly pointed out, it doesn't seem that Nicky will be happy anywhere because he will always find something to be frightened of: 'It's a place that Lily can be really comfy in and very

Lily's mother and father always like to hear what she has seen on her walk.

Figure 3.3 From *Lily Takes a Walk* by Satoshi Kitamura

happy, but Nicky can be like "Ooh this room!"' There's just something about everything that he can get very scared about.'

Doonan notes that 'The omnipresence of musical and artistic instruments reveals Kitamura's focus upon the inner life, as well as providing intertexual reference to the artist's own creativity, and indicates a source for the self-reliance and independence of his characters' (1991: 108). Although there are no musical instruments to be seen, Lily's room is decorated not only by a Kandinsky-like poster, a calendar and a seagull mobile, but also by her own drawings (or maybe original Kitamuras?) and her table is covered in art materials and a sketch of Nicky. Perhaps Lily, unlike Nicky, channels her imagination into her drawing, making her unafraid of encountering monsters on her walks.

Reading further into the picture

As readers and researchers walked along with Lily and Nicky, the responses gave us an insight into the more complex discursive aspects of this book in particular and of picturebooks in general. As we have noted, the most distinctive feature of *Lily* is the counterpoint between perspectives and it was this aspect we were keen to explore with the readers. In other words, we wanted to find out how they made sense of the interaction between words and pictures. Other responses that provided insights in relation to this main aspect were the following: readers' appreciation and awareness of visual features of text and artistic intentions; the implied reader and the children's own reading-viewing process and appreciation of the significance of the book as a whole.

Interaction between words and pictures

Almost without exception, the children thought the pictures were more interesting than the words. They felt that the book would still be good if you only had the pictures, but if there were only words it would be boring, especially, they added, for 'children'. There was definitely a belief that books with pictures (lots of them) were for younger children and the amount of pictures in books decreased in inverse ratio to the words as books were intended for older readers. However, some children did realise that only having the words would change the meaning of this particular book. Hugh's (9) comment about having only words was typical: 'you wouldn't be able to see what was happening'.

About the relationship between words and pictures in *Rosie's Walk*, Nodelman says, 'In showing more than the words tell us, the pictures not only tell their own story; they also imply an ironic comment on the words. They make the words comic by making them outrageously incomplete' (1988: 224). A similar interaction is taking place in *Lily* and it means that the reader must link not only the two different narratives – that of the printed text and that of the pictures – but also what the pictures are telling us about the printed text. As Nodelman says, they are showing them to be incomplete and therefore enhance the comedy of the narrative. It is not surprising that most of the younger readers struggled to express their understanding of this inter-action; what is surprising is that some of the older ones managed to explain it quite clearly.

I: Do you think the pictures are telling the same story as the words?
SELMA (11): Yes plus a bit more ... [the pictures] seem to bring out the story.

When asked if the words and pictures told the same story, most readers found it hard to separate them and answered yes, but some of the more engaged ones recognised they were different:

I: Do the words and the pictures tell the same story?
KATHY (7): A bit of a yes and a bit of a no because it doesn't say that like Lily is pointing to the leeks or something, but it does say 'today she ... '
I: So if the words are telling that story, who's telling the rest of the story?
KATHY: The dog.

The older pupils were more able to articulate the difference between the meanings derived from the written text and the pictures. For example, Flavia (10) pointed out that 'the pictures tell you about the monsters and the words just tell you what Lily thought'. Keith (10) described this in more detail, weighing up the contribution of both words and pictures:

[If it were only the words] it wouldn't be good because it would just be a happy book because it doesn't say anything about anything being scary. It's just saying she's not scared and she'll do her shopping, she looks at the stars, she walks past someone's house and waves. You wouldn't see the bats or any of those things that make it scary. ... Some books are better without the pictures because then you can make up your own thing, but I think this is better with the pictures … the words need the pictures more than the pictures need the words.

Invoking his previous experience as a reader, Keith recognises the difference between the two signifying systems and how they work upon the reader (the pictures make it scary). His statement also shows us the analytical process by means of which he arrives at a conclusion and makes a judgement on the value of these systems. It is an indication of the processes that are going on in the reader/viewer's head as they attempt to construct a story structure using different kinds of 'building blocks'.

Appreciation of visual features and artistic intentions

Questions about visual features were asked throughout the interviews with prompts about colour, pattern, perspective and body language. We also asked if they had found similarities with other Kitamura picture-books. Most of the children mentioned colour, and referred especially to the different shades of sky (later, many of them made an attempt to portray these skies in their drawings). They also noticed the cartoon-like patterns of the 'wobbly' lines, the uneven bricks, the flat wheels and the crooked windows. One 10-year-old boy described this style as 'realistic but not realistic'. This 'cartoon-like' style helps widen the distance between the straightforward textual narrative and the fantastic images. Other visual features that were mentioned included perspective (how the trees became smaller in the distance); where the characters were placed (for example, that Lily is always on the side furthest from the monsters and Nicky is nearest); and intertextual references (to Kitamura's *A Boy Wants a Dinosaur*).

The less experienced readers tended to provide less plausible expla-nations (with no basis in the text) for the way in which Kitamura draws lines. For example, they said the steps were wobbly because: 'they belong to a witch', 'they've been there for thousands of years' or 'a heavy man stepped on them'. The more experienced readers tended to give reasons that had more to do with logic (rightly or wrongly) than with the author's intention. Kathy (7), for example, said: 'It is hard to draw steps so he might wiggle a little bit 'cause he is worried about it, that he's going to do it wrong, so he's a bit shaky.' And Martin (7) considered how they added to the atmosphere, 'it's to make it scarier and to stand out more'.

Other children commented on the atmosphere created by the continual appearance of dark colours, the blank windows and empty cars. They described it as 'spooky' and 'upsetting'. Carol (10) spoke of the difference between these dark backgrounds and the way in which Lily and Nicky 'brightened it all up'. Martin (7) also remarked on this contrasting effect:

> It's very good, his use of colour, because he's like used all bright colours on her. ... I reckon he could have picked different [flowers] like roses or daffodils ... but he probably just chose a really bright colour: yellow. And he's chose a really dark colour for the houses.

Both Kitamura's characteristic colour and line were reflected in most of the children's drawings as they attempted to recreate the atmosphere in his pictures. Further examples can be seen in chapter 6.

The implied reader and children's own reading-viewing processes

Perhaps because the 10- and 11-year-olds had little opportunity to look at picturebooks both at home and at school, *Lily* was initially considered a book for younger children. This was also true of some of the 8- and 9-year-olds, because, they argued, if it were for older children it would have more writing and 'a bit more detail'. However, by the end of the interview day, this opinion was revised by many of the older readers, such as Peter (9):

> I think this book's interesting because ... children enjoy picturebooks but I think it's also better for older people because if they read it carefully they can like spot things, like what we're doing now, they can sort of have fun with it and spot things.

This and other answers show how their previous experience of books and their knowledge of the type of fiction we were reading comes to bear on their responses. Kitamura's cartoon-like style was an indication that it would be both a fictional and humorous book. Anne (9), for example, when asked if the monsters were real or imaginary, said: 'Well in books really anything can actually happen, it's just your own imaginary world so that could actually be happening.'

Asking a reader to describe what happens when he or she reads is always fascinating, especially when they are young children who are searching for a way to describe it (these processes are described further in chapter 9). Many answers revealed the importance that detail has for them. The older children described how they spot 'the problem' or the unexpected and then return to the 'normal' and put the two together:

PETER (9):   I look carefully and I see what may be the problem because you see the dog notices things that the girl isn't noticing so then I split the book into half and I see what Lily's seeing and really what she's saying … seeing and doing, and I will look at the dog and see what he's doing.

I: So you get sort of one side and then the other side?

PETER: And try and put them together.

Peter's description of what is going on in his head as he reads give us an indication of what children are noticing as they look at pictures. As they read, they are looking at the whole picture and connecting it to the words, as well as seeing through the characters' eyes and trying to pull all this information together. Their processes of deduction involved both imagination and common sense. Judy (6), for example, spoke of looking for clues to 'get things right'.

Readers were aware that they were joining in a kind of game which allowed them to go back and forth through the book to look for details they had missed in order to solve the puzzles. In this case, they had to work with two different characters, comparing and contrasting their actions and words (at least Lily's words) with the written and pictorial narratives (which also meant imagining what Nicky would say if he could). They were willing to work hard at making connections and coming up with explanations; evidently they were deriving great satisfaction from participating in the meaning-making process by piecing the picture together.

Significance of the book as a whole

One of the most difficult tasks for any reader is to be able to stand back from a text and view it as a whole; it is perhaps even more difficult when we are dealing with a book where two different discourses must be dealt with at the same time. Yet the children in the study showed that they were beginning to consider overall meaning at various levels. To begin with, we asked children whether they would describe Lily as 'funny' or 'serious'. Many of the younger readers said it was simply 'funny', while some of the older readers said it was both. They pointed out the humorous elements of the picturebook and the way in which Kitamura 'makes you laugh'. Hugh (9) summed it up by saying 'It's funny because the dog keeps getting scared and the little girl smiles.' In the children's drawings, Nicky is depicted as worried and Lily always smiles.

As the interviews and discussions progressed, the children raised moral and ethical issues which demonstrated that they were able to perceive more profound implications of this deceptively simple story. This occurred mainly in the group discussions. Often the researcher led up to some of these issues, but in other cases the readers arrived at some surprising conclusions as they discussed possible and alternative meanings. For example, in the following extract from a group discussion, 6- and 7-year-olds are debating whether the 'monsters' were really there or if they were a product of Nicky's imagination:

KATHY: I think he's just looking at it and then he thinks 'Oh no!'

JUDY: No, because it is in the dark, because he's staring in the dark and it makes them look different to what they really are.

JOHN: No, I think he's been watching TV about all this stuff. ... He's thinking of all this stuff and when he looks he sees them there, when they are not really there.

MARTIN: (Maybe it's a) person holding things up ...

SEAMUS: I think that it's that he looks at them and then he imagines that they're scary.

The children put forth their hypotheses, trying to explain it to themselves and the others, based on their own experience of dealing with imaginary terrors. Together they are struggling to reach beyond the literal to a level of understanding that shows psychological insight into the dog's behaviour.

The environmental issue was raised by some children who noted that litter appears in many of the pictures. Carl (8) read this as a message Kitamura was trying to put across through his book: 'he might be trying to tell people in just a picture in a little way to clear up your rubbish ... he might be saying to people who read the book to clear up your rubbish'. This idea was also brought up in the group discussion between 7- and 8-year-olds, and for one girl it involved an important consideration about viewpoint and perspective:

I: So the dog does notice all the rubbish doesn't he?

LAUREN: Because he's so small he might see it more, because it's a bit bigger than him.

By means of the two stories running alongside, Kitamura leads us to understand that the world can be seen from different perspectives. Selma (11) applied this idea to the fact that the 'vampire' and Lily's dad look quite similar. It is interesting to note that she also speaks of the importance of looking carefully at the text in order to notice this sort of detail and understand what she called 'the moral': 'People may look different in a different suit but they could be the same person. Some people may not realise that, they just look through it and they don't actually see the dad.'

The interviewer picked up on the idea of 'the moral' and as the children worked collaboratively, they reached a more satisfying explanation of what is going on in the book:

I:　Would you say that there were any other morals in this book?

LAUREN (11):　People believe in things but not everybody.

ANGUS (9):　From the dog's point of view when you are little things scare you more than when you are bigger … when you are little sometimes your imagination just wanders and then when you are older you can tell things look like that or not.

The last statement shows a grasp of how characters' perceptions can be different and how these differences may be responsible for their emotions and actions. It also shows an analogical understanding of how the ability to discern between reality and fantasy develops with age. Like Angus, by the end of the group discussions, many other children were showing signs of a much broader comprehension of the picturebook.

Looking and walking with Kitamura

In English schools, picturebooks are not often re-read and re-discussed because of the constraints of the curriculum. This means that many children remain at a more literal level of comprehension, in which they understand the plot sequence, facts and details, but find it difficult to construct meaning at a more critical level. We found that at first the children were trying to make literal sense of the gaps and incoherences, instead of being able to take a step back and comprehend how they worked within the whole of the story structure. The reading of books like Lily confounds the reader's expectations in a playful and at the same time thought-provoking manner. It forces even older readers such as Keith to look more carefully, resulting in a greater understanding of how the visual and verbal narrative can work together as well as a greater enjoyment of the text.

We also found that some of the children who were considered by the teachers to be 'struggling readers' turned out to be some of the more experienced and articulate interpreters of the visual; even those students who had particular learning disabilities were able to make meaning and in some cases actually expanded the possibilities of Kitamura's pictorial text. Such was the case of Charlie, whose slight autism made him speak slowly and not very distinctly (his extraordinary drawings are analysed in the vignette). It was Charlie who reasoned that Lily's white face, the fact that the family were drinking the same tomato juice as the vampire and the father's resemblance to this vampire, meant that Nicky was, ironically, living with a family of ghostly monsters. No wonder Lily wasn't afraid of the dark!

An earlier version of this chapter appeared in M. Anstey and G. Bull (eds) (2002) *Crossing the Boundaries*, Sydney: Pearson.

Vignette – 'getting the pictures in my head' (Charlie 9)

Charlie was not one of the four children interviewed individually about Kitamura's *Lily*. I first met him for the group discussion, where his extremely slow and hardly intelligible manner of speaking, as well as his reluctance to meet my eye, made him stand out from the rest of the children. He spoke so slowly that he was constantly interrupted (something he seemed to be used to) and it was a struggle to make the others let him finish. I was intrigued, however, by his interventions – short as they were – and particularly impressed when I saw his drawing. So much so, that I decided to re-interview him five months later after a brief talk with his teacher. She described him as 'slightly autistic' and said that he was registered as having special needs. However, she added, 'although he's slow, it's all up there'.

Charlie's first drawing is based on the 'tunnel monster' picture, where Lily is looking up at the stars (see figure 3.4). All of it is drawn with thick, determined lines. The left half of the picture is dominated by a brick lined arch filled with vivid turquoise blue pencil crayon. On either side of the arch stand two lamp posts bent inwards underneath the top of the arch giving the impression of two staring eyes. Inside stand two nearly identical houses with a perfectly balanced window and door in the centre of each. Nicky's state of mind is revealed by the squiggly, uncertain line that is his mouth. As with the rest of the drawing, Charlie has paid great attention to detail and the dog is carefully patterned with spots and black paws. Both Lily and Nicky are drawn in profile and this is particularly interesting because only a few of the other children attempted to draw the characters from this perspective. In his attempts to get it 'right', Charlie has rubbed out Lily's face once before carefully redrawing her hair and the shape of the side of her nose.

At the beginning of the re-interview, I asked Charlie why he had chosen to draw this particular picture. He said it was because that page 'looked really spooky, because it looks like a horrible monster, like the mouth'. It was also his favourite picture in the book because of 'the way the path goes like

Figure 3.4 By Charlie (9)

into the mouth' and the way Kitamura had drawn the lines. As these comments reveal, Charlie was very perceptive about Kitamura's actual drawing style. He mentions the 'lines' twice and also that 'the colours are good and like that's quite scary … because her [Lily's] skin is very white.'

The other aspect of Charlie's reaction to the pictures revealed by these comments was his sensitivity to the atmosphere in the book. He explained that the lines made things look scary, 'and the black walls too, the rubbish on the ground is also scary, and kind of crooked tyres and crooked sticks'. He mentioned that he often had trouble going to sleep after watching a scary video. Kitamura's images also haunted him: 'When I read this book it made me think of bats when I was in bed.'

During the group discussion he scrutinised a copy of the book, pointing out the monsters to the others. After several interrupted and unintelligible remarks, he pointed out that the father in the penultimate picture looks 'just like' the man in the poster and that Nicky was feeling 'a bit sick and thinking, "No, go away!" to those horrible things in his mind'. When at the end of the discussion I asked the children what they would like to ask the artist, Charlie said 'Well I'd like to ask him if that was Lily's Dad and were these things actually really happening or Nicky was just thinking he'd seen them.' It seemed to worry him whether the monsters were 'real' or just a product of Nicky's imagination. When I spoke to him five months later I asked him what he remembered most about the book. He said: 'the looks of things … they look like spooky things'. I asked him what Kitamura wanted to make the readers think. He replied: 'that the town is haunted … he's trying to say that there are monsters and horrible scary things, or maybe he's [Nicky] just imagining them'. Charlie thought he could make out more monsters in Lily's room (made of windows) and claimed: 'If [Nicky] looked out the window he would see more scary things.'

During the re-interview, I read the book to him slowly, letting him comment during the reading if he wished. Then I asked him the same questions I was asking the other re-interviewed children but tried to give him as much time as possible to answer. Even so, he did not say very much because of the effort it took him to speak, and much of what he said was refining the ideas he had tried to put across during the group discussion. He had no problem under-standing what the story was about: 'Lily is having a good time but Nicky is not having a very nice time on the walk ... the pictures tell his story and if he tells it the people wouldn't believe him.' So he has noticed that the words and the pictures are telling different stories.

The picture he chose to represent in his second drawing is the one with the 'vampire' man and the bats, which had evidently made a strong impression on him and, like the first one, it shows an outstanding ability to draw as well as an understanding of Kitamura's style (see figure 8 in plate section). In this drawing there is also an example of his hand-writing, which reveals his meticulous interest in shape. The letters have been laboriously delineated as if he had been thinking carefully about each of them. The drawing bears many of the characteristics of Kitamura's original drawings such as the accurately hatched blue sky which dominates the composition. Apart from the predominant blue colour, the picture is drawn almost entirely in black felt tip, with a red sea of tomatoes on the poster spilling down onto the pave-ment.

In this drawing Lily has become more 'ghost-like' because only her yellow hair and red shoes are coloured. The man coming from the poster is very similar to that of the original, with his round cartoon eyes, U-shaped nose and arching semi-circle smile – again, carefully thought-out shapes. Lily and Nicky are drawn in a similar position and profile to the first picture but here is a more accurate depiction of the side on view with only one arm showing. Charlie's drawing also shows development in terms of movement (another aspect which few pupils tried to depict) with Lily's back leg bending at the knee as she walks forward.

Of all the drawings we showed him, it was Charlie's that most caught Kitamura's eye when he saw them; he even said he wished he had thought of the composition himself! Kate Rabey, who analysed the other 'Lily' drawings in the study (see chapter 6), also found that Charlie's art work stood out, particularly in its attention to detail (e.g. the lamp on the post is shaped exactly with pointed pattern on the top, split into two panes and anchored on three triangular-shaped supporting struts). She was also surprised by the boldness of his line and use of colour, suggesting it reveals a confident, definite use of drawing materials. She surmised this must be a child who draws a great deal (noticing, for example, the repeated schema of the house and the figures, almost identical but subtly improved in between the two sessions). It also seemed to me that he was carefully trying to reproduce the menacing atmosphere which so impressed him.

Not surprisingly, Charlie told me that he prefers pictures over words 'because they help you with the story, only words would be boring'. When faced with books without pictures, his approach is to 'get the pictures in my head, imagine them'. He certainly did not lack imagination, especially when he reasoned that Nicky was so afraid because he realised the whole family were ghosts! He came up with this idea after pointing out Lily's face is 'white' (colourless), that the father is like the 'vampire' and that the family were drinking tomato juice.

Fortunately, Charlie's teacher was aware 'it was all up there' and the fact that she selected him for the interviews meant she was confident that he would have something to say about pictures. The obstacles in verbally expressing himself completely disappeared when he communicated through the visual. His engagement with the picturebook was intense and it is this intensity he manages to express to us only through his drawings.

Notes

1   'Dependent on the degree of different information presented, a counter-pointing dynamic may develop where words and images collaborate to communicate meanings beyond the scope of either one alone' (Nikolajeva and Scott 2000: 226).

2   Nikolajeva and Scott (2000 and 2001) include a section on *Lily* both in their book and in an earlier article. Their insights on the word/image dynamic is useful for understanding *Lily*, however, we differ in the interpretation of some of the images, as they see the 'monsters' as more menacing than humorous and seem to have misinterpreted some of them, such as the 'giant', which is not emerging from a shop window but from an advertising poster (and playing with advertising billboards is a common feature in Kitamura's work).

3   *Lily* was read in two of the seven primary schools that participated in our project, one in Cambridge and one in Essex. Only one of the interviewed children had read the book before, and only a couple remembered other Kitamura books they had read. The interview schedule for *Lily* can be found in the Appendix.

4   Keith was described by his teacher as of 'middle ability'. He was a bright, articulate boy who spoke of *Lily* as a book for younger children, yet he became more and more involved in it and particularly in the relationship between words and images. He is therefore frequently quoted throughout this chapter and is an example of the way in which picturebooks can stimulate older children's understanding of visual literacy.

5   When asked about this particular point in the interview, Kitamura admitted that he might have made the reference unconsciously. See chapter 10.

6   Harvey (7) recreated the flap in his own drawing.

Chapter 4

A gorilla with 'grandpa's eyes'

How children interpret ironic visual texts – a case study of Anthony Browne's *Zoo*

I always remember pictures. I sometimes forget words.

(Amy 5)

He doesn't just want to say the animals want to be free – blah, blah, blah. He leaves you to find it out a bit better ... makes you keep thinking about things.

(Erin 7)

A visual analysis of *Zoo*

The story is an account of a family visit to a zoo, which interrogates the ideological concept of zoos, and of man's relationship with animals, delivered in a multi-stranded narrative. ... The family and its backgrounds are depicted in comic book style, with clean outlines, minimal modeling and (with the exception of Mum) in plenty of bright, saturated hues, in lightly framed pictures generally, which occupy about a third of the page area. The animals and their enclosures are portrayed in black framed full plates, painted in Browne's meticulous non-photographic realist style, with intense care to selected details and textures. Each animal has a grave and beleaguered natural beauty set in contrast with unsympathetic materials – concrete, brick, cement shuttering – from which their environments have been structured. ... The composite text both questions the value of caging wild animals for the casual pleasure of the majority of visitors, and at the same time communicates the sad truth that humans also construct metaphorical cages through the ways in which they construct the world.

(Doonan 1998)

With her usual flair, Doonan gives a telling description of Browne's prize-winning book. The dramatic cover features black and white, vertical, wavy lines which most children interpret as reference to a zebra which is, in fact, missing from the list of animals encountered in the book. 'Well, it's just like a zebra, the stripes of a zebra I think and … that's kind of symbolising a zoo really' (Joe 10). It is also suggestive of the sort of puzzling optical illusions so favoured by artists like Escher. It could be a postmodernist joke, as *Zoo* is an unstable text with surrealistic fantasies side by side with hyper-real illustrations. Instead of zebra stripes, those lines could represent the bars of cages dissolving before our eyes. Nothing is what it seems. From the cover in, it is clear this is not going to be a conventional family outing (although that is more or less what it is in the written text) and the reader will be taken on a confusing but rewarding journey.

There is also a book-shaped insert of the central family on the cover with an oversized father, a small, young-looking mother, plus two boys. The male family members are in the foreground looking happy and confident, wearing bright, colourful jerseys, whereas Mum (reminiscent of the mother living in a sexist household in Browne's *Piggybook*) almost disappears into the background, looking straight at the reader with a serious face. Unusually, the only lettering on the front or back cover is the title and the name of the author which are in large, white, bold print. The typography hints at eyes (gazing on the reader?) in the two 'O's of ZOO. In contrast, the word 'Zoo' is picked out in black lettering on the title page, which also depicts a hamster in a cage full of colourful accoutrements, the same colours as the clothes of Dad and the boys.

The dominance of black and white is further emphasised in both endpapers, one side white, the other black, an unusual choice and clearly there for a purpose. It suggests there is going to be a debate going on in this book; or perhaps it is raising the issue of right and wrong, good and bad, two sides of the same coin? It is for readers to decide by analysing the pictures; Browne raises questions rather than providing answers and the story told in words is often at odds with what is revealed in the pictures. Young readers soon learn (if they haven't already discovered from earlier encounters with Browne's books) that everything in the visual text is significant and they are going to have to work hard to carve out the meaning for themselves. Fortunately, this is an enjoyable process, as Browne is extremely funny and children laugh a lot as they read the book.

Ironic picturebooks

Most children read *Zoo* as a book which is severely critical about animals being held in captivity, but there is no reference to this in the written text except for Mum's final comment: 'I don't think the zoo really is for animals. I think it's for people.' Otherwise, all the evidence for an authorial stance critical of zoos comes from the pictures. For children to judge that this is a book about how humans treat animals and about captivity and freedom, they have to be able to interpret irony and read moral ideas into pictures.

Zoo could be described as a prime example of an ironic picturebook as Kümmerling-Meibauer explains: 'Ironic meaning comes into being as the consequence of a relationship, a dynamic, performative bringing together of the said and the unsaid, each of which takes on meaning only in relation to the other' (1999: 168). This irony makes demands on the reader to use inference to detect contradictions between what is said in the written text and illustrated in the picture. She goes on to underline the difficulties irony poses for younger readers, suggesting that:

> children do not acquire a full understanding of this concept in comparison to other linguistic phenomena until relatively late. ... The groundwork for understanding irony is often laid first not in verbal but in graphic images that act as visual equivalents to tone in oral storytelling and that can serve to play with or cast doubt on a straight-faced text.
>
> (1999: 167)

Nodelman (1988: 222) devotes a whole chapter of *Words About Pictures* to consider irony in multi-modal texts: 'They come together best ... when writers and illustrators use the different qualities of their different arts to communicate different information. When they do that, the texts and illustrations of a book have an ironic relationship to each other.' While Nodelman argues that picturebooks are 'inherently ironic', Kümmerling-Meibauer prefers to emphasise the reader's role in recognising irony through paratextual clues and other visual hints which often contradict or subvert the written texts. These operate as triggers to suggest that the viewer should be open to other possible meanings, thus encouraging the development of metalinguistic skills. She also emphasises the hard intellectual work involved in interpretation of such indeterminacy which forces the reader 'to prise open the gap between the text and the pictures, working on the relationship between them' (1999: 167–76).

Nikolajeva and Scott (2001) also talk about the tension between the two different sign systems creating 'unlimited possibilities for interaction between word and image in a picturebook', also using the term 'counterpoint' to describe the dynamic between them. They go on to outline different kinds of 'counterpoint', many of which apply to *Zoo* – i.e. counterpoint by genre (e.g. realism and fantasy side by side), style (e.g. use of different artistic styles), in perspective (e.g. contradiction between ideologies), of paratexts (e.g. titles and covers). It was evident in our study that most of the children, even the very young, were aware of, and responded to, tensions within *Zoo* and that this was one of the features of the book they found so intellectually challenging and absorbing.

Seeing and thinking

Browne uses surrealist techniques to make connections between human beings and animals; people begin to metamorphose as the visit progresses. At first there is just the hint of a tail, a banana, or a fur coat, but soon we have people growing webbed feet, hooked noses and monkey faces (see plate 3). On most double spreads animals, often alone, are presented within their cages with the colours, light, caging and body language emphasising their isolation. On the left-hand pages, in contrast, Dad, the boys and other visitors to the zoo appear in bold colours, often in bright sunlight under a blue sky with billowing Magritte-type clouds, something the children always notice. The visitors often behave thoughtlessly, intent on their fun and dismissive of the animals. Throughout the book the animals are portrayed sympathetically in contrast to the bizarre-looking humans, displaying (often most amusingly) shallow and boorish behaviour. Although the zoo is newish, architect-designed and relatively clean, the emphasis is on harsh, synthetic materials; the reader is positioned outside the cages until half-way through the book when the standpoint moves just inside for an even closer experience of the misery of captivity.

What came over most forcefully in the interviews and group discussions based round Browne's *Zoo* was the children's engagement with the text and their willingness to spend time analysing its meaning.[1] What we saw, even with the young children, was what can only be described as intellectual excitement with the ideas raised by the book and aesthetic pleasure in the images. It was as if *Zoo* offered an invitation that children felt compelled to take up. Here are Lara (10), Joe

(10), and 5-year-old twins (part of the pilot study) explaining why the pictures were a priority for them.

LARA: The writing doesn't explain everything what you think about …
the writing only explains what the book is about and what is
happening, but it doesn't explain what you feel and what they feel.
So I like the pictures better because then you can think more stuff [our
emphasis].

JOE: I think I found the pictures more interesting really because the text
does help me to know what is going on in the family, *but the pictures
show what it's really like* and what's going on with the animals [our
emphasis].

R AND F: Pictures are better.

F: 'Cause we can understand it more. We can't read very well, but *we
can understand it by the pictures* [our emphasis].

Motivation was high from the moment children started looking at the
front cover of *Zoo* and, almost without exception, they were eager to
engage with the book after it had been read to them by their class
teachers. Although this enthusiasm was evident in all the children
(whether they had seen the book before or not did not seem to make a
difference), those below the age of 7, unsurprisingly, found it much
harder to answer the questions in interviews than those of 7 and above.
Furthermore, children below the age of 7 were usually satisfied with
seeing things in the text; older pupils wanted to pursue the how and
why of Browne's artwork.

By the group discussions at the end of each interview day, it was always
evident that the children's thinking had moved on. Aspects of the book
that individuals had failed to comprehend in interviews were often
sorted out when they began talking together. Group dynamics were interesting. For example, Joe was regarded by his teacher as a very good reader
and was the most academic of the 10- and 11-year-old children. He made
thoughtful responses in interview, but held back during the discussion.
This could be for reasons of personality; perhaps he was confident enough
to form his own opinions without voicing them aloud, or perhaps the
more forceful members of the group held him back? However, if there was
any doubt about his emotional investment in *Zoo*, a glance at his
powerful drawing of an elephant would cast it aside (see plate 4).

The children were assiduous at noticing details in *Zoo* and were
keen to interpret every last image. They all enjoyed the humour, but

thought the book more serious than funny. This is probably one of the reasons for Browne's popularity with young readers: the combination of intellectual challenge, aesthetic pleasure, amusement and intriguing 'puzzles' to unravel.

Perplexing features of visual texts

There were some instances of imagery which adults tend to find straightforward, once they have been pointed out, but which proved perplexing to most children. For example, on the first page a snail is poking out of the top right-hand section of the picture, ahead of the traffic jam leading to the zoo, while cars and people acquire animal characteristics. This is presumably an ironic joke by Browne, saying that the traffic is moving so slowly that even a snail could go faster. We should not have been surprised that children found this difficult since Kümmerling-Meibauer reminds us that such irony requires sophisticated metacognitive awareness and, perhaps, familiarity with metaphorical linguistic terms and their application, such as 'going at a snail's pace' or 'the traffic was crawling along'. Children came up with every conceivable suggestion for the snail's role on the opening page. Here are some examples by groups of 5-, 8- and 10-year-olds:

YU (4): To make it beautiful.
ASHOK (5): Because *Bear Hunt* had lots of different things and perhaps he thought he could put lots of different things into this book as well [a nice example of intertextual awareness].
PAUL (5): I think he's jumping off the roof.
ASHOK: Because he wanted to get to the lions first.

SOFIA (8): Well, the man in the van must have like pushed him off.
EYLEM (8): It shows you to like … change the page.
I: It tells you to … go to the next page. Is that what you mean?
EYLEM: Yeah [a good try, but incorrect].

MIKE (10): Well he might like snails.
GIOVANNI (10): 'Cause he can see the traffic jam, people shouting and arguing and it gives you an idea of the snail is fed up and he's trying to get away from it.

In the final discussion, most children of 7 and above solved the snail conundrum together with some guided questioning by the interviewer. The children's problems with interpreting the snail[2] serve to highlight the extraordinary analytical ability shown elsewhere by so many children about other pictures in the book.

Affective and moral dimensions of Zoo

One of the reasons the children were encouraged to work at an analytical level in examining *Zoo* is that they were emotionally involved with the book. Vygotsky taught us about the interrelationship between the intellect and emotion, arguing for 'a dynamic system of meaning in which the affective and the intellectual unite ... every idea contains a transmuted affective attitude towards the bit of reality to which it refers'. Vygotsky believed that thought processes were inevitably linked to 'the fullness of life, from personal needs and interests, the inclinations and impulses of the thinker'. And he goes further: 'Imagination and thought appear in their development as the two sides of opposition ... this zigzag character of the development of fantasy and thought ... reveals itself in the "flight" of imagination on the one hand, and its deeper reflection upon real life on the other' (Vygotsky 1986: 10).

There were some features of the book that most children, regardless of age, were able to comprehend and articulate. Perhaps most noticeable was an empathy with the suffering of the animals, often linked to statements of personal analogy. This was generally accompanied by criticism of the way humans behaved towards animals. Joe (10) summed up the book's message neatly. 'I think he's trying to get across that we are more like animals than animals really ... like it says on the last page ... the zoo is more for humans than animals.' Most of the children interviewed were critical of the poor conditions in which the animals were held and very concerned about their apparent unhappiness. (Again, this is never mentioned in the written text and has to be inferred from the pictures.) The older the children, the more concerned they were with the ethics of keeping animals in captivity. This strong moral viewpoint was also evident in the drawings of this age group, which either showed humans and animals in role-reversal situations or pictures which contrasted the misery of the animals in captivity with the joyousness of freedom, expressed in the use of bright and dull colours. Sue (10) joined the discussion, but was not an interviewee. She had only had one quick reading of *Zoo*, but she quickly gets straight to the heart of it:

SUE: Well, it was about how lonely (the animals) were in the zoo ... and the people were being nasty and just wanted to look at the animals. ... They didn't seem to realise how miserable the animals were ... it is not just a trip to the zoo. It is thinking about how the animals feel and how the people. ... They should be given more freedom. ... The animals are acting better than the people. The people are acting like animals or what we think animals act like.

The children read emotion in Browne's pictures with great subtlety and their empathy was often extended towards the mother who shows concern for the animals' plight and appears ashamed of the bad behaviour exhibited by her husband and children. Here's Sue again, observant of Mum, and understanding what it means to show rather than tell: 'Perhaps she felt sorry for the animals, because all the way through it suggests it.' Les (10) also noticed that Mum might be disapproving as 'she's just standing there and everyone else is smiling'. Even 5-year-old Amy was able to articulate in her second interview that 'Mum is sad – she thinks the animals should be going free.'

AIDAN (10): She doesn't like the animals being in the cage 'cos when they was looking ... I think it was at the gorilla or something like that ... she said 'poor thing'.

I: Right. So she doesn't ... like the animals being caged in the zoo?

MIKE (10): Because she's a very serious-looking lady that she er thinks the animals should be free, so she probably ain't in that picture because she's like wandering off all upset that the animals are trapped.

Many children found the image of the orang-utan very moving (see plate 2). Browne emphasises a sense of desolation as the animal crouches dejectedly in a corner of a domestic-looking cage with his back to the jeering visitors. The only objects in its space are bits of faeces and empty shells. In contrast, the increasingly animal-like visitors (who include Magritte, Catwoman and D. H. Lawrence!) bang on the glass in derision. Here is an extract from the discussion of 10-year-olds who humanise the orang-utan, perhaps for greater identification with him:

SUE: Because he is sort of similar to a human, he should be treated like a human.

LARA: Because he looks like he's got hair coming down ... it has got really long hair.

SUE: And it has got hairy ears.

TONY: And it has got grey hairs like an old person.

SUE: He looks like he's got his hair in a bun at the top and like ...

I: How do you know he's sad?

JOE: Because you don't just crawl up into a corner, just turn away, for no reason. You can't be happy when you're like that, you can tell that he is not happy.

A 7-year-old in interview showed how she could read the environment:

I: How do you think the orang-utan is feeling?

ERIN: Very sad.

I: What makes you say that?

ERIN: Well if he's not showing his face then it might be because he's sad and he just doesn't feel like it.

I: Is there anything else that suggests he might be sad?

ERIN: Well if you look really, he hasn't got anything around him. Like the elephant, no natural habitat.

The 4- and 5-year-olds in interview also realised the orang-utan was unhappy:

I: How do you think the orang-utan is feeling?

AMY: Sad.

I: You think he's feeling sad? And what makes you think he's feeling sad?

AMY: Because he's sitting in the corner.

Analysing visual imagery

Kümmerling-Meibauer discusses the textual markers and paratextual clues that encourage readers to recognise irony in picturebooks operating 'as triggers to suggest that the viewer should be open to other possible meanings, thus encouraging the development of metalinguistic skills' (1999: 168–76). What follows in the next few sections are some examples of children recognising textual markers, noticing switches in artistic styles, analysing colour imagery, noting changes in points of view and filling in semantic gaps.

Younger children were fascinated by the changes that kept appearing in Browne's humorous, comic-style art work. They also kept commenting that reading this text was like solving a puzzle.

ARJANIT(10): You know where the 'em the gorilla is ... that looks like a puzzle and it's like ... he's puzzled they're looking at him like that.

I: Why do you like his pictures?

AMY (4): Because he hides things.

There were many examples in the transcripts of the children's understanding of how Browne used frames to emphasise the captivity theme. Doonan (1998): 'There are hand-drawn frames thin as threads (depicting humans), their outlines wavering and bulging at times almost like breathing. ... There are rigid frames (for the animals), black save for one yellow, and one grey. The apparently small detail like type of frame becomes a vital sign in the discourse.'

I: Why do you think he puts that big black line round the animals?

AMY (4): Because the edge of the cage is black.

ERIN (7): They're all barred up like they can't get out, and it's not very nice.

TINA (10): Yes, on the little picture there is hardly any, but then on the big pictures (of the animals) there is a big, black outline round the pictures ... on this page it hasn't got a border at all, so it is like he's an animal and he is also free.

The children were also able to talk about how the viewer was positioned, confirming their hunches about the text with reference to Browne's use of colour imagery, perspective and body language.

TINA(10): I've got two things to say. That the big animals have got little bits of wood and the things like the gorillas and the monkeys and the lions have all got bars, so really they haven't got much freedom. And it doesn't look very healthy around there, because it is all really grey on the page.

SUE (10): He's chosen quite pale colours and nothing too bright ...

TINA: It is like the giraffe; it's got all dull skies around it, so it seems like there's a factory somewhere near the zoo and letting lots of fumes just near it.

They were also quick to notice Dad's behaviour linked to body posture.

SUE: Because he's a more dominant person and he's shouting and bossing people about all the time.

TINA: He's always big in pictures and there's one picture where he is standing up and he's got two clouds like that and he looks like the devil.

Figure 4.1 From *Zoo* by Anthony Browne

The children had no difficulty in analysing most of the visual metaphors. For example, Browne is clearly making a pointed analogy when he paints a butterfly, perching freely on fresh green grass in identical colours to the tiger who paces across the parched grass of his high metal cage (figure 4.1). This was not lost on some 10-year-olds.

LARA: He is kind of like saying the butterfly is free but the tiger isn't.
TINA: It makes you think the tiger has been walking around that bit for ages and made a shape of himself.

The 7-year-olds:

ERIN: Well outside they're free and happy, but inside he's really sad.

And the 4- and 5-year-olds:

AMY: The butterfly's the same colour as the tiger.
I: Why do you think he put a butterfly out there on the grass?
AMY: Because butterflies live outside.
I: And do you see the colour of the grass there [lush green outside]? But what about the colour of the grass in his cage [dull green inside]?
PAUL: Because it's like a desert inside his cage.

This example shows development of visual understanding linked quite clearly with age. The youngest children have noticed connections between the butterfly and the tiger and the first glimmerings of understanding that they represent the concepts of captivity and freedom. Although this is a sophisticated idea for 4- and 5-year-olds to grasp, we believe their responses show that they do. This is backed up in the children's drawings. Five-year-old Amy observes the size differentials between the family members looking at the tiger with fierce claws dwarfed by his large cage. She also notices the grass outside the cage. Ten-year-old Bella is trying something quite sophisticated and 'Brownesque' as the tiger's stripes appear to be melting into the background. Both depict the butterfly outside the cage. (The children's drawings appear in chapter 6.)

Paul's analogy, likening the grass to a desert, shows his imaginative interpretation of the picture. By the age of 7, children were able to provide a simple explanation, linking freedom with happiness and captivity with sadness. (The word 'sad' was probably the adjective used most frequently in relation to *Zoo* by children from every age group.) By the time they reach 10 years old, children are capable of articulating the visual dichotomy. 'He is kind of like saying the butterfly is free but the tiger isn't.'

A gorilla with 'grandpa's eyes'

The image of the gorilla is one of the most powerful in *Zoo* (figure 4.2), partly because he gazes directly at the reader/viewer and 'you are required to enter into an imaginary relationship with the gazer', as Doonan puts it (1998). This dignified, wise-looking gorilla seems young at the top of the picture and older at the bottom, depicted against a structure which could be a cage or a window, but also forms the shape of a cross. (Browne himself once described this picture as 'my first crucifixion'.) Adults may be familiar with such symbolism from religious paintings and visits to churches, though most do not see the connection until it is pointed out to them. None of the children were aware of the religious iconography

Figure 4.2 From *Zoo* by Anthony Browne

suggested by the gorilla framed within a cross during individual interviews. Joe (10) came closest and did notice it in his interview, but he wasn't quite ready to go one step further to make the connection with the crucifixion.

JOE: I think it's interesting the way they've made a white cross right through the middle of the picture and I think it's to show that he's trapped inside this cage. That he drew this thick line to show the cage lines ... and he can't get out and he looks ... he's got a really sad expression on his face.

I: What might the cross symbolise?

JOE: I think it symbolises that he's just ... he can't get out because there's all these wires stopping him ... and he just doesn't have the freedom and he can't run around in the wild. He can just sit there while there's all these people staring at him.

One researcher did not pursue this line of questioning in the group discussion since none of the children had made reference to it. The other researcher, however, was very interested in the symbolisation of the gorilla as a Christ figure. Consequently, she was tenacious in her questioning on this issue, not least because she believed the children themselves were aware of some symbolic meaning, judging by their voices and their body language. After discussing Browne's use of frames, cages and bars in the group discussion with the 10-year-olds, she draws their attention back to the cross:[3]

I: Look at this shape. Does it remind you of anything else? We've said windows; we've said bars of cages. Is there anything else this shape reminds you of?

TINA: It reminds me of a sad thing that happened, when Jesus got crucified on the cross and like the monkey is thinking that he might ... [voice tails off]

Children as young as 7 eventually noticed the connection in the group discussion.

I: Yes, but there's something else. There's something else. Look at that cage. There's something else in that cage.

ERIN: There's been no white bits in between ... because like it looks sad and kind of like he don't want to see in his ...

CHLOE: It's like Jesus's cross.[4]

Finally, here's Amy (now 5) and Yu on a second interview, answering the question, 'Why do you think Browne makes us look at things this way in the gorilla picture?'

AMY: It's like a cross ... makes me feel sad ...
YU: He's got like ... a grandpa's eyes.

Empathy and personal analogy

On the final spread, the boy who is the narrator of *Zoo* sits with head in hands while the bars of a cage are shadowed against his body (figure 4.3). All the mischief seems to have ebbed out of him and we are left with a small boy in a subdued and reflective body posture. On the opposite page, we see the zoo buildings in silhouette, dwarfed against a beautiful moonlit sky with two wild geese flying off into the distance. The buildings are angular with straight lines; there are, perhaps, echoes of concentration camps – even a tree appears to be imprisoned – which contrast with the soft roundness of the moon and the curved lines of the geese in flight. The images made a big impact on young readers. Here is Chloe (7), an inexperienced reader who is struggling to articulate her thoughts.

I: What do you think the last two pictures are about?
CHLOE: Like he's a little bit sad because we're leaving the zoo now ...
I: How do you know he's sad?
CHLOE: Yeah, because you know he's going like that (points to his crouched position and bent head) he don't feel very well.
I: So you're reading his body posture, aren't you?
CHLOE: Yeah ... and he feels like sad because he's like left the zoo and he's like thinking like a dream. He's thinking like a dream. He's like thinking about the gorilla and he's dreaming about it at the same time.

Similarly, Dan (7), also an inexperienced reader, felt a sense of moral injustice on reading *Zoo*, again linking it sensitively with his own experience.

DAN: He's in a cage and been all sad and all that lot.
I: Do you think the boy was feeling bad about the visit to the zoo?
DAN: Yeah, and sometimes when your worst dreams, you like cry in the middle of the night and all that lot. ... I like this page because it's all black, dark and all that lot. And then birds come along and

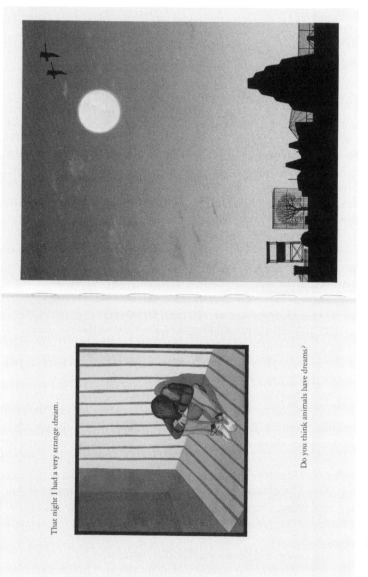

That night I had a very strange dream.

Do you think animals have dreams?

Figure 4.3 From *Zoo* by Anthony Browne

fly away. And it's nice and peaceful in the dark, I find it is, and I just like these mountains and all that ...

I: What do you think Anthony Browne wants us as readers of the book to feel about it?

DAN: Well I think they should read it ...

By the age of 10 some children, like Joe, were able to express their ideas more forcefully.

I: What do you think Anthony Browne wants us as readers of the book to feel about it?

JOE: He wants us to stop and think about that zoos may be fun to go to and look at all the animals but it's really horrible for the actual animals ... they need to be happy. But they're just stuck in cages for our own entertainment.

I: Do you agree with him ?

JOE: In the end I agree with him and when I go to zoos I just don't stop and think about how they might feel.

As we have tried to demonstrate, a significant finding from the research was that, while some children who were fluent readers of print were also good at reading image (such as Joe), it was also noticeable that many children in this study labelled as below average readers (such as Lara) were capable of subtle and engaged analysis of visual texts within an enabling environment: with an interested, experienced reader who listens carefully to their responses and gives them time to think; in a situation where the emphasis is on talk and image rather than written text and writing; where carefully constructed questions supportively challenge their thinking; through the facilitating process of talking in a focussed yet open-ended way with peers and a teacher/researcher with high expectations of what the children could achieve; using a text that is intellectually, affectively and visually interesting and that motivates engagement and scaffolds learning – in other words, a text that teaches (Meek 1988). Indeed, as we read the transcripts, it is almost possible to watch the children working through their particular zone of proximal development into deeper understanding.

LARA: It's a good book because it gives you the feel of what it's like, because I never thought what it would be like in a cage.

I: You've never thought of that before.

LARA: No, but then when I read this book it made me feel different. *It's a serious book* [our emphasis].

An earlier version of this chapter appeared in *Children's Literature in Education*, 32 (4) 2001: 261–81.

Vignette – 'I think she feels the pain of the animals' (Lara 10)

Lara was impressive from the outset. She listened and watched eagerly as her teacher read *Zoo* to the class and clearly couldn't wait to contribute to the discussion. Her answers showed her to be alert, sensitive and fairly articulate. As I knew that one of the two girls I was interviewing must be an experienced reader, I assumed (wrongly as it turned out) it was Lara, and was very surprised to discover later that she had literacy problems. Lara was eager to be interviewed and took an active part in the group discussion later in the day. Her drawing in response to *Zoo* was ironic, featuring a defiant, fashionably dressed woman with a bare midriff behind bars, shouting 'What's everyone looking at?' as families of pigs, foxes and bears jeer at her with cheeky, speech bubble remarks – 'Look at that thing!' 'Hey kids, look at that.'

The most noticeable aspect of Lara's response to *Zoo* was her empathy for the animals' plight which she often highlighted through powerful personal analogy. Looking at the picture of the penguins, she remarked, 'If I had to live in a cage, I would live in the penguins' cage because it has got nice turquoisy colour water and it looks like it's been looked after.' Speaking about the elephant which she has described as 'lonely … because it is in the dark in the corner doing nothing', Lara goes on to say: 'I think he [Browne] is trying to make us feel what you would feel if it was you being trapped in a cage.' She imagines the orang-utan 'is missing his family and wants to be at home where he used to live instead of being trapped in the zoo, because most probably he doesn't want everyone looking at him all the time … and staring and shouting and waving and looking at him all the time. He just wants to be left alone.' Unsurprisingly, Lara was sensitive to Mum's feelings: 'I think she feels the pain of the animals. They want to be left alone and not pushed about and shouted at.' And later: 'The Mum is looking very miserable still because she has got dark patches around her eyes.'

This attention to pictorial detail also helped Lara analyse visual metaphors. She realised that Browne created a dramatic cover for visual impact: 'it makes it different from other books'. She correctly identified the imagery of wild geese on the final page: 'making it look like they're free, but the animals in the cages aren't'. She was also able to read the silhouette of bars against one of the boys: 'they've swopped around, so the boys are in the cage instead of the animals'. Lara was strongly aware of colour symbolism and the emotional intentions of the artist.

I: How do you think Browne shows us the elephant's loneliness?

LARA: Because it is in the dark, in the corner doing nothing. It is all bright then they just go to into this other page and it's all dark ...

I: And do you think Browne did that deliberately?

LARA: Yeah, to make you feel what it is like to have everyone looking at you ... it doesn't look a very nice place to be in, so that makes you think what would you feel if you were trapped up all the time in a horrible little cage.

Lara's teacher was surprised that she had made such a positive impact on our research, yet the extracts above show that she was deeply involved by the ideas in the book and articulate in exploring them. Did this largely pictorial text enable Lara to show what she was capable of when not held back by problems with decoding print? Did the images provide an enabling structure in which she could develop her ideas? By analysing a sophisticated picturebook (unlike the relatively simple fiction she could manage on her own), was it the case that, for once the complex ideas, images and issues thrown up by this text matched Lara's need for challenging literature? She was so absorbed by this book that it led us to question the diet of texts struggling older readers like Lara exist on, how many chances they normally get to engage with satisfying texts, and whether visual texts should not have a greater part to play in reading development? It also raised questions about whether the short, highly focussed approaches to text in the Literacy Hour had replaced more ruminative exposure to literature, where there was more time for young readers to explore texts in their own ways.

We had intended to re-interview Lara, but on the day in question she had the chance of taking part in a special maths game and chose that activity above ours. (Another child was re-interviewed in her place.) It was a useful corrective for a researcher all too ready to make assumptions about Lara's passionate commitment to picturebooks!

LARA: How would you feel ... trapped up in a cage and everyone looking at you, staring at you, shouting at you. Treating you really bad. ... If you think about it, if you had to be put in a cage, that is where you would stay. You would stay there and I can't imagine living in that sort of conditions.

I: Did you think of that before you read the book?

LARA: No, I just thought about it a moment ago.

Notes

1   This research was carried out in two contrasting schools, one located in Cambridge in a mixed catchment area which included council housing, prosperous private housing and the range in-between.

2   They had equal difficulty with suggesting why there was a caged hamster on the title page.

3   This was certainly a leading question, but one that the interviewer had used regularly with adults on other occasions, many of whom had failed to see the connection.

4   This shows the difference the knowledge and preferences of teachers can have on learning outcomes even in a situation where teachers were trying to follow a common script.

Chapter 5

'Letting the story out'

Visual encounters with Anthony Browne's *The Tunnel*

I: Why do you think the ball and the book are together on the final page?

SENTHURAN (5): Because now the ball and the book can cuddle.

Sinatra defines visual literacy as 'the active reconstruction of past visual experience with incoming visual messages to obtain meaning' (1986: 5). This simple definition emphasises that visual skills are essential for encouraging an active and even critical interpretation of textual and visual information. In proposing to investigate how visual texts are read by children, we attempted to find out what skills children already possess, how they think about image and participate in the meaning-making process and how this participation can be extended. *The Tunnel* provided an ideal means of exploring these areas, given that the printed text and the richly detailed illustrations only release their story when they are linked to other narratives and pictures. Yet because of Browne's careful use of symbols, even children as young as 4 are able to make these links and find meaning in *The Tunnel*, perhaps even better than many adult readers who have lost touch with the fairy-tale world in which Browne immerses his reader.[1]

We found that even in their earliest impressions of *The Tunnel*, it was evident that the children were drawing on their previous experience of books and their knowledge of the world. For example, one of the youngest children, Luke (5), spoke of things that couldn't happen in real life, 'but in books they can'. More importantly, from their reading experience – especially of the picturebook genre – they brought the expectation that what they saw carried meaning and that they would have to look for and construct it from the illustrations. Thus Simone (10), speaking of the first set of endpapers, said rightly: 'I think it might mean something that might be there later on in the story ... it might mean the meaning of the story.' Even those children who were not familiar with Browne's work realised that they would have to look carefully in order to make sense of the story.

Gemma (9), however, was familiar with Browne's picturebooks and spoke of him as one of her favourite authors. She provided an example of how an experienced reader approaches a picturebook. She had read *The Tunnel* at home and also done some work on it at school 'for our literacy'. From her interview, we can gather that she lives in a house where reading and talking about books is commonplace. She writes stories, and visits the library every weekend to 'do some research on my favourite children's books'. When asked what was special about the illustrations for *The Tunnel*, she summed up the three most outstanding characteristics of this book: 'detail', 'characters' and 'colour'. In what follows these characteristics and the way in which they were linked by the children to the characters and overall meaning of the story will be discussed at length.

Entering the tunnel

All the children regardless of age were enthusiastic about reading the book, and those who had not read it before were intrigued by it from the beginning. On the front cover a young girl can be seen, halfway into a dark tunnel; next to the entrance is an open book with drawings suggesting fairy tales. The children described the cover as 'interesting', but also as 'exciting', and arousing 'suspense'. It suggested something strange or wonderful would be found inside or at the other end of the tunnel and this made them want to read on:

> It makes me feel like there's going to be a fantasy story. ... Like there's going to be like lots of stuff happening in there. And it's got really good titles [so you] know it's going to be a really good story.
>
> (Matt 8)

The narrative tells us about the resolution of the conflict between siblings. As the protagonists – Rose and Jack – are introduced, a visually alert reader will have begun to make connections between the girl and the boy and the book's endpapers which are striking because of their contrasting patterns: leaves and flowers on one side and a brick wall on the other (upon closer inspection both of them turn out to be wallpapers). These images enhance the textual description of a sister and brother constantly at odds with each other because of their different temperaments: she likes to read and dream indoors on her own; he likes active games outside with his friends. We learn more about the children in the next spread where Jack is playing on Rose's fear of the dark by coming into her room with a mask. The wolf shadow cast by the boy, a red cloak, a picture inset of Little Red Riding Hood by Walter Crane and a lamp in the shape of a fairy-tale cottage are the first of many intertextual references to fairy tales the reader encounters in this book (see plate 5). As Doonan points out, all of Browne's picturebooks require 'knowledge of other texts and discourses – folk and fairy tales, classics, and his own works, fine art, cinema, comics, advertisements; the intertextual process is his whole business' (1998: 1).

When they are sent outside by their mother, Jack finds a tunnel in a bit of waste ground and decides to explore. Rose becomes so worried when he does not return that she puts aside her fears and follows him through the dark and damp tunnel. On the other side is a wood that soon becomes a terrifying forest, with strange shapes on the trees and other objects reminiscent of fairy tales. After running through the forest, Rose arrives at a bleak clearing to discover a stone statue of her brother. Tenaciously she hugs him and smiles in triumph as he recovers his human form and hugs her back. The dark woods have become lighter and less dense, the sky is blue and the ring of small stones around Jack has become a ring of daisies. In the last picture, a happy, knowing Rose smiles at her brother. We read (because Browne does not show us Jack's face) that he smiles back. Their hair mingles and the warmth of the light from the window is reflected in her face. Rose has confronted her fears and conquered them through love. The ball and the book, pictured together on the endpapers underneath the brick pattern, confirm the siblings' new-found closeness.

As we read and talked together, most of the children recognized the motifs that keep appearing throughout the book, such as the ball and book, the leaf and brick patterns and those related to the story of *Red Riding Hood*. In some cases, listing these and other objects sidetracked them from discussing the significance of the particular images, but more often it led them on to speculate why the artist had put them there. Some children, for example Mark (8), proposed that Browne was playing a game to involve the reader: 'It makes you look at the picture [and] you use your imagination.' Other children suggested that he was creating a certain atmosphere: 'making it scary', such as Simone (10) who said that Browne 'included bits of stories into his book to make it have more feeling [...] that scary feeling and all sorts of feeling.'

During the interviews the children were fascinated by the many 'details' as they called them and kept pointing them out – especially in the woods and the waste ground. As Dave (8) said, 'the more you look at it the more you find'. The significance of these details and their connection to the narrative usually began to emerge as the interviews and group discussions progressed, sometimes aided by the interviewer's questions. The following excerpt from the group discussion in School A, with 9–10-year-olds, shows how the pupils build upon their peer observations to make meaning and also relate this meaning to their own life experiences. It is also an example of the way in which they analysed visual imagery and linked it to the characters' different temperaments:

SEAN: Look, salt and pepper!
I: What about the salt and pepper?
SEAN: The pepper's black and [is interrupted]
CORINNA: And the salt's white! It's kind of like they're having an argument therefore they see things in a different way.
TAMSIN: Like me and my sister when we argue about something [see figure 5.1].

As well as intertextual references, there are intratextual ones. The text and illustrations keep referring back to themselves and this leads to re-readings and moving back and forth between the pages, and between the words and the pictures in order to make yet more connections between the incoming visual messages. Browne skilfully uses his craft to make these intratextual references, using colour, pattern and symbols. All these references are there for a purpose, as Browne himself says, 'whenever I put anything in like that [an image or reference within a picture] nearly every time, it's there for a purpose, it's there to help to take the story somewhere else, to tell something about the story'.[2] In *The Tunnel* these 'puzzles' (as Browne calls them) must be taken seriously and put together like a jigsaw in order to make the story meaningful. In order to arrive at a deeper understanding of this story, the bits and pieces of fairy tales which appear throughout the illustrations must be 'puzzled over' and sorted out. The next section reveals something of the children's reconstruction processes and how they contributed to the meaning of the story as a whole.

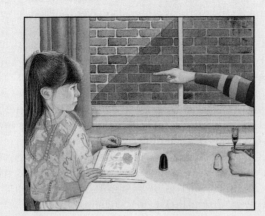

Whenever they were together they fought and argued noisily.
All the time.

Figure 5.1 From *The Tunnel* by Anthony Browne
Source: Illustrations from *The Tunnel* copyright 1989 Anthony Browne.
Reproduced by permission of Walker Books and Random House Inc.

Fairy-tale land

The children's responses revealed their familiarity with the fairy-tale
genre in their recognition of the intertextual references (especially to
Little Red Riding Hood, but also to *Hansel and Gretel* and *Jack and the
Beanstalk*). They used their knowledge of the genre in constructing
explanatory narratives; for example, Gemma (9) pointed out that
Rose's fears come from reading a lot of 'bad fairy tales'. Another
example was when they gave explanations for Jack's statue-like form,
such as that a witch or 'mythical character' (like 'the Medusa') had
put some kind of magic spell or curse on the boy and 'marked their
territory' with the stones. Another explanation was that Jack and the
flowers had been 'frozen', probably an unconscious reference to the
boy's 'cold' attitude to his sister. Several children contrasted his coldness to her warmth, and although they seemed to mean it literally, it
is not difficult to see that they have a sense of the children's person-
alities:

Because her body's warm-blooded she hugs him and then because she's warm all of her sweat and body makes the stone go away.

(Shanaz 8)

Maria (8) literally linked his freezing to not having a coat (unlike his more sensible sister) and the dampness of the tunnel. This girl's imagination also led her to create a whole additional story line where the witch's hat and black cat outside Rose's window were 'warnings' about what might happen to her brother, and the animals in the wood were 'giving her a message' that her brother was hurt. This imaginative but implausible deduction can be contrasted with the metaphor Gemma (9), the experienced reader we mentioned above, struggles to use in order to explain her more subtle grasp of the sibling relationship. Although at first glance her comments seem confusing, closer scrutiny shows Gemma has caught the tension in the relationship quite well.

Maybe two things that didn't agree with each other bumped in and then like water doesn't agree with a computer because if you knock it down then ... the computer'll go funny so if two things aren't happy with each other then something bad will happen.

Some explanations for the stones turning into flowers were integrated into the fantasy narrative although a few were also quite literal. Stewart (11) thought the stones or rocks were preventing the plants from growing, so when Jack moved they were able to shoot up again. Simone (10), like several others, thought the sun melted the stones. Gokhan (8) was the only child who mentioned God: 'Maybe God done it 'cos God was happy what she'd done. She saved her brother.' And Tamsin (9) was the only one who interpreted them as symbols:

Because the [flowers] are beautiful. Or because maybe the artist thinks that rocks are not that peaceful because people throw them at things and they get breaked and flowers are peaceful because kids make chains as presents.

This kind of imaginative deduction, trying to thread together the events and objects in the pictures was an ongoing process. The readers were determined to make sense of the story, to try and explain why things appeared in the illustrations, to fit it into a coherent whole (within or without the folk/fairy-tale genre). This coincides with Gardner's description of the child's early development with respect to art: 'As the child gains facility in using language and reading pictures, he manifests a very strong tendency with respect to these symbols. Put directly, the child searches for meaning or reference in every perceived symbol or object' (1973: 156). This was especially apparent in the interview with a recent immigrant from Africa, Sam (11). He had no knowledge of European fairy tales, yet because of the strong visual images, he recognised the genre and worked hard to assemble the pieces of the story, grafting these to traditional tales from his own culture that deal with magic and witches (a more detailed analysis of his interview can be found in chapter 8).

When the children got hold of an idea that began to make sense of all the 'details' and the general story, they became very excited, as in the group discussion below (with 8- and 9-year-olds). They all began speaking at once, racing ahead of each other with their ideas:

BOBBY: In that picture ... that could be the Candy Cottage or something, it could be like a fairy-tale picture like, and they could have crawled into the picture.

MARIA: That's what I said, I said that!

RUTH: Well as they went into the tunnel, it might be like they're going into the fairy tale as well ...

BOBBY: Yeah, oh no, maybe everything's the other way round in here.

DAVE: Yeah, it's a different world, everything's got the other way round. It's a fairy tale. He [Jack] must have gone into the pictures!

This group developed the fairy-tale motif more than other discussion groups did and, in the example above, it is clear how they encouraged each other towards an understanding of the story. They are also using previous readings to imagine that Rose and Jack 'entered' another world, one where 'everything is the other way round' (a reference to *Through the Looking Glass?*). Although only a few children like those in this group actually described the other side of the tunnel as 'fairy-tale land' or described Rose's adventure as a fairy tale in itself, it is evident from all the responses that there was a continual exploration of the possibilities which would help construct a schema for interpretation. As the children saw more intertextual references, they refined this mental schema, actively extending their own, and in some cases, others' understanding of the story.

Brothers and sisters

The character of the siblings and their relationship is the other focal point of the book. In some cases the children reduced the plot to a simple 'they didn't like each other and now they are friends' but in others there was a more complex understanding of their relationship. Many children made immediate analogies between the relationship in the book and their own experiences of these relationships (fighting, making up with their siblings):

> Like me and my sister. We don't actually get along very much, because we fight a lot, well when she's upset, I really, well I don't feel good.
>
> (Ruth 8)

Here we have the bridging of life experience with the visual experience, a text-to-life link that also allows the reader/viewer to create meaning from art. It is also life experiences that the artist builds on and in this case we have Browne's recollections from his childhood, not only of a dangerous game he used to play with his brother, swinging their legs over an abandoned tunnel, but also of being left alone in the woods.[3]

Although at the beginning not everyone was able to say what the wallpapers represented, by the end of the book most linked the patterns that appear throughout the illustrations to the differences in the children's characters. Even Polly, who had just turned 5, was able to see this: 'I've noticed that the boy always has bricks there and the girl always has patterns.' From the picture of the waste ground, readers were also able to infer something about the sibling relationship and their insights went well beyond the obvious ones based on body language (not facing each other) and symbolic objects (the pipeline or pole that physically separates their spaces). For example:

> Well [the picture] tells you that the brother don't like the sister because the sister's sitting like far away from the brother. The brother's standing quite far away. You can see the brother don't want her near, because you can see the pole and he don't want his sister to cross it.
>
> (Matt 8)

Because of the contrast between the siblings, the story lends itself to gender analysis.[4] In one school, during the reading of the story, a few boys snorted when the teacher read that Rose was scared to go into *The Tunnel*. Like Jack, *they* would have gone inside with no hesitation! Some of the older boys also seemed impatient with her fears about witches and goblins and, like her brother, probably thought she was being a 'baby'. The wallpaper patterns were considered to represent the children because 'girls like flowers' and boys play football on the 'grass' (the green bit of carpet). Reading was definitely felt to be a 'girl thing' and playing football, a 'boy thing'. Cliff (10) said that looking around in waste ground was also a 'boy's thing: 'I think he's more at home there because I know that boys like exploring in a junk yard.'

The most profound insight into the general question of gender and the fairy-tale genre was made by Dave (now 9) during the follow-up interview. When asked to talk about the last picture (when Rose is smiling at Jack), he seems suddenly struck by an idea:

> She thinks she's been to a fairy-tale land and she's like [long pause] instead it's the other way around! It's usually the lady who gets stuck and the boy who rescues, usually, and here the girl rescues the boy. Like in nearly every fairy tale when the lady is stuck in the tower, a man comes along and rescues her or she gets chased by the fox and the woodcutter chops his head off another man. And this time it's a girl. [Browne's] changed it [Interviewer: Why?] To make it feel, don't know, like if this little girl … she might feel she couldn't do anything so now she can do something the boy can't.

Revealed in Dave's response is one of the achievements of Browne's artistry which can be described in Grumet's words, 'the work of art simultaneously draws the viewer to it; engaging expectations, memories, recognition, and then interrupts the viewer's customary response, contradicting expectations with new possibilities, violating memories, displacing recognition with estrangement' (quoted in Sinatra 1986: 31). Dave's expectations of gender roles were contradicted and hopefully these 'new possibilities' will lead him to 'see' further or keep an open mind before applying the usual gender stereotypes. Although the other pupils did not seem to be aware of this change of roles, with further guidance from a teacher,[5] most of them would probably be able to achieve similar insight into this and other gender issues in *The Tunnel*.

Another aspect that strengthens the bond between the siblings is that at the end of the story they share a secret, a secret that is kept from their mother. They are smiling in the final page, not only because they like each other now but also because no-one else knows what happened and it will be their special secret. This was also a matter for empathy and analogy:

> She's smiling because their mum don't know what happened, and they do. That's the kind of look I have when I steal some ice cream from the kitchen.
>
> (Tamsin 9)

For most of the readers, it was the sibling relationship which was seen as conveying the main message of the book. One child who came from a family of Jehovah's Witnesses managed to find 'a lesson' in the book: 'So it must have been like a lesson, maybe. [Interviewer: What sort of a lesson?] Maybe you should always like your family and enemies, your friends.'[6] Dave (8) did not say it was a 'lesson', he just boiled the thought down even further: 'Don't be angry with people, be friends.' In general, when the children were asked if the book could be described as 'funny' or 'serious', although some parts were found to be 'funny' (such as where the brother scares his sister with the mask), because of this message or 'lesson' the book was mainly considered 'serious'.

In the initial endpapers only the book appears, but both ball and book sit side by side in the final endpapers. Their explanations for the change of focus in the endpapers were sometimes quite literal, such as that he was outside playing with it or 'maybe the brother didn't like football then' (Shanaz 8). Although some of the younger children still missed the point about the ball and the book on the final endpapers, most realised they stood for a closer relationship between the siblings, as Natasha (10) said: 'Because they're together, that means they're getting along.'

Watson, reading *The Tunnel* with 4½-year-old Ann, also tells us that she recognised the symbolism of the ball and the book: 'Ann knew at once that the illustration was a metaphorical representation of reconciliation, or friendship, or what she thought of as *kindness*.' Watson points out that this interpretation involved 'more than an instant revelation about an image; it involved a kind of "backward reading" and the ability to hold in her mind a full and holistic sense of the story and the way the narrative web is strung together' (1996b: 148). This stringing or piecing of the narrative was being done all along the way, gathering force as the readers had more time to think about it and make more connections. The way in which certain visual features, such as the use of pattern and colour, helped strengthen these connections (book/flowers and ball/bricks) will be discussed in the next section.

Drawing 'the real' and other visual features

The visual features mentioned most often by the children were colour (particularly the use of dark and light) and the hyper-realist style of the illustrations. They make Browne's work easily recognisable and memorable. Matt (8) immediately compared the two picturebooks he was familiar with: 'In *Zoo* he uses colours quite light, and in *The Tunnel* he uses them quite dark.' According to the children, it is these two features that make a 'good' artist: the colours make the pictures 'stand out' (e.g. Rose's red cloak and the wolf's red eyes) and his detailed and what they saw as realistic style make them 'lifelike'. The use of shadows – another of Browne's trademarks – also provoked positive comments. Some children (probably echoing adults) praised him for 'staying in the lines', colouring them in 'nicely' and 'not smudging'!

Several respondents revealed a keen interest in the technical aspects of his drawing, such as his use of different kinds of paints and brushes. Although they may have been incorrect in supposing what kind of brush Browne actually used, it perhaps made them think of their own artistic experiences and it is clear how much they would have benefited by discussing the pictures with an art teacher. One of the children who spoke most about Browne's techniques was Maria (8). Her comments show how carefully she had examined each picture. Asked to talk about the first set of four pictures (where the characters are introduced), she referred to colour and tone:

> [On the girl in the room and the boy outside] I like how he's mixed them colours up. Like there's light green, then a little darker then really dark and then lighter again. He's mixed all the colours up together to make them look like they're from the sunlight [as] it's shining onto the curtains and you can see the shadows as well, from the boys [outside].

She also spoke of the transformation caused by the use of light and dark in the sequence when Jack turns from stone back into a boy, regaining his own colours while the sky goes from grey to blue. Like many of her peers, Maria easily linked this change to the mood of the narrative: 'Then instead of being dark, it comes to … light and then more light, and then light. That's why I like that, because they probably done that because of the happy ending.'

Tamsin (9) was another discerning viewer and both she and Maria tried to explain how the perspective in several pictures worked. Although precise technical terms are not used, we have a detailed appreciation of Browne's artistic techniques as well as value judgements based on his ability to capture reality through body language, colour and detail as well as perspective:

MARIA: I like (Browne's) bird's eye view from up above.
TAMSIN: It looks like it's a really long way, the picture [of Rose entering the tunnel]. But it's just one piece of paper and you're looking down.

In developmental models of aesthetic experience, the middle childhood years are usually considered to be a time when children express a preference for realism. This could be one reason for children's attraction to Browne's style, as things are drawn as they supposedly really look. Benson questions this theory by citing Goodman's distinction between 'pictorial fidelity' and 'pictorial realism', fidelity being the representation of the object corresponding to the properties which are ascribed to it and realism depending on 'how easily this information (in a picture) is yielded to the viewer by the picture' (1986: 125). Benson argues that middle childhood is characterised by both pictorial realism and pictorial fidelity and this is related to their first experiences with literacy in school where they are encouraged to understand the word–thing relationship as denotative, thus reducing the ability of pictures to mean if they do not clearly denote objects or actions with which they are already familiar.

It is interesting that Browne's hyper-realist drawings were frequently compared to other types of visual media with which the children were familiar, for example: videos, 3-D ('not just a flat picture'), film and a 'play'. Simone talked about the way Browne 'set out' the picture of Rose going into *The Tunnel* as if it were 'in slow motion'. Dave liked the way the graffiti on the walls looked like 'proper spray'. References to the way movement looks in real life were made about Rose running in the forest. Children talked about 'smudging', 'all the bits going off' and how colour contributed to this effect: 'Because when you run … you can see the colours, they kind of run away' (Tamsin 9).

This raises questions about the value children accord to what they see as 'realistic' and what many of them also enjoy but is definitely 'unrealistic', such as cartoons. Could it be that in the case of *The Tunnel* a more 'realistic' style of drawing allows them to relate to the characters in more depth? Further research is clearly needed in this area to understand how children read and value different styles, not only in the technical sense but also in terms of their emotional and intellectual response.

Following Benson's line of thought, although Browne's picturebook apparently 'yields information' quite easily to the viewer, it then causes a disruption in their expectancies of narrative because readers are forced to consider objects that, although 'realistic' in style, denote something beyond themselves – such as the ball and the book. The objects in the waste-ground picture are a good example too, because of the eagerness with which the children identified them, and also because they had to consider why they were there not just as 'junk' but as symbols of the siblings' relationship (like the pipe or pole that divides them) as well as intriguing intratextual references (the shoes, the cat face). With the interviewer's prompting, many of the pupils in this study did consider the links between these references (and many of them appeared in their drawings, see chapter 6).

'Describing' words and 'helping' pictures

In *The Tunnel*, the relationship between the words and the pictures is more straightforward than in some of Browne's other books (such as *Zoo* or *Voices in the Park*). The written and pictorial texts reinforce one another, with the pictures adding symbolic and intertextual dimensions to the story. The children, especially the younger ones, found it hard to differentiate the stories told by the words and the pictures. Most of them thought the pictures were more interesting than the words; they felt that the words without the pictures would be 'boring', whereas the book could still be good without the words. However, some of the older children considered the words equally important. Stewart (11), for example, said Browne was a good illustrator but he also 'throws these little words in very well'. The pictures were considered aids to understanding and a better way of showing details which would take too long to describe in words, as Kemal (8) explained: ' 'cos if it doesn't say she's running, on the pictures you look, you can see her running'.

Jason (9) had an interesting theory about the different narratives (textual and visual): that the forest picture was 'from the girl's point of view ... because she's scared and if you're scared, you imagine stuff like that.' Simone (10) also attempted to explain the difference:

> They tell different stories because there it says they went to a piece of waste ground and here you can see it but you could actually tell it in a different way to the writing (because) he can get more descriptive words and you can see the pipes and all sorts of stuff.

Gemma (9) was one of the few who talked in more detail about the written text and found it hard to choose between one or the other:

> He's very good at illustrations and the words he used to describe things and the nouns he puts in makes it look ... makes you want to read more [Interviewer: What kinds of nouns make you want to read the book?] He doesn't just sleep softly, he sleeps soundly. He doesn't just sleep normal. So the words he used are very effective. Well I couldn't really choose between them [words or pictures] because the illustrations are excellent and the words he uses just capture your imagination and then if it didn't have any pictures you would still understand because the words he uses describes it very well.

Even though Gemma seems to actually be referring to adjectives rather than nouns, she reveals an understanding of the interaction of words and pictures and how both of them move the story along.

According to the children, having pictures make it easier for the book to appeal to younger audiences. They seemed to agree that *The Tunnel* would be 'good' for all ages ('from age 1 to about 13' according to Dave) because both younger and older children would enjoy looking at the pictures. Jason (9) recommended the picturebook 'for parents to read to their children when they're quite young, about 5 or 6', because if the children were 'beginners', the pictures would help them understand the book better. Natasha (10) added: 'They will be able to read the pictures because children have a good imagination.'

Conclusion: rites of passage

In his interview, Browne commented that, among the many letters he receives from his readers, the ones about *The Tunnel* are the most interesting and that children seem to be 'really thinking' about this story. Our study confirmed that children 'really think' as they read and look, so much so that, as Watson writes of 4-year-old Ann also apropos *The Tunnel*: 'Reading illustrations was not a mere list-making activity or an inventorying of her observations; it was a complex and dynamic process, mediated through conversation' (1996b: 151). Throughout the interview day (and in some cases in the follow-up interviews) it was possible to observe how their thinking processes developed and their mental schema changed as they became more familiar with the story. Many of the children, for example, tended to get 'stuck' in their 'inventories' of the objects in the pictures. Once they had taken their time to look and had been gently prodded by the researcher's questions, they were able to consider how these objects contributed to understanding the 'bigger picture'.

Doonan uses the words 'psychological journey' in a possible interpretation of *The Tunnel*,[7] and Browne speaks of the story being about the boy and the girl 'coming together in some sort of balance'.[8] Although the children obviously did not have the knowledge and experience to articulate these interpretations of the story, their responses showed that, through the dialogue with the interviewers, they were widening their Vygotskian 'zone of proximal development' and beginning to appropriate more mature structures of meaning.

Gardner grants the status of 'audience member' to children when they reach the age of 7 because they are capable of 'experiencing pleasurable sensations and changes of affect in the presence of symbolic objects, by appreciating the difference between artistic illusions and real experiences, and by achieving some understanding of the symbol system' (1973: 234). However, he stops short of according 'critic' status to children because, although 'the genuine antecedents of the critical faculty seem dependent upon some degree of competence with symbols', they cannot articulate their reactions and evaluations in a systematic manner (1973: 118).[9] Our study indicated that all of the children in the study could be considered 'audience members', including those under the age of 7, and that some of the more experienced 'viewers' required only a little help in order to become 'critics'. These are precisely the abilities and skills that need to be taken into account in a curriculum which claims to emphasise 'literacy'.

As Sinatra says: 'The visually literate are those who have acquired the ability to make viable judgements about the image they perceive' (1986: 56). Just consider the following comment by Tamsin (9), which reveals acute observation of artistic features, emotional involvement and critical appraisal:

> [About the siblings at the table:] 'Cause the way the shade's done on that, it's lighter then it gets darker, cause the sun is on the part of the roof, it makes this part dark and this part light and how it's just chosen like, the arm is going around and it's not just like flat. I think it's really wonderful the way they've done the shadow, it's good.

The children were definitely learning to be 'visually literate' and only lacked the words to express their aesthetic experiences. In fact, in

some ways their choice of words – notwithstanding grammatical structure – went further in describing aspects of the work than many adults
would probably do. Gemma (9) best summed up Browne's accomplish-
ment in *The Tunnel* as: 'the way he does the illustrations, it just lets the
story out'.

An earlier version of this chapter appeared in *Reading* 35 (3), pp.
115–19.

Vignette – 'If you can read the pictures you can tell another story' (Dave 8/9)

As I was writing this vignette, I glanced at the answers Dave
gave to our questionnaire on reading habits and preferences.
They were no different to those of most of the 8- or 9-year-
old boys in the study (in brief, he liked reading picturebooks,
comics and stories but preferred computer games to books),
except that his handwriting was more illegible than most
and, where I could read it, his spelling seemed based on his
own particular phonetic rendition of a word: 'Bloow peter'
(*Blue Peter*), 'Benow' (*Beano*), 'Supooer Mareeyow' (*Super
Mario*), 'Dinsi pichus' (Disney pictures). I had not seen this
questionnaire at the time of the interview, nor did I know
that he was a pupil who 'struggled with reading and writing'
as his teacher later told me.

As we went through the interview questions and looked
at Browne's *The Tunnel*, I was struck by Dave's engagement
with the narrative, his capacity for noticing pictorial details
and his frequent references to visual techniques (including
terms from other visual media such as comics, photography,
film and computer games). It was obvious that he found the
images compelling from the very beginning:

> The pictures just look so good. You just want to read it …
> you think, 'Oh, what's going to happen to her, is she going
> to die, is she going to live, what's going to happen?' It just
> makes you read it.

Dave grasped not only the basic plot but also some of the finer details of the narrative after just a couple of readings, an achievement many of his fellow pupils did not manage immediately. He realised the differences between the siblings, he recognised the allusions to fairy tales and summed up Browne's message: 'Don't be angry with people, be friends.' During the group interview he went a step further in his interpretation: 'It's a different world. It's a fairy tale. [Jack] must have gone into the pictures.' Five months later during the re-interview he came up with the most insightful interpretation of the book of all his contemporaries, in terms of Browne's subversion of typical gender roles: 'It's usually the lady who gets stuck and the boy who rescues, usually, and here the girl rescues the boy. He's (Browne) changed it ... like if this little girl she might feel she couldn't do anything so now she can do something the boy can't.'

Dave's interpretation of the story was based on his attention to detail and his ability to make sense of it within the narrative. During the group interview he said he liked the details because they 'make you look at the picture [and] you use your imagination'. He noticed the flowers on Rose's mat and the explosion on Jack's as they sit at the table, as well as the line between them created by the shadow on the wall. He linked it to the different wallpapers which show 'they don't have nothing in common' so 'they hate each other'. Then, speaking of the coming together of the siblings at the end of the book, he says 'the stones mean hate and the flowers mean love'. But he's also noticed other significant details:

> The pictures have got detail in them because if you look in this picture there's no trees, but when the sister comes to get him there's like some trees, like they just re-grow ... when she touches him. [It's] gloomy, then lighter and lighter. Look here, she's nearly avoided it, like her brother, going into the ring.

The last sentence refers to a 'detail' I had not noticed and which I presume few readers of *The Tunnel* ever notice: there is a shadow which one can assume is of Rose's head, just at the edge of the circle of stones where her brother has been 'frozen'.

On several occasions Dave described Browne's style as 'realistic' and this realism extended to other aspects such as 'the way they [the characters] stand'. When asked how Browne made things look 'real', he showed me the entrance to the tunnel as an example and explained that it was of 'all the creases ... and all the shading, it looks like 3-D not just a flat picture, it goes darker'. These details were painstakingly reproduced in his own drawing of Rose going into the tunnel, where he attempted to show these creases as well as the shading. He was particularly sensitive to different textures, the graffiti on the waste-ground wall, for example, looked 'like proper spray, it's smudged'. He also noticed the tiny blue dots covering the image of the boy lying on his bed and speculated that Browne had used a blow pen for spraying it.

Because Browne is such a 'good artist', according to Dave, he could make a picturebook without words and 'you'd still know what's going on'. The problem was when you had a book with just words, because 'it would be a lot fatter book because there'd have to be more writing, describing and everything'. Dave said that before he could read, he'd 'make up the words in my head', but he also said that he'd recently had trouble 'making up the pictures' for a book for 'older children' which he had found difficult to understand.

It seems Dave's extraordinary capacity for making sense of visuals was not helping him face the printed word. However, during the interviews he mentioned another of Browne's picturebooks, *Voices in the Park* and it was evident he had been struck by the different print fonts which distinguish each character's version of the story. In this case, the letters themselves had become visual objects:

[*Voices*] is good because one person has different writing and speech, like one has slanty writing ... some is printed like on computer, some big bubble letters, some was writ [*sic*] quite small.

Would it be possible to use these sorts of observations to make print more accessible to Dave? Could this be a way forward for helping Dave in his reading and writing? But would his teacher notice and, even if she did, would she have the time and knowledge to build upon these visual skills? Finally, I ask myself, during his schooling, will anyone realise there is 'another story' to be told about Dave's literacy skills?

Notes

1   This picturebook was read in three of seven schools that took part in our research: two of the London schools (both of which had a significant ethnic minority population including refugee pupils) and one in Cambridge, serving a mainly working-class council estate. Altogether, 72 interviews were conducted on *The Tunnel*. The interview schedule can be found in the Appendix.

2   All quotes from Browne are from an interview we conducted in January 2000, see chapter 10.

3   The first incident is mentioned in Doonan (1998: 2) and in Browne's various talks about his work; the second was mentioned in his interview, see chapter 10.

4   In discussing *The Tunnel's* setting as support for characterisation, Nikolajeva and Scott comment that: 'we must accept that there is considerable gender stereotyping in this book' (2001: 105). It seems to us that Browne is actually using these stereotypes in order to make a point about how they can be subverted.

5   Such as the work done by Davies (1993) in *Shards of Glass*.

6   A reminder of the children in Roadville who were expected to find the 'moral' in stories, in Brice Heath's 1983 study, *Ways with Words*.

7   Doonan (1998: 2–3): 'The story may be interpreted as a psychological journey of male and female principles moving towards integration, or the unity of ego and id, or as contrast between conscious and unconscious worlds, or simply as being about two children of different temperaments of either sex.'

8   Browne (interview): 'I think it's also a book about coming to terms with different aspects of your own character. In a way it's about a brother and sister, but it's also in a way the two aspects of oneself. I mean I think, I identify with both the boy and the girl in that. And in the end you have them coming together in some sort of balance.'

9   Gardner also says the critic must have the capacity to perceive essential features of the work and the symbolic media, which, as we have seen, most children were able to do.

Chapter 6

Thinking aloud

Looking at children drawing in response to picturebooks

Kate Rabey

> However it works, drawing is thinking aloud, a powerful route into knowledge.
>
> (Sedgwick and Sedgwick 1993: 29)

> Sometimes I practise when I draw. I draw a lot and it gets much better, I hardly scribble now, you see. I love drawing and colouring in 'cause it's really fun.
>
> (Polly 5)

Polly's comments show one young artist drawing, talking and 'thinking aloud' in response to Browne's *The Tunnel*. Both quotes demonstrate the role of thinking in the creative process, but Polly also captures that unique pleasure that young children can derive from drawing. In this chapter I will look at how the children in this study drew in response to *Zoo*, *The Tunnel* and *Lily*. Through their drawings, we can see them 'thinking aloud' and begin to understand more about the metacognitive processes involved in creating visual texts.

Children can communicate what they see through their drawings and their drawings, in turn, reflect their responses to the visual stimuli they encounter. In *Art as Experience* Dewey states that:

> Thinking directly in terms of colours, tones, images, is a different operation technically from thinking in words ... because the meaning of paintings and symphonies cannot be translated into words. ... There are values and meanings that can be expressed only by immediate visible and audible qualities, and to ask what they mean in the sense of something that can be put into words is to deny their distinctive existence.
>
> (1978: 73–4)

A visual experience demands a visual response true to its original form. From Rousseau onwards, we have seen an unprecedented interest in children's art, which has been both celebrated for its aesthetic qualities and explored as a tool for understanding cognitive development. Psychologists such as Arnheim (1966), Kellog (1979) and Gardner (1980) have demonstrated how children draw to make sense of the world around them. In simple terms, the toddler starts by drawing the world she knows and a waxy, circular scribble with two dots eventually becomes her mother's face. Early drawings form a bridge between the concrete world of experience (mummy) and the abstract world of symbols and signs (waxy scribble) and open the way into the other forms of symbolic representation such as reading and writing.

My involvement with the project came as a class teacher and art specialist. This chapter is both a description of my experiences working on Zoo with my own class of 4- and 5-year-olds and an analysis of the drawings of the other children in the study. As the only teacher/ researcher, my pupils had the advantage of being able to spend more time thinking about one picturebook. Our work formed a mini-project where the children were given the opportunity to look at and discuss the illustrations and text in great detail and make their own 'zoo' stories through play and art and craft. I was also able to watch them drawing. As well as working on Zoo at the time the researcher visited my classroom, we returned to it a few months later and spent further time discussing the text and drawing our responses.

Analysing the drawings

I have divided my analysis of the drawings into several sections, based on categories adapted from Davis (1993), Parsons (1987) and Lewis and Greene (1983). I start by looking at *literal* understanding, which constitutes a basic level of response, whereby the child draws people or events from the text to communicate story and content. Next I looked at the *overall effect* of the drawings, considering qualities such as the aesthetics of the image and a discussion of colour, tone, form and line. Finally, I looked at the *internal structure* of the drawing, examining the composition for balance and the relationship between objects or characters and their relative scale. I found that some of the most interesting *developmental differences* appear somewhere between overall effect and internal structure. (I will explore these differences later in the chapter, focussing in particular on one exceptional class of 10-year-olds.) Through their individual details many of the young artists move closer to what Parsons describes as the final autonomous stage of appreciation and judgement (see chapter 2). A case study of an exceptionally gifted child, Yu, exemplifies some of these categories in more detail.

Literal responses

Children drawing in response to all three books showed literal understandings of their narrative content. The vast majority of children studying *Zoo* picked up on the central issue and drew animals trapped in cages. At all ages children highlighted the contrast between the worlds inside and outside the cages. In many of the drawings of the younger children an animal subject formed the focal point, often occupying a large part of the centre of the picture plane. Amy's drawing (figure 6.1) was made in response to her first reading of *Zoo*. On a literal level her simple pen-and-ink sketch indicates that she knows that the story is about a family visit to the zoo. Both animal and humans are given equal status in the composition and occupy the same space.

The majority of drawings in response to *Lily* and *The Tunnel* also depicted people and events from the texts, communicating the children's understanding of the narrative. Many of the *Lily* drawings showed a child walking a dog, often placed within an urban scene and

Figure 6.1 By Amy (4)

Figure 6.2 By Seamus (7)

feature many of the strange monsters such as the snapping pillar-box, the river monster and the grinning tree (see figure 6.2). Drawings inspired by *The Tunnel* picked up on the sibling relationship and focussed on references to fairy tales and physical environmental features, such as the tunnel, the bedroom and the woods.

Overall effect

The overall effect of each of the three books is very different. In Browne's books the illustrations are painstakingly drafted and contain meticulous detail of everything from the stripes on Dad's polo shirt to the stony pattern on the surface of the tunnel. Browne's almost photographic realism and skilful control of the composition give a solid overall effect which is heightened by sensitive use of colour. In *Lily* Kitamura uses colour and line in a very different way. His pictorial style is more direct and cartoon-like with black pen lines encasing a wash of bright primary watercolours. In all three books colour, pattern and line communicate a strong sense of mood and atmosphere and open up many avenues for discussion. Looking at the drawings it does seem that the children have picked up on some of the different stylistic qualities of these two artists.

Figure 6.3 By Will (9)

Will's (9) drawing evokes a disturbing overall effect and vividly characterises Dad from *Zoo* as the devil using light, unstable pencil strokes; the big empty eyes and dark grimacing mouth form an eerie focal point (figure 6.3). Will also captures Dad's brightly coloured shirt which contrasts with the nightmarish features on his face. As a finishing touch Will captions the drawing, 'dad the devil are you scared?'

Tony (10) drew one of the most articulate emotional responses to *Zoo*.[1] It is also worth noting that he was one of the children judged to be an inexperienced reader by his teacher and his interview was hesitant and uncertain. A black line down the centre of the page clearly divides the picture into two halves which stimulate very different responses. On the left-hand side he uses a faint pencil line to draw a small human figure and a pig. The figure appears behind long vertical bars whereas the pig is positioned outside the bars and is carefully coloured in a soft pink crayon. On the other side of the picture a large tree marks the division, negating the existence of any bars in this new world. A large hairy gorilla stands smiling underneath the tree in the centre of gentle, curving arcs of warm light coloured in yellow, blue and red. This side of the picture is coloured in bold, bright felt tip and the overall effect is a potent image of containment versus freedom.

Both Will and Tony have moved away from a literal representation of the story and added their own evocative details.

The younger children's drawings in the study were generally freer and less inhibited than the older pupils' in overall effect, and they often used the space more boldly. In response to *Zoo*, for example, Sara (4) (figure 6.4) recreates the family, each member occupying equal space across the horizontal picture plane. Her lines are curvaceous and free, enclosed and protected by a large beaming sun in the left-hand corner, complete with a stretch of sky punctuated by one cloud and a flock of round-shaped birds. Her simple pen drawing is happy and spontaneous and the four smiling faces beam out at the viewer.

After reading *Lily* Janet (4)[*] explored the expressive qualities of colour. The top left-hand half of her first picture is covered in a coloured stripe. The first section is made up of thinner strokes of purple, blue, red and brown before a square of intense black and then yellow. Cutting into the yellow square is a large green vertical form which echoes the long neck of the sea creature in the river in Kitamura's story. The green form stands in a large purple square. Janet has worked with a great degree of care and control and the resulting image is both imaginative, original and highly symbolic. Her detailed explanation of the composition backs this up; she described the hori-

Figure 6.4 By Sara (4)

zontal stripe of colour as representing her curtains, the black square acting as a dark window and the final yellow square showing light pouring through a window. Her second drawing* three months later is made with the same concentration, but now shows more interest in planning. Her drawing has become an exploration of forms laid out horizontally across the page, highlighted by a thick purple stripe of night sky along the top. Drawing this time in felt tip, Janet again uses colour to articulate feelings but her drawing has become more realistic as she experiments with and re-creates the twisted shapes of Kitamura's lamp posts, clock towers, buildings and trees.

Internal structure

Many of the drawings collected in the study show children beginning to experiment with structure to introduce new viewpoints. Christina (8) (figure 6.5) starts by drawing a large orange tiger in the centre of the page and, having rubbed out her first attempt, tries hard to make her picture as realistic as possible. Although she has clearly had difficulties with the head, which is large and awkward, the hind legs and tail are drawn with greater accuracy, with the far leg placed behind the front leg in a convincing way. This thoughtful drafting corresponds

Figure 6.5 By Christina (8)

with her interview when she talked about the way in which Browne positions a baboon to show it is sitting: 'I think the way he draws the baboon that's sitting down like a lion with his mouth open. He draws all the fur first then he draws two legs and draws two more legs on the front to make it seem that it's sitting up.'

The tiger's tail and paws are carefully shaped, as is the butterfly fluttering outside the cage. The threatening grey felt-tip bars of the cage stretch vertically across the whole piece of paper and are reminiscent of the thick black lines around the animal pictures in *Zoo*. Although Christina has drawn green grass in the cage she makes a clear distinction between inside and outside by the position of the butterfly, shaping the grey felt tip so as not to cover its pink wings. It is also interesting to note that she has continued these games in the top right-hand corner of her picture where she has written 'ZOO', doodling eyelashes and eye balls on the two 'O's. On a third line she has written, 'enjoy' a neat little joke of her own which demonstrates not only a real understanding of her drawings as means of communication, but also an understanding of the role and position of the viewer.

Several children drawing in response to *The Tunnel* depicted the boy turned into stone, one of the most haunting and compositionally

Figure 6.6 By Bobby (8)

sophisticated images in the book. As in the original drawing, Bobby (8) (figure 6.6) has framed the image in a rectangular box, and the reader, peering in on the scene, empathises with the girl's sense of loss and isolation as she finds her brother 'still as stone' and sobs, 'Oh no … I'm too late.' Bobby has drawn in grey pencil except for a thin stripe of blue on the horizon blended into the grey clouds. The internal elements in the drawing have been placed with care: the jagged grass in the distance, the tree stumps and the circle of stones around the boy's feet. The figure has been redrawn several times, but Bobby has successfully depicted the boy frozen in motion, arm and leg outstretched to run away and, most chillingly of all, mouth and eyes wide open in fear.

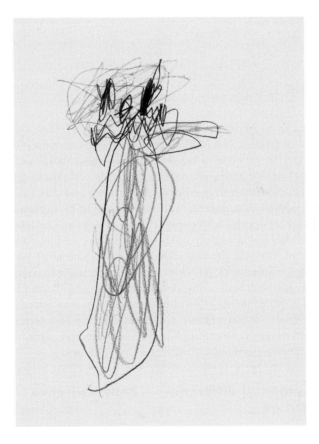

Figure 6.7 By Ashok (4)

Figure 6.8 By Anne (9)

Ashok (4) and Anne (9) chose the grinning tree from *Lily* as the central point in their composition, but a comparison of their drawings demonstrate the differences between the two ages. Ashok draws with great energy and his large green scribble tree is placed in the middle of the picture, complete with its menacing black mouth and dark eyes (figure 6.7). The picture is as graphic and direct as might be expected in the drawing of a young child. In contrast Anne has drawn the tree as only part of the whole composition (figure 6.8). Repeated rubbings out around the figure of Lily and the dog show that this young artist has placed considerable emphasis on 'getting it right'. Her colouring in is more accurate and controlled, and, unlike Ashok, she uses careful, solid blocks of colour. The arrangement of the internal elements is more worked out and more skilfully arranged and executed. However, her drawing lacks the direct aesthetic response of Ashok's tree. This deliberate planning brings us to an interesting point about developmental changes.

Developmental differences – Polly 'switches her brain on'

In *Artful Scribbles*, Gardner's young son explains the difference between the drawings of older and younger children: 'As you get older,

I think you look differently. You look more carefully at things. Also you think a lot, you plan before you actually make the drawing' (1980: 17). This notion of the role of thinking and planning in drawing comes through in several of the interviews and is evident in the pictures made by some of the older children, such as Christina, Bobby and Anne. However, we found that even younger children such as Polly and Janet were capable of engaging in the metacognitive processes involved in the creation of images. Here are more of Polly's (5) comments whilst drawing (see plate 6)[2]:

> I'll just switch my brain on ... that's the house in the distance that's why it's really small. ... Now here I am going to use another green. Isn't grass two different shades of green? This is a lime shade of green ...

Unfortunately, Polly's was the only transcript which captured a child talking aloud while actually drawing, but Erin's (7) comments to the interviewer also capture an awareness of the role of thinking and planning in the production of images, as well as showing her enjoyment of picturebooks:

ERIN: I really love his books.
I: I want to know why you say that, Erin.
ERIN: Well he doesn't just say, 'I'll just write a story, I think I'll do it about this' and then he writes it. He actually thinks about it. Or he plans it ahead and then he really does good pictures and the pictures tell a different story, the same story only in a different way.

Erin's first drawing (figure 6.9) uses bold colours and composition and is emotionally direct. However, by the time of the re-visit, her drawing had lost some of this earlier confidence becoming more concerned with a moral message (like most of the older children) than creative expression. This developmental change can be described in terms of a move away from an emotional and aesthetic response towards a greater interest in the internal structure of the composition.

Davis (1993) explains this change in terms of 'U-shaped' development. In middle childhood (8–11) children reach the trough of 'literal' translation and are held back by the desire to capture the 'realness' of an object; they are no longer satisfied with a drawing which provides the essence or an impression of what they see. Benson (1986) also

Figure 6.9 By Erin (7)

describes this period as an important time of conventionalism, a preoccupation with the rules of language and of graphic representation. The expressive qualities of the younger children's drawings are, perhaps, a direct result of a lack of restraints and rules. Gardner suggests another possible factor:

> Once writing mechanics and literary accomplishment have advanced sufficiently (as they ought to have by the age of 9 or 10), the possibility of achieving in words what was once attempted in drawings comes alive: the stage is set for the demise of graphic expression.
>
> (1980: 155)

Gardner suggests that the child's drawing is affected not only by the development of concrete operational thinking and increasing awareness of the self and its surroundings, but also by teaching methods which emphasise the primacy of the written word as a means of communication. Echoing Gardner, Davis fears that, 'Although artists thrive and survive the literal stage, most individuals are lost in the trough of the U' (1993: 90). The desire for realism is impossible to achieve and only a few very gifted artists ever attain the degree of pictorial accuracy so craved in middle childhood. Most children are defeated by pictorial forms of representation, thus considering themselves unable to draw. This can be seen in the majority of the older children's drawings in the study which seem more constrained than those of the younger children.

The humanities project

As the U-shape model suggests, middle childhood does not necessarily have to herald 'the end' of aesthetic artistic response as long as children are given opportunities to continue to explore, accept and understand the uniquely expressive qualities of art and other aesthetic forms of communication. One class of 10-year-olds in the study proved it was possible to emerge from the 'U'. Working with an experienced and charismatic teacher, these pupils had taken part in an extended humanities project: over the course of the year they had examined the portrayal of refugees from World War II – and more recent conflicts – in a variety of media texts including photographs. The drawings they produced in response to Zoo were powerful and visually fluent, as their characters scream and glare out of the picture plane, demanding attention. Their interviews also showed that the children understood and used a wide variety of visual terms:

MAL: … she probably feels sorry for the animals …
I: So how do the colours signal that?
MAL: 'Cos she's wearing that black and dark … dull and dark colours.
I: So what does that mean? Black, dull, dark colours?
MAL: They're like … you usually wear black for funerals.
I: Right. So you wear black for funerals. And what do black and purple represent?
MAL: Sad and sorryness.

They also discussed compositional devices such as the use of different borders around pictures:

BELINDA: It's like saying that like he probably says that the humans aren't really important, so he put like wavy lines round the picture. That the animals are more important than the humans so he's put like a straight border around the picture …
AIDEN: The animal pictures are all edgy and it's like you know, it gives the … really there's a tension …

This knowledge of picturing devices and techniques is also evident in their drawings. Sally (10) has attempted a complicated composition inspired by the close-up image of the caged gorilla in Browne's original text (figure 6.10). She has drawn the cruciform bars of the cage so that

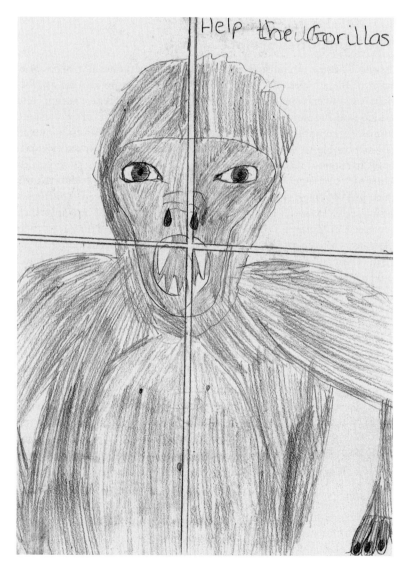

Figure 6.10 By Sally (10)

they show up white against the grey fur of the gorilla and form a cross two-thirds up the vertical picture plane, deliberately positioning the gorilla's eyes on each side of the top section of the cross. This careful composition is strengthened by her clever use of colour. The drawing is executed entirely in graphite pencil apart from the deep brown eyes and gaping red mouth which form the focal point of the picture and draw the viewer in.

In Belinda's (10) drawing (figure 6.11) she experiments with the striped pattern of a tiger. Browne's style is characterised by his attention to the minuscule details of the daily world and many of the children's drawings echo this sensitivity to pattern and design; like Belinda, they experiment with stripes and marks on the animals' coats, playing with ideas about camouflage. A large number of children depict striped animals, tigers or zebras, which echo the bars of the cages, the black and white cover of the book and even the stripes on Dad's shirt. In Belinda's drawing the stripes have slipped off the tiger and metamorphosed into the cage itself, providing an interesting metaphor for the relationship between environment and animal. As it loses its stripes the tiger becomes unclassifiable to the human eye and the cage takes on a strange, organic and fluid quality of its own. This is cleverly juxtaposed by a lonely butterfly which has been positioned on

Figure 6.11 By Belinda (10)

the bare white paper underneath the cage. The issue of camouflage and the naturalness of the surroundings are the key to many of the drawings from this class and show an understanding of composition, content and message as well as the deeper philosophical and moral implications of the story.

Many of the drawings by these pupils explored the moral dimension of *Zoo*. Some show a clear visual portrayal of human versus animal viewpoints and incorporate words into drawings to increase impact. One unsigned drawing (figure 6.12) is divided into two parts named FREEDOM and ISOLATION. On the 'freedom' side of the page, a monkey swings upside-down on a banana tree prophesying, 'no cage will spoil the world!' A smiling, colourful earth is drawn next to a person wearing clothes bearing slogans 'I hate zoos' and 'I hate animals in zoos'. This person says, 'it's great not to be in a cage'. The 'isolation' side shows a caged black-and-white earth with a mouth drooping downwards. Although the images in this drawing are strong and eloquent in their own right, it is interesting that the child felt the need to back up his or her moral view with the written word. This ties in with Gardner's point about the move from visual to verbal forms of communication.

Figure 6.12 Unsigned drawing

All of the drawings by these older children contain striking individual details representative of the particular interests and motivations of the artist. They show the effects a gifted teacher and an in-depth analysis of visual image can have on the way children think, write and draw. As Gardner says, 'The capacity to consider various intellectual and social possibilities confers fresh powers on an individual's artistry' (1980: 213).

The *Zoo* project

As my class's understanding of *Zoo* developed, so too did the sophistication of their drawings and I can see many parallels between their work and the work of the 10-year-olds described above. This change took place in the context of a series of visual exercises and experiments which were designed to encourage the chidren to deepen their existing understanding by talking, looking and making. Their work also demonstrates the cognitive link between seeing, doing and knowing.

During our re-readings I talked to the children about Browne's pictures using direct questioning, and I also allowed the children to ask questions in return. One of the strongest compositional devices and the easiest for the children to see is the juxtaposition of the two worlds inside and outside the cages. We also talked about the way in which the artist uses the left- and right-page spreads to illustrate the two different sides of the zoo debate. As our discussions about the book continued, many children began to place different emphasis on the relative size of animals to humans.

In addition to our focussed work on *Zoo*, the class had wide experience of creating their own images, both from their imagination and in response to familiar objects, pictures and stories. Over the course of the year we carried out a series of experiments with colour, pattern, tone and form which encouraged the children to develop their own visual vocabulary. They were also encouraged to draw their own stories, make books and use their own images as a starting point for writing. This particular class was also characterised by a wonderful capacity for focussed looking and great concentration. Just as they were happy to sit for half an hour on the carpet analysing a picture or a book, a simple pencil exercise could occupy them for a whole afternoon. During class drawing sessions they were often so absorbed that they worked in total silence. Our return to *Zoo* enabled my class to use their newly acquired visual skills, having developed the confidence and control to produce drawings that were closer to their actual understanding.

Revisiting Zoo

After the initial in-depth study, I wasn't sure how the children would respond to Zoo several months later. When they came in from lunch many of them spotted the book resting on my board and a few started a discussion about which Browne book was their favourite. When I re-read Zoo with them I was conscious of a strange shift of power and felt that they were reading the story to me, often eager to interrupt my reading of the text with knowledgeable and confident observations and suggestions. During the initial sessions we had talked about the gorilla picture in some detail, although none of the children had drawn it afterwards. This time they were obsessed by it and one of the most striking observations was made by a normally silent child with special needs, Louis (4), who talked to the class about the compositional similarities between the gorilla picture and the family portraits at the start of the book (see figure 4.2).

Lyle (4) was an exceptionally articulate child; in the class discussion he talked in depth about the visual symbolism in Browne's book, particularly the penultimate page which focusses on the gorilla's face. The children noticed how the page is split 'like the bars of a cage' and described the gorilla as 'looking like a king' and 'his eyes look like a person'. When I asked the class whether it reminded them of anything, Lyle responded, 'Jesus. Jesus died on a cross.' When asked why the artist had chosen to draw the gorilla like that he replied, 'Because God made Jesus and God made all the animals.' The children also compared the animals and people: 'The gorilla looks wiser, more like a person.' Lyle concluded, 'I think the animals are becoming wiser and the people are like animals.' His comments tie in with his own deeply religious home background. In Art and Illusion Gombrich writes: 'Whenever we receive a visual impression, we act by docketing it, filing it, grouping it in one way or another, even if the impression is only that of an inkblot or a fingerprint' (1962: 251).

Lyle has drawn on his own bank of visual experience, something all readers do in their own idiosyncratic ways when interpreting or responding to image. Although this particular child was frustrated by his attempts to communicate what he saw and understood visually, his verbal responses showed a proficiency in interpreting and understanding visual references and metaphors. This is a good example of what Kress is saying in Before Writing where he describes reading as a transformative action in which the reader 'makes sense of the signs provided to her or to him within a frame of reference in their own experience' (1997: 58). The reading process is multi-modal and, as we have seen, visual meaning can be communicated and interpreted in many different ways.

In *Zoo* the facial expressions and body language of the family and the animals are powerful communicators of the isolation and pointlessness felt by Mum and the apparent lack of concern of Dad and the boys. As we have noted elsewhere, many of the youngest children were able to talk about facial expressions and body language. My class and I discussed in detail how individual protagonists within the story were feeling. Initially only a few of the children were able to articulate these feelings in their drawings, a finding backed up in research cited in Gardner (1980). However, on revisiting *Zoo*, I was intrigued to see that the children now had the confidence and skills to depict some of the more challenging and complicated images from the book. Many chose this time to draw the image of the gorilla within a cruciform frame. Louis (4) made a quite outstanding drawing of the family and the caged gorilla (figure 6.13). Although his figures are still very immature and tadpole-like, he has deliberately drawn bemused frown lines on Dad's forehead. A strong white crucifix separates the gorilla from the family and his eyes have been skilfully placed on either side of the top section. Louis has also attempted to write the title of the book. Many others made similar developmental leaps to achieve levels of

Figure 6.13 By Louis (4)

expression and fluency unusual in such young children. The confidence evident in the discussion is also reflected in the children's drawings as they explore the theme of suffering on the cross – one of the most distinctive and poignant images of the western world – and relate it to the gorilla in the cage. The children were symbolically representing captivity and suffering in their drawings and communicating empathy for animals (and elsewhere for people, especially Mum). This finding runs contrary to beliefs about the egocentric perspective of the pre-operational young child.

The final drawings are by Jane (5), who made a quite remarkable leap between the two sessions. Her first drawing shows a literal understanding of the story and depicts a grinning elephant centred on the page inside a square box surrounded by a happy but androgynous 'tadpole' family (figure 6.14). Her later drawing is an attempt at the gorilla's face seen through the crossing bars of the cage (figure 6.15). Jane has made a deliberate decision about the composition and internal structure of her drawing and has halved the page horizontally and vertically with two thick bars in the shape of a cross. Her drawing focusses on the gorilla's eyes, placing each in a top quarter of the page. She works in graphite pencil to capture the texture of the gorilla's fur, hatching tiny lines in different sizes and directions, using darker,

Figure 6.14 By Jane (5)

Figure 6.15 By Jane (5)

stronger lines on the bottom half of the face to emphasise the gentle sadness of the eyes. Her drawing explores not only Browne's dramatic composition and viewpoint, but also his realistic rendering of every tiny hair on the gorilla's face. In both drawings Jane uses the compositional devices of the cage to communicate entrapment. However, in the later drawing she is intrigued not only by the positioning of the humans to the animals, but also by the psychological dimension. The detail in the fur and the eyes reveals how important she understands the individual animals to be. Her sophisticated composition creates drama and pathos articulated by skilful attention to texture and detail. By experimenting with and talking about artistic devices and conventions Jane has developed her visual knowledge and is now trying out these devices in her own work.

Final thoughts

> Children's hands and eyes must be active for intelligence to develop.
>
> (Kellog 1979: 13)

Looking at the drawings in this study has demonstrated to me that even the youngest children can interpret, comprehend and communicate the visual – far beyond what they might be assumed to know. The young artists in my class came to a deeper understanding through their visual explorations. What seems to happen when we draw is similar to the process that we experience through writing: by doing we come to understand.

Although many children draw spontaneously from a young age, adults have a role to play by allowing space for experimentation and practice. By focussing explicitly on external visual elements such as composition, line, form and colour, the teacher can develop children's capacities to internalise this visual language and, in so doing, come to understand and communicate through their pictures. These explorations should take place through looking at art, as well as developing children's graphic skills. Our study provided opportunities for children to explore what they saw through playing, talking, making and drawing, thus enabling them to demonstrate the sophisticated thinking of which they were capable. Drawing is a serious enterprise for young children; combining drawing with careful looking offers the intrinsic pleasures derived from all creative activities and the special way in which art nourishes 'the invisible realms of our mind' (Gombrich 1962: 239).

Vignette – 'it makes you feel you are trapped in a cage' (Yu 4)

Of all the drawings in the study some of the most interesting in terms of overall effect, content and understanding are by Yu (4). She is a quiet and thoughtful child and, although both her reading and writing are advanced for her age, she said very little in the interviews or the class discussions. However, her drawings communicated a deep response to *Zoo* and an indication of some of her own preferences, feelings and experiences. In many of her early drawings the figure of Mum is drawn particularly carefully. As middle child of a young family of five children, her drawings perhaps indicate the importance and power of her own mother as primary carer.

Yu's early drawings reveal that she has understood the main themes in *Zoo* by depicting the family side by side with animals caged inside their enclosures. Yet she also shows a striking level of sensitivity to visual elements such as composition, design and characterisation. Yu's first drawing shows a giraffe and a large tree fenced in by a bold, three-barred gate (figure 6.16). On the other side of the fence, to the right of the tree, stand Mum, Dad and the two boys who take up the last vertical quarter of the picture. Yu's composition shows an understanding of the contrast between the freedom of those outside the zoo and the unnaturalness of the animals' enclosures. The tree and the fence form a clear barrier between the animals and humans while a small, smiling bird sits on the fence next to the giraffe.

This distinction is reinforced by environmental details. A large sun, a few clouds and birds in the sky of the animal section form a marked contrast to the bars which separate them from the human protagonists. There even appears to be fruit on the giraffe's side of the tree and on the floor of its enclosure is a nondescript shape, reminiscent of the dirty cages in *Zoo*. Yu has taken greatest care over the figure of Mum, who is drawn bigger than the rest of the family with

Figure 6.16 By Yu (4)

details such as her eyes which are drawn with lashes and tiny pupils. Yu skilfully controls the relationship between the different actors in her story by placing one in front of the other. Cox (1992) and others have discussed how very few young children achieve this partial hiding or occlusion in their pictures and will draw, for example, the whole object rather then partially obscuring a hidden object. Luquet used this example to demonstrate that 'children draw what they know rather than what they see' (quoted in Cox 1992: 88).

Later on the same day as the interview, Yu began her second picture, which is an example, not only of her widening understanding, but also of the way in which children continue to explore what they see through drawing (see plate 1). Sitting at a table with a group of other children, she began with an exploration of bubble writing which she placed in the top horizontal section of the picture. (I had noticed before how children enjoyed experimenting with typographic conventions and bubble writing is a good way of exploring both the shapes and conventions of text.) Next Yu started drawing an animal, a cheetah, which was then carefully contained in a cage, along with the bubble writing. As she drew in the bars of the cage she tried not to go over the lines on the cheetah before adding a few thin, dusty strokes of black dirt to the base of the cage. By now she had filled nearly the whole piece of paper, so she reached for another piece on which she redrew the family. Again the tree forms a powerful divide, this time between the parents and the boys who are now squeezed into the left-hand vertical plane of the picture.

As with the first drawing, Yu reapplies carefully practised schema for her figure drawings. While the boys are treated in exactly the same way in both drawings and are nearly identical, once again it is the figure of Mum who receives the greatest attention; she is the largest character, occupying nearly half the picture plane. However, the figures of both Mum and Dad demonstrate changes in her schema. Mum is drawn in profile with her back to the children and her arms outstretched towards Dad to whom she is saying, 'Come back!'. Drawing figures in profile is very unusual in young children's drawings as once again the child is required to draw what they see rather than what they know. A long, diagonal sweep of hair draws the character in towards the rest of the family. Mum's hands, arms and hair are emphasised, whereas on one of the boys the arms have been forgotten altogether. Dad's face is drawn in greater detail, his eyes are big and open and he has an angry, fuzzy mouth and expressive, upturned eyebrows, more reminiscent now of the father in *Zoo*. While Mum looks at Dad, Dad looks out of the picture towards the viewer. As in the book, he is fooling around and making silly noises, as do the children. Finally, Yu went back to the drawing of the cheetah and added a speech bubble for the animal, 'ha, ha ha'.

Three months later Yu drew again in response to *Zoo* after re-reading the book in the classroom (figure 6.17). In this drawing, a large rhinoceros stands alone in the centre of the page in a dirty, barren enclosure. The cage has no bars and is bare except for the grey bricks of the top right-hand corner and a few mouldy, insipid green patches on the floor. The cage is dirty and scratched with graffiti. Yu has placed the viewer in the cage with the animal, a compositional device employed by Browne in *Zoo*. The most significant change in this later drawing is the facial expression of the animal. This time the eyes are slanted and angry, its mouth is open and teeth bared. The total effect is both unsettling and disturbing – similar to feelings evoked by the neglected, lonely orangutan in *Zoo*.

In the final drawing after the second interview, Yu depicts a tiger and four birds (figure 6.18). Three brown baby birds sit inside a nest perched on top of a palm tree while a much larger, rainbow-coloured bird flies towards the right-hand side of the page, pointing in the same direction as a dramatic, elongated tiger. Yu's positioning of the bars of the

Figure 6.17 By Yu (4)

Figure 6.18 By Yu (4)

cage gives an ambiguity to her picture, as the reader is not entirely sure whether all the creatures are inside or outside the cage. Such indeterminacy is, of course, a feature of Browne's work.

Since Yu's first reading of *Zoo* she has spent time studying not only this book but other natural history books. In her later drawings the animals are more anatomically correct and individual for each animal type. The tiger is depicted in profile and is angry with a long, wavy mouth and upturned eyebrows. Yu is now working in felt tip and the bright blues of the sky and careful, multi-coloured pattern on the bird produce a powerful aesthetic response in the viewer.

Yu is clearly a gifted artist and her mature understanding of the story is communicated through sophisticated, detailed drawings. She has begun to grasp some of the complex rela-tionships between the actors in the story and her drawings show a striking degree of sensitivity to the emotional state of the main protagonists and the beginnings of characterisa-tion. It is very unusual for such a young child to draw a figure in profile, to represent movement and to layer the composi-tion by deliberately placing one object behind or in front of another. By continuing to provide her with opportunities to express herself visually, to draw what she sees, Yu will be able to communicate her considerable knowledge as well as adding to it. She is also able to express her powerful reac-tions to *Zoo*, strong feelings which she was unable to communicate in any other way.

Notes

1   Unfortunately this drawing is not included as it does not show up in black and white. We will use [*] to indicate when this is the case with other draw-ings.
2   Polly uses bold colour and line to represent Rose and Jack in the forest, the figure of the wolf in the tree, the tunnel and the siblings' mother shouting, 'Children', (written by the interviewer at Polly's request) from her house at the top of the hill.

Part III

Listening, talking, thinking and learning

Chapter 7

Putting yourself in the picture

A question of talk

Helen Bromley

'What is the use of a book,' thought Alice, 'without pictures or conversations?'

(*Alice in Wonderland*, Lewis Carroll, 1865)

Introduction

A good story's got to have a problem and the problem's in the pictures.

(Kathy 6)

Picture, if you will, the following scenes. Running her fingers over Kitamura's evocative blue sky in *Lily*, Kathy says softly, 'Back in Majorca we had some colours with that all across the sky ... and also in the sand, blending.' Judy ponders the reasons why Kitamura has drawn steps with wobbly lines and says, 'They are very old. My church is very old and it has steps like that.'

These snatches of conversation illustrate the power of the picture-book to stimulate children to reflect on their past through the window of the present. Invited into the miniature world of the illustration, children and indeed the adults who are prepared to take time to look, contemplate and talk with them, have access to both individual and shared histories. The illustrations in the book encompass the individual's past within the present time and everyone's experiences are authenticated. In this chapter I shall look at how this shared context created by the pictures provided a foundation for some fertile and reflective conversations.

Tell me ...

In discussing *Lily* with the children, both as individuals and as small groups, I became increasingly conscious of the role that the pictures played in creating a shared world. Although the memories which the pictures triggered in me could not be identical to those of the children, it became clear that through the pictures it was possible to find 'common ground' – areas of experience which, despite the differences in our ages and personal histories, overlapped and formed a shared foundation for conversation – a site for genuine collaboration. The creation of this shared context was supported by the pace at which the interviews were conducted. It was as if the pictures were being shared, savoured and relished in the manner of friends looking at photographs, rather than as a lesson in looking.

How might all this appear in practice? Here is Kathy (6) discussing with the interviewer a double-page spread which shows Lily and Nicky standing on a bridge. Lily looks at the ducks on one side of the bridge, while on the other Nicky is aware of an enormous dinosaur. His legs are moving frantically; we know this through Kitamura's use of the conventions of animation – numerous legs on the dog, and movement indicated by small lines around his paws. The text on the page reads simply 'She stops by the bridge to say good night to the gulls and the ducks on the canal' (figure 7.1).

The discussion went as follows:

I: Tell me about this picture.

KATHY: She might have found some things in the bag that the ducks might like to eat. And she is throwing them out and Nicky is looking at them and I think it might be a dinosaur, it might be a big duck!

I: You see that as a big duck?

KATHY: But it hasn't got any wings.

I: No it hasn't got any wings, yes it is the funniest-looking duck I have ever seen, I have to say!

KATHY: It hasn't got any beak.

I: No. No beak. I think we can safely assume it's not a duck.

KATHY: It might be a dinosaur.

I: It might be a dinosaur.

KATHY: But how could there be a dinosaur in the water and also, there wasn't people when dinosaurs were alive. But there was a couple but I suppose they killed 'em to eat the meat.

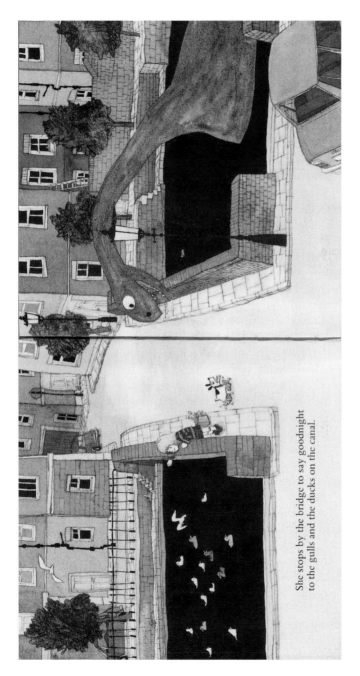

She stops by the bridge to say goodnight to the gulls and the ducks on the canal.

Figure 7.1 From *Lily Takes a Walk* by Satoshi Kitamura

I: Oh, well the dog's got problems in that case. How do we know then that he is moving, this little dog, how do we know he is moving?

KATHY: Because he is going like that [waving arms in the background]. He might be doing the can-can …

Chambers says that the words, *Tell me*, 'suggest a desire for collaboration, indicating that the teacher really does want to know what the reader thinks, and that it anticipates conversational dialogue rather than an interrogation' (1993: 49). This certainly seems to be true in the example above. By this point in the interview Kathy has been asked to tell the interviewer about other pictures in the book and so realises that her views are valued, and that there are no right or wrong answers. In fact she feels so secure that she is able to make jokes and enter into a playful relationship with the interviewer. What is not apparent from the transcript is the mischievous grin and the tongue-in-cheek tone as she says, ' It might be a big duck.'

In the conversational exchange that follows (where both participants use irony), the joke is played around with, and indeed various possibilities explored, until Kathy herself suggests that it might be a dinosaur. The adult's responses are also important here. To have closed the exchange at this point, and decreed that the creature was indeed a dinosaur and that Kathy was 'correct' might well have closed the conversation down. What came next might not have been heard at all and yet is one of the most interesting parts of the conversation. She knows that the likelihood of there being a dinosaur in the water is slim for a number of reasons; there aren't dinosaurs now (implied, but not stated) and they did not roam the earth at the same time as people. However, what she can see in front of her is indisputable; dinosaurs and humans in the same picture. This juxtaposition of remembered facts prompts the sanctioning of the widest range of possibilities. What is apparent here is a child 'turning around' her own schema. Her memories of what she knows about dinosaurs have to be reconstructed in order to fit the context in which she is working. Kathy has what Bartlett (1932: 206) would describe as 'the capacity to turn around (her) own schemata and construct them afresh'. In the conversation in which she is participating no single type of knowledge is privileged over another – thus creating an atmosphere where Kathy feels that she is able to reflect on and manipulate her memories to solve the problem that the picture poses.

Kathy's humorous approach continues when the adult returns to the interview schedule to ask about the dog's legs. The sort of complex concepts that Kathy is dealing with and the way that she deals with them are made manifest through her conversation. In order to subvert facts, you need to feel secure in your knowledge of them, and she does this remarkably well. What we have here is visible thinking. Kathy's ability to use her remembered knowledge and make connections between it and the context in which she is currently working are as worthy of note as her interpretations of the picture. The *Tell me* focus has effectively given Kathy permission to ask and answer her own questions.

It is important, too, to note how identities and roles are created through the discussion around a picture. In this small piece of transcript Kathy positions herself in several ways: a dinosaur/prehistory expert; an animation expert; a user of irony; a thinker; a conversationalist. She does not position herself in the traditional role of 'pupil' – a receiver of knowledge. The identity that she creates for herself (through talk) is of someone who is on equal terms with the adult in the conversation, who is confident to take turns with the adult, and who can manipulate the pictorial symbol system assuredly. There is a genuine non-competitiveness about this exchange which makes it all the more worthwhile. Both participants co-operate in the negotiation of meanings, which no doubt encourages Kathy to talk about her ideas. As Wells points out, ' It is the collaborative approach ... that encourages children to explore their understanding of a topic and gives them the confidence to try out their ideas without the fear of being wrong' (1986: 115).

Judy (6), another child from Kathy's class, also used her prior knowledge to make meaning of this particular double spread. Asked to tell the interviewer about the picture she begins:

JUDY: He is in the water, he must be swimming but he can't put his neck in there because he is too big he might knock all the houses down. He [the dog] is scared because there is one of them [referring to the dinosaur].

I: How do you know he is scared?

JUDY: Because he is big and she is looking at the ducks. They're looking different ways again because he probably doesn't like duckies and they're probably scared of the dog. She has put the flowers down.

I: She has put the flowers down. I suppose it is difficult to feed the ducks if you are holding the flowers. Why is he drawn like that though?

JUDY: He's gonna run away from that probably.
I: So what does it mean then?
JUDY: He is shouting.
I: Mmm. Dogs don't have eight legs do they, so why has he got lots of legs in that then?
JUDY: Is it because his legs are shaking?
I: Yes, I think you are right.
JUDY: That's what happens, because I had this thing and she only had two wings and arms and when they ha! turned around and then she had lots [Judy is referring to a toy].

As with Kathy, Judy clearly demonstrates how problems can be solved through conversation. Importantly, she was asked to explain how she knew something. This supplementary question led ultimately to Judy being able to explain a complex visual phenomenon (persistence of vision) and how it can be represented in two dimensions and not three. Judy continues to speculate about the picture for some considerable time, discussing such wide-ranging topics as the possibility that all the houses are empty (because their occupants are at the pub), and what would happen if the dog was to be eaten by the dinosaur. Throughout her interview Judy was able to use her experiences of life to interpret the miniature world encapsulated in the pictures of Kitamura. Her answers and interpretations are even more remarkable when one considers that she was positioned in the 'lowest ability' group in that classroom.

It is fascinating to look at the different types of experiences which the girls draw upon in interpreting the pictures. In both cases they use their own first-hand experiences – feeding the ducks in the park, for example, or playing with a moving toy. There are also those experiences whose reality is of a different nature. Kathy's knowledge of life in prehistoric times comes from books read, films or TV programmes seen or museums visited. Looking at Judy, one can see the same types of knowledge being used: the reality that was her spinning toy, the reality that is feeding the ducks, and the knowledge about dinosaurs – their size and strength. This thoughtful and reflective dialogue with their past provides the children with a powerful means of moving forward in their thinking.

It is talk which empowers this. Asked to *Tell me* about the picture through writing, it is certain that for Judy at least, such complex understandings would never have been revealed. The task of writing would have masked her considerable ability to reflect on the pictures in front of her. Dialogue is also important – while a writing journal, or a 'thinking book 'would have gone some way towards supporting and enhancing these behaviours, the teacher would also have needed to be an equal partner in the written dialogue.

The pictures are undoubtedly the key to the children's success. Both participants in the dialogue have equal access to the ideas represented by the illustrator. This would not have been the case had we been discussing written text. Trying to hold the ideas presented by the written word and reflect upon them would have been too demanding for both Judy and Kathy. More importantly, dealing with the written word, the adult would have undoubtedly been the expert. Pictures provide a landscape in which minds can meet for contemplation rather than competition.

Griffin and Cole, quoted in Edwards and Mercer, say that 'a zone of proximal development is a dialogue between a child and his future; it is not a dialogue between the child and an adult's past' (1987: 164). It is interesting to consider this quote in the light of the children's discussions. It is obvious that the children's past histories are of considerable importance to them as ways of constructing meaning. It is as if the pictures act as a trigger for a host of memories – each one personal to that child. The adult's past is also important in these discussions. It is the overlapping pieces of these autobiographies that help child and adult understand each other, finding commonalities of experience as well as being able to explore differences. The possible worlds created by Kitamura, child and adult, overlap. Each participant in the discussion has their experiences widened through incursion, not only into the worlds of the picturebook, but also into the remembered vistas that are the landscapes of memory.

Reading together

Kathy, interviewed for a second time, is prompted to draw upon a whole new referential framework to discuss the pictures in *Lily*.

> Bats flitter and swoop in the evening sky. 'Aren't they clever, Nicky?' says Lily. 'Not far now.'

KATHY: I don't really like bats.
I: Don't you?
KATHY: NO.

I: We get some in our garden sometimes. I think they're quite curious.
    They move very funnily.
KATHY: My nan gets foxes, well she used to.
I: Does she? Did she used to feed them, Kathy?
KATHY: No.
I: No. Do they come for her dustbins?
KATHY: Well, once actually, my Dad was sleeping over my Nan's for
    some reason I don't know, and he left his trainers outside and the
    foxes came and sort of bited the laces and stuff and it was all
    horrible. And there was all holes in his trainers and everything.

This vignette of family life so powerfully provided by Kathy may at first
glance seem to consist mostly of 'off task' talk; however this is not the
case. The comment prompted by the picture of the bat is picked up on
and the discussion enlarged, and culminates in the sharing of an
amusing anecdote and, less importantly, an insight into the habits of
urban foxes. It is as significant as the contemplation of the meaning
behind the picturebook or Kathy's comprehension of the story. This
type of talk builds relationships and creates shared contexts which may
act as reference points for future learning.

    Knowledge about the children as individuals can only be gained
through conversations such as these. Through these spoken stories
Kathy's ideas and interpretation of events are available with an inti-
macy, immediacy and authenticity that would be difficult to match in a
conventional activity. Yet it is too frequently the case that, in the
classroom situation, the adult needs to drive on with the 'educational'
agenda of the day, hiding wisdom and understandings such as those
displayed above. Conversations like these also build the relationships
needed for children to feel emotionally secure and predisposed to learn.
How good to know that the grown-up with whom you are working is
interested in you as a person, and not just as a recipient of an adult-
designed and -delivered curriculum. Wells (1986) speaks of how 'the
content of the curriculum becomes increasingly to be presented
symbolically through uses of language that are more characteristic of
writing than of conversation'. He goes on to argue that children for
whom it is difficult to cope 'with the linguistic representation of ideas
that are disembedded from a context of specific personal experiences'
become less able to meet the demands of the school system, and
become judged as academically limited'. The use of pictures overcomes
these difficulties.

    The older children in the study tended to be less conversational in their responses. While studying the picture of the dinosaur that gave the younger children such food for thought, the older children's comments included: 'Lily's looking at something nice ... all the swans and ducks swimming around, but all Nicky sees is a big dinosaur' (Tina 8). Unlike Kathy, Tina returns directly to the book in her description of the picture, but on this occasion chooses not to expand on the theme of the dinosaur. Seamus (7) pursues a line of thought prompted by the drawing of Nicky: 'I like the way where they've put the dog. You've got like four legs at the front and four legs at the back and he's trying to get away. The water's kind of really dark. ... A little bit of black, not exactly blue.'

To Seamus and Tina, the juxtaposition of the dinosaur with a human being does not pose the problem that it does for Kathy. For Seamus, the picture simply amuses him; and we could argue that Tina also 'got the joke'. Their reflections, however, did not seem to take on the dialogic nature of either Kathy or Judy's comments. This may be, of course, because some of the dialogue has become internalised. Transcripts alone cannot show the way that the children examined the picture, their heads to one side in contemplation.

Looking at the same picture, Lauren (10) comments: 'There's a bridge in the middle page with houses in the background and then Lily is looking at the ducks and she might have been feeding them or something like that. I mean on the other side where Nicky is looking it seems like there is a dinosaur, a Loch Ness Monster.' Lauren makes reference to her knowledge of mythical monsters, but does not feel it necessary to pursue that line of thought. However, as with the younger children, she is interpreting the picture through the use of remembered experiences – in her case knowledge of the Loch Ness Monster. In common with the other interviewees, she recognises that the large number of legs on the dog signifies movement and can attribute her knowledge to media texts. In response to the question 'What is Nicky doing?' she replies 'Getting really scared. Like in cartoons, and they run with their legs.'

It is in comparing this response with that of Judy, who used the flying toy to interpret the picture, that the different learning styles of the children become apparent and how important it is for all experiences to be brought to bear on a problem-solving task. Judy has undoubtedly watched cartoons, but it is clear that playing with the toy has been the most powerful tool for her interpretation of the picture. Neither child is more 'right' than another. Knowing their different ways of thinking would undoubtedly help teach them more effectively.

Making pictures

Throughout the conversations with the children it became apparent that they were as interested in how the pictures had been constructed as they were in their content. The children's appreciation of colour, depth and tone and of the way in which Kitamura had constructed the pictures suggests that this is an area which should be developed further in schools. Discussion about how illustrations are made have parallels with deconstructing written text – in both cases children are contemplating the use of tools and of symbol systems, as well as thinking about the efficacy of the whole and its relevance to them as people.

Here is Kathy (6) in discussion about the colours in the book:

I: What do you think about the colours in this picture, how do you think he has used the colours?

KATHY: Maybe the sky might be sort of like he might have got some dark colours and then made it lighter and then lighter, and maybe he didn't put no water on it for a long while.

I: Yes. I think that you could be right there. How do you think the colours make you feel?

KATHY: Like back in Majorca, because back in Majorca we had some colours with that all across the sky … and also in the sand, blending.

Kathy is not only able to speculate on the possible construction of the picture, but also to link the colours in it to her prior experience – in this case a happy family holiday. The wistfulness in her voice suggests a longing to relive that experience, something that many of us could identify with. There is no doubt that the colours in the book are evocative – the use of blue was mentioned by most of the children and there was a determination to replicate this colour in their own drawings. Their comments included the following:

I like the way the sky … like it's gone quite dark and into the light.

(Lauren 10)

They are well done because they are like … the sky has been done very well. Like dark and erm light blue, and I like how it has been done.

(Judy 6)

I like the way he's done the colours, and made them really blue and swirly colours and it's a bit like black.

(Seamus 7)

Seamus in particular made comments which showed how he understood the role that the pictures played in helping to tell the story, rather than merely showing us what is happening. His comments arose through being asked why he felt that Lily and the dog were constantly looking in different directions.

Erm, I think Nicky, it's getting dark, so I think he's a bit worried so he's going to look around and make sure nothing tries to snatch him or anything. See, because at the beginning it's broad daylight and she's out for the whole day. If you turn the pages, it gets darker and darker and darker.

Seamus was also asked about the lines in the illustrations. Reflectivity on the part of the children was supported by the conversational nature of the interviews and the time given to them to formulate their answers. His reply is a good example of the way in which all the children pondered their initial responses and built on them, offering supplementary answers:

I: How do you think he [Kitamura] used lines?
SEAMUS: It doesn't look like he used a ruler or anything.
I: No, that's true, it doesn't look like he used a ruler, no.
SEAMUS: I don't think he knows about rulers, it's a Japan thing.
I: I wonder why there are so many lines. Because there certainly are, aren't there, on each of the pages?
SEAMUS: He's put a lot of them in. I don't think he knows of a word called blank!

It is interesting to note that the children related their own ability to discuss the construction of the pictures (materials, perspective etc.) to the knowledge of art that they had gained from watching children's television. Programmes such as Smart, Art Attack and Blue Peter were mentioned by the children and creating their own works of art at home was obviously an important pastime for many of them.

The pictures and the type of questions asked about them clearly supported the children in formulating personal responses to Lily. Martin and Leather (1994: 48) comment that 'Perhaps we need, as teachers, to indicate much more clearly the kinds of response that are possible, so pupils see that it is a natural part of reading to make links between the book and the 'real' world. Drawing significant moments from a book offers children one such alternative response.

The 'pleasure principle'

It was apparent throughout the interviews that the children took great pleasure in the pictures in *Lily*. Interestingly, what was initially rejected by the older children as an 'easy book' had its hidden depths revealed by closer inspection:

> When [the class teacher] read it out loud to us I thought, 'Oh, no, why is he reading us this baby book? But then the jokes got more and more and I realised it wasn't a baby book.
>
> (Selma 11)

With this realisation, Selma allowed herself to take delight in the book, particularly the pictures, which are where the jokes are told, and then was able to respond to them through speculation and reflection. In these discussions pleasure was not denied; indeed, it was validated and encouraged. The enjoyment of the text was linked to the pleasures that existed for these children outside school – family holidays, trips to the market, watching television, reading the *Beano*, to name but a few.

These pleasures formed part of the unique experience that was each child's response to the text. As Evans, quoted in Martin and Leather (1994: 117), writes, 'It is no part of the teacher's business to reduce that uniqueness to uniformity.' Fortunately, neither art nor language provides the security of a single interpretation. However, as adults working with children, we need to provide the security for multiple interpretations to be shared and made explicit. As soon as children think that there is a 'correct' or true answer to be had, then diversity vanishes and along with it children's willingness to take risks and to develop their use of spoken language as a tool for thought. The conversations with the children around the pictures in this book were some of the most enjoyable that I have ever had in twenty years in schools.

For all the children in the study the pictures provided a means by which they could move from using talk for appreciation, to using talk for critical understanding, particularly through the group discussions.

This is a very important development for them to make. As Bruner (1986: 129) tells us:

> The language of education, if it is to be an invitation to reflection and culture creating, cannot be the so-called uncontaminated language of fact and 'objectivity'. It must express stance and counter stance and in the process leave place for reflection, for metacognition. It is this that permits one to reach higher ground, this process of objectifying in language or image what one has thought and then turning around on it and reconsidering it.

For the children who participated in these discussions, invitation was key. They were quite literally, invited to take part, invited to share their views and invited to participate in group discussions. The language of the conversations was never going to be that of fact and objectivity – the nature of the questions prevented this. Children expressed stance and counter-stance in many ways: these included debating issues with themselves (for example, Kathy and the dinosaurs), debating issues with the interviewer (Seamus and Kitamura's use of rulers) and, of course, with each other during small-group discussions.

Many children came to the group discussions full of enthusiasm for the renewed opportunity to reflect on the text and to create new understandings. In returning in this way they had been given space to reflect on their initial comments and to sound out their ideas in the company of their peers. Many of them quoted their earlier interviews: 'Do you remember when I said ... '; 'I said about the sky didn't I ... '; 'You liked it when I said about the lamp posts. ...' These comments indicate how important the discussions had been to the children.

The shared memories of some 10-year-olds led to profound interpretations of the book which no child on their own had managed to make. This is just a small extract from one discussion.

I: A lot of you noticed the rubbish in the book. What do you think the significance of the rubbish is?

SELMA: I think all the bits and everything makes it a bit more amusing.

ANGUS: I think it is just because the monsters are around that all the rubbish is in the book. I think it just adds things to the picture.

I: If we think about what Angus said, there might be a relationship, there might be something to do with the monsters and the rubbish. How do you think they might be related?

SELMA: I think it is like all the monsters making the rubbish, so like they are knocking everything over.

ANGUS: I don't think Lily has seen any of the rubbish.

I: Do you think it says anything about the way people treat the planet?

SELMA: Yes, they are a bit careless, not minding what they are doing and just not bothering about anything, just making all that rubbish and not bothering.

ANGUS: It is teenagers. They think they are big stuff and just throw their rubbish where they want.

I: So the dog though, he does notice all the rubbish doesn't he?

LAUREN: Because he is so small he might see it more, because it's bigger than him.

Supported by the interviewer and working within each other's 'zone of proximal development', the children elaborate their interpretation of the text. Although the adult provides the focus for discussion, it has come directly from observations that the children have made on their initial readings of the book. Their responses support and enhance each other, moving thought processes forward to 'the higher ground'. Look at how Lauren, through a series of statements, builds on her first thoughts and encourages Angus to offer personal opinion and develop his own earlier ideas. It also becomes clear in this discussion that Lauren, who does not contribute as frequently as the other children, nevertheless makes a pertinent point which contributes significantly to the way that this discussion continues: that animals are more at risk from a polluted earth than humankind.

Seven-year-olds worked in a similar way to allow Seamus to reach this conclusion: 'It might be because erm … because they might be quite erm. … As well as showing this they might, he might be trying to tell people in just a picture in a little way to clear up your rubbish.' The tentativeness of the way Seamus offers his opinion powerfully demonstrates the crucial significance of involvement in such a discussion. He is developing and redrafting his thoughts as he speaks. For children like him, the group discussion provides an opportunity to listen to the ideas of his peers, and to feel safe to offer his own thoughts. Children were also able to pool their individual expertise. Each child was differently aware of the dramatic potential of each picture. As each of these double-page spreads was a fragment of narrative that formed part of the wider story, bringing the children together in discussion was rather like completing a jigsaw puzzle of meaning. They could support each other in putting missing pieces into place, literally putting the whole picture together.

Implications for teachers

The significance of carefully planning questions to use with the children was key to the success of the project. Asking questions which tantalise children and which provoke thought is not a new or revolutionary idea, yet in practice very little planning for questioning takes place. In his book *Teaching Thinking* (1998), Fisher discusses at length how to use stories for philosophical enquiry, and how cognitively demanding it is for children not only to answer questions of a philosophical nature, but to think of such questions for themselves. He also proposes creating a 'community of enquiry' in the classroom. This research project provided the opportunity for the children involved to be part of a modest community of inquiry. The interviewers gathered valuable insights into children's motivations, ways of thinking and learning styles, as well as sharing personal anecdotes which cast valuable light on the children and their lives.

Quality conversations such as those described by Wells (1986) were evident throughout our research, only a few extracts of which are shared here. It is apparent that the children were committed to these conversations and answered at length, in stark contrast to recent findings about the discourse of the Literacy Hour (Mroz and Hardman 2000). (Children involved in conversations about the number of phonemes in 'pig', for example, have a limited option of possible answers and little likelihood of showing the thinking skills so clearly demonstrated by the children here!) Teachers need time to hold such discussions with children, either individually or in a group. They also need time to contemplate the questions they might ask, getting to know books well before using them with the children.

Our discussions were clearly held in high regard by the children; most of those who were involved in the re-interviewing process quoted themselves, or opened statements with 'When you came before I said …' And they were generally right. How often do we allow children to return to a topic of discussion months, or even weeks later? After participating in this research, I have no doubt of the value of revisitation, particularly for the purpose of developing metacognitive skills. In his re-interview Seamus looked at the final page of *Lily* where a lift-the-flap device is used and exclaimed: 'Oh, now I get it. …' and leant back in his chair with great satisfaction. We need to build in more opportunities for children to savour their learning in this way. As Bruner says: 'Much of the process of education consists of being able to distance oneself in some way from what one knows by being able to reflect on one's own knowledge' (1986: 129). The discussions about the picturebook provided the children with a meaningful context to reflect not only on what they knew, but most significantly on how they knew it. The research project allowed for such reflectiveness to be made possible over a period of time. Children were able to distance themselves from their initial readings of the text and, through interacting and talking with others, were able to reflect on their own learning.

The significance of being able to discuss the pictures was neatly summarised by the oldest children. I asked them to try and remember how they felt when the class teacher first held up the book.

I: What exactly was in your head at that moment, have you changed your thoughts from this morning?

ANGUS: I don't think I really saw the Spooky Surprise Book, and I thought it was a book for Year 2.

SAUL: Now I have read it I thought it was quite good, but at the start when Mr. Smith held it up, I thought 'Oh no, another boring story.'

ANGUS: From where I was sitting, I couldn't see any of the pictures, so I didn't know what it was about, apart from what the words said.

I: Now you have had a chance to see the pictures your opinion's changed …

SAUL: Yes – they seem to bring out the story.

Putting yourself in the picture

When asked if she placed herself in the book as one of the characters when she read, 10-year-old Lauren came up with a very powerful description of the reading process. 'No, I'm not one of the characters. I am in there though, but I'm watching them.' Kathy (6) was asked not only about how she read, but also 'What happens in your head when you read?' Her responses were very illuminating. '[When I read] I'm always thinking, "I wonder what's going to happen next", "I wonder what's going to happen next", even though I know it's already been decided.' Asked if it was the same when she watched television or played computer games, she was able to shed further light on how she copes with the complexities of being a literate child in the twenty-first century:

When I play solitaire [on the computer] I'm thinking, 'Come on, come on', especially when I need something I'm wishing would come. When I watch TV it's usually with a friend and I would say, 'What do you think's going to happen?', something like that.

Thus Lauren deals with such intricate thought processes as prediction, problem-solving, the joint construction of knowledge and, of course, the toleration of uncertainty that all readers face, whatever the text. As well as showing how they could read images, during the research I was also aware of children's facility to paint pictures with words, regardless of age or academic ability. Each time the curtain rose on Kitamura's pictures, the scene was set for new characters to populate the narrative. The props in the pictures, from shopping bags to ducks and dinosaurs, required concentration and experience. Readers used these props to put themselves and those around them 'in the picture'. To do so, they drew on the frozen fictions of their minds – re-creating moments of the past to interpret the present. I hope that the pictures painted in words throughout this book by the children in our study will empower educators to give image the same status as words in their discussions with pupils. To return to *Alice in Wonderland*, I would add, 'How much *more* use is a book with conversations *about* the pictures.

An earlier version of this chapter appeared in *Reading* 35 (2) pp. 62–7.

Chapter 8

'The words to say it'
Young bilingual learners responding to visual texts

Kathy Coulthard

The transformative power of visual narrative

The teacher was nearing the end of the story. As she revealed the final page of *The Tunnel*, Sam's (10) face was transformed by a smile so immediate and engaging that I neglected to observe the reactions of other pupils. What was it that Sam had seen? What had spoken to him so directly to cause this involuntary expression of empathy and under-standing? Tantalising questions, as Sam had arrived in this English classroom from Tanzania only three months ago. It was easy to assume an incongruity between Sam's experience of growing up in a different tradition and the Englishness of Browne's book, but something had transcended language, place and culture to enable Sam to find himself within and be touched at the deepest level.

The Tunnel tells the story of Rose and Jack, a seemingly ordinary sister and brother who are 'not at all alike'; and it is Browne's represen-tation of this difference in the endpapers that gives us the first clue about Sam's engagement with the book. These endpapers portray two patterns which, on closer inspection, reveal contrasting wallpapers, one with brick and one with leaves and flowers. A closed book lies in front of the latter. Pointing to the brick and then the flowery wall-paper, Sam expresses his understanding of the endpapers as a way into the book and goes straight to the symbolic meaning: 'this means the place where the boy is playing. And here means the girl where she likes sitting and reading the books because she likes flowers.'

His response to the night-time scenario suggests that he is looking at this text in the light of his own experience. We see Jack creeping into his sister's bedroom wearing a wolf mask with the deliberate inten-tion of scaring her. As in all Browne's books, this picture reveals so much more than the written text. Sam notices the red coat hanging on the side of the wardrobe, the shoes arranged in a sinister way, the tail under the bed and the 'scary' picture of a 'wolf talking with a lady'. The story of Red Riding Hood is not part of his oral or literate tradition but other folk and fairy tales are and it is this genre experience that enables him to clue into the menacing intertextual messages:

> This picture means the brother is ... at night. Because the brother knows her [his] sister. She's afraiding of dark. Now she [he] always comes down. Sometimes night she[he] comes and make her to afraid and cry. That's why. And then she [he] goes away [see plate 5].

His response, however, demonstrates an understanding that goes beyond the immediate situation. He knows exactly how to scare someone like Rose:

> Because you know how she's afraid of him because she [he] just come and stop here in the shadow and makes her afraid. Because she doesn't see a person. She just see a shadow and the shadow doesn't show this.

Both the written and visual text deal with the here and now and neither hints at a possible outcome but Sam can predict how this drama will end: 'When they [he] goes she starts crying. The boy goes away and says I'm not the one, I'm just sleeping.'

To arrive at this state of 'innerstanding' (Heathcote 1983) Sam has to mediate the cultural differences between himself and Jack and Rose. The obvious differences are in appearance and the context and land-scape in which they live, of which he has no intimate knowledge. There must be numerous cultural motifs beyond his experience and textual features to be reconciled but, despite cultural differences, he understands why the characters act as they do and the consequences of their actions. Although he stops short of analogising, there is a powerful resonance of personal experience in his interaction with this particular visual text.

And now we arrive at the final page of the book and the reso-nance is even more powerful in Sam's involuntary reaction when presented with a smiling Rose facing both her brother and the reader. They have been through a transformative experience. Rose has conquered her fear; the sibling bond has been tried and held fast. Sam chooses this as his favourite picture because 'they look happy and are happy to each other' and explains their mutual smile in this way (see figure 8.1):

> Because they love each other now ... are ... he ... because the sister showed the ... the brother that I like you. I like staying with you. And if the brother was interested with her [his] sister then he ... she ... the sister couldn't rescue the brother. The brother could stay there always they could find they couldn't see. You see now that's why they were smiling and they will be together everywhere.

Following our session together, I learn from his teacher that Sam's sister had died in a tragic accident in Tanzania only weeks before. Sam did not talk about this but his involuntary smile during the class reading and his struggle to unlock and communicate the symbolic meaning of Browne's secret images attest to a profound critical engagement with this story of sibling relationship. In discussing the

Figure 8.1 From *The Tunnel* by Anthony Browne

Source: Illustrations from 'The Tunnel' copyright 1989 Anthony Browne. Reproduced by permission of Walker Books and Random House Inc.

complex nature of narrative, Rosen (1989: 159) writes: 'Even so stark an ending as death is only an ending when we have made a story out of life.'

Is Sam engaged in making a story out of their life together and has Browne's text helped him to revisit, remember and reassess? He is so eloquent in articulating the symbolism of the ball and the book lying next to each other on the final endpapers. His words go straight to the heart of the story that Browne (see interview in chapter 10) has defined as 'coming to terms with different aspects of your own character' and the siblings 'coming together in balance':

> I think this football and book means when they like each other now the sister and the brother she made a friend the book and the football like each other now. They don't chase each other so they'll be playing or they'll be setting time to play of them. … To play football at the same time. Or maybe the brother will tell the sister play football after half time maybe they start to read a book telling each other about their book.

Cummins (1996: 91) stresses the absolute importance of texts that second-language learners can relate to their own personal histories or their understanding of the world, but equally important is the opportunity to have one's voice heard. Sam's first language is Kiswahili, which he also reads and writes. When he arrived in school three months ago he had neither oracy nor literacy in English, yet so engaged is he with *The Tunnel* that he struggles for an hour to make himself understood in a language that is not his own. He uses every resource available: gesture, mime and facial expression are as valuable as words and intonation. He takes enormous risks as the drive to communicate meaning takes precedence over correct use of language. Sam has something to say and finds the words to say it.

Why did he bother to make the effort? The choice of text must go some way towards answering this question. For Sam, *The Tunnel* is an emotionally powerful text to which he can respond from inside his own life experience and, significantly, the focus on making meaning from the visual image enables him to do this. Another possible reason is that the interview context is authentic. I genuinely want to know what Sam is thinking and he enters into a dialogue about his understanding in the certain knowledge that he is not being assessed on his ability to decode unfamiliar words or the extent of his developing sight vocabulary in English. The interview questions exemplify reading as a quest for meaning with an invitation to Sam to take the role of active meaning-maker. It is in this quest that we observe him working at a higher conceptual level than his current literacy in English would suggest. To demonstrate this, he has needed a book worth reading, the opportunity to explore and time to think and reflect. Under these conditions, the effort seems to be worth it.

From 'intimate' to 'extra personal' responses

Unlike Sam, Mehmet finds the interview situation overwhelming and takes refuge in silence despite the presence of a Turkish-speaking inter- preter whom he knows. He is just 6 years old and has only been in British mainstream schooling for two terms, so clearly does not feel comfortable to be away from the support of his teacher and friends. The interview is abandoned. I am surprised but delighted when he chooses to join the group discussion at the end of the day although there is no interpreter available. At the time of the discussion Mehmet is a beginning reader and learning to read in a language that is not spoken in his home or community. He is unable to read the words of *The Tunnel* but has listened attentively and been engaged in looking at the pictures during the class reading. The focus on reading pictures is significant as it removes a barrier in terms of the written text and puts him on a more equal footing with the rest of the group. Visual literacy, however, is no easy option when the text being read is as complex, multi-layered and fragmented as *The Tunnel*.

At one point in the discussion I focus the group on the bedtime scene as their individual responses had been predominantly descrip- tive. They had noticed details such as Jack wearing a wolf mask, a wakeful Rose, Crane's picture of Little Red Riding Hood and the open book lying on the bed, but had not perceived or attached significance to these and other deliberate hints of menace (see plate 5). In discussing how readers bring meaning to text, Smith (2000) suggests a primary stage in which the responses are 'intimate' based on 'who I am' and 'what I know'. This is especially true of young, inexperienced readers. The children's initial response to this visual text came from inside their own experience of bedtime.

The questions are now framed to support the group in discovering another layer of meaning, by helping them to see and reflect on images that had been previously unnoticed or which had been treated as benign. I draw their attention to the shoes under the bed. The explanations are still pragmatic: 'Because she's gone to bed. If she put them in her wardrobe she would maybe forget where she put them' (Alison 6); 'You should put your shoes together in a dresser then you wouldn't get mixed up' (Tosin 6).

It is only when the children's attention is drawn to the position of the shoes that the schema about this night-time scene flips from one of domestic familiarity to one of menace. Mehmet notices that they are lying at an awkward angle and remarks: 'I think someone's under the bed.'

It is his response to this pivotal question that leads the group into greater awareness and insight: 'There's a man under the bed' (Manisha 6). The floodgates open and they begin to notice a wider visual vocabulary. Luke's (5) eyes travel to the other side of the bed and see 'a sort of rope hanging out' which Mehmet elaborates on: 'Somebody can be under it [the bed], it's supposed to be a monster.' Tosin clarifies that it is a tail and this prompts Michael (5) to suggest that what is also lurking under the bed is more likely to be an animal such as a lion or tiger. With the growing realisation that these images are extremely significant, the cosy bedtime scene ceases to exist. The group has moved from the 'intimate' to the 'extra personal', Smith's second layer of response, in which we observe them reading the images and constructing meaning beyond their personal experience but within their knowledge of how the world can work.

There is now the distinct possibility that another story is unfolding and this leads the group to a further layer of response, the 'intertextual'. Mehmet makes an observation that shapes the group's expectation about the nature and narrative possibilities of this story. He spots the picture above the bed and recognises it as Red Riding Hood, a folk tale found within his own cultural tradition and which he has obviously experienced in Turkish. He demonstrates his familiarity with the story:

I: What's scary about the picture?
MEHMET: A wolf and Red Riding Hood
I: What happened in Red Riding Hood that was a bit scary?
MEHMET: The wolf was trying to eat Red Riding Hood

The realisation that Red Riding Hood is haunting the scene influences subsequent readings as the children bring their narrative experience to Browne's carefully planted motifs. Attention now turns to the red coat hanging on the side of the wardrobe. It looks particularly menacing

Figure 8.2 By Tosin (6)

with the pointed hood shaped like the head of a fox or some surreal creature. Mehmet makes the intertextual association: 'I think it's Red Riding Hood's and it might come in real life'. His syntactic error is powerful in fuelling Tosin's imagination. *Coming in real life* rather than *coming to life* suddenly moves this scenario from the world of books to the world of the mind. So completely has she entered into this pictorial text that the line between fact and fantasy becomes blurred and she is filled with foreboding. The hints of menace are potent. She wants to stop: 'I don't want to do this. It's scaring me.' Tosin's fears are reflected in her simple but striking drawing of the open cupboard, a strange creature lurking by the door and the girl in bed (see figure 8.2).

Seeing, talking and thinking

This small section of the transcript opens a window on a group of 5- and 6-year-olds developing their individual and collective responses to this visual text. We witness their initial observations of the images and their movement through a zone of proximal development, from 'seeing' to 'thinking', led by a guide who points out significant landmarks along the way and allows those on the quest time and space to explore. With limited experience of English and schooled literacy, it would be easy to assume that Mehmet would take a more passive role but the transcript tells a different story. Out of a possible one hundred speaker turns, he takes twenty-four and, far from being passive, he is pivotal at certain points in leading the group to greater insight and deeper layers of meaning. He clearly did not feel confident in the interview but, surrounded by his classmates and with the emphasis on enquiry, he feels safe enough to speak out. At times this requires him to use some quite sophisticated aspects of English, most noticeably when he is engaged in expressing insights or feelings. Responding to questions about the waste-ground picture, Mehmet communicates his thoughts about Jack's character and intentions, drawing on intratextual references to Rose's fearfulness and her brother's obsession with football:

> I know why the brother brings the girl here. Because the brother wants to scare the girl. … The brother, yeah, cares about the sister not coming with him so that he can play football if he wants or so that he can go down the tunnel.

These are complex issues. He is having to piece together the jigsaw of images and hypothesise their significance in relation to this page specifically and the story in general. He then has to articulate his thoughts in English, a language he has been learning for only six months. Since the questions are open-ended and invite discussion, he is involved in producing more extended explanations than single-word answers. The task is cognitively demanding but the contextual support in this pictorial text and in the collaborative group ensures that Mehmet is positioned to succeed. We are reminded that this is exactly the context in which cognitive and linguistic growth is stimulated and second-language learners (indeed all learners) flourish:

> At a cognitive level, writing about or discussion of complex issues with the teacher and peers encourages students to reflect critically and refine their ideas. As learners connect new information with what they already know, their cognitive power increases. They are enabled to understand more of the content and language that they hear or read.
>
> (Cummins 1996: 81)

It is not only Mehmet who benefits from being part of this community of enquiry. Manisha (6) is a French speaker from Mauritius who arrived in school two terms prior to the research. She is at the beginning of her journey into linguistic competence in English and, like Mehmet, is learning to read for the first time in an unfamiliar language. She is understandably reticent in the early stages of the discussion and her responses tend to be literal, fragmented and expressed in single words or short sentences. It is when the group begins to explore the bedtime scene that she becomes more actively engaged, searching the page for images and expressing her own thoughts about their significance.

I first notice her engagement when she extends Mehmet's insight that there is someone hiding under the bed by clarifying who the 'someone' might be: 'There's a man under the bed'. When prompted to link this response to what she knows about Rose's character, she responds in this way: 'The sister has put something under the bed, like a monster.' At first reading this response seems literal but subsequent readings begin to suggest a deeper, more informed interpretation.

She has heard the story read aloud at the beginning of the day and has formed an impression of Rose which she is bringing to the discussion. There is no way of knowing what her impression is as Manisha was not interviewed but there is little doubt that these first thoughts are being nourished and moulded by the exploratory talk in the group. Browne provides numerous visual clues to Rose's character. The first is on the cover in the image of a book abandoned at the entrance to the tunnel. It is open at a double-page spread, with a picture of a witch and a rather indistinct figure wearing a crown suggesting that the story is a fairy tale. Manisha does not volunteer an opinion about the cover but hears Mehmet explain why he likes it: 'When the girl said 'witch' and there's a witch there … It might carry me away'. She then hears Tosin (6) making an explicit connection between Rose, her reading and the abandoned book:

> I like the cover because the girl's in the tunnel, yeah, and I think, and because she's saying that there's witches and stuff like that and then because there's witches in her book.

When we return to her tentative suggestion that Rose has put 'something under the bed, like a monster', is it possible that she is expressing an unconscious thought about this fearful sister who lives in the world of the imagination and feeds her fears with narrative? Does she have a sense that the feet sticking out from under the bed represent a paralysing terror of the dark and 'the noises of the night'? I am not suggesting that this knowledge is conscious; rather that her simple words may suggest an unconscious thought that Rose's fear is self-induced and it is Rose herself who has put the threatening creature under the bed. Manisha may not have been able to articulate why she believes Rose would do such a thing because she is only 6 years old and has limited English-language resources at this time, but I would have liked the opportunity to have explored this with her. So often these very young children expressed thoughts whose significance I did not immediately grasp, but which left me with a nagging impression of a deeper interpretation.

The Tunnel is about conflict and reconciliation but it is also about facing fear, a major human emotion familiar to all children. As Manisha becomes more engaged in the discussion there is a strong sense that she is living through the story and using her own experience of fear to integrate the images on the page. The group pore over the picture for more and more menacing clues and Manisha suddenly turns her attention to the immobile figure in the bed. All that is visible of Rose is a small head and two timid little hands clutching the duvet. Her mouth is obscured by the bedclothes which we can imagine muffling her terror. The written text complements this wakeful image by telling us how 'she would lie awake, listening to the noises of the night'. Despite these clues, Manisha announces: 'She's waking up!' Encouragement to look again for menacing clues is ignored as she cuts across me and insists: 'She could be scared, she could be.'

Constructing virtual texts

In discussing the kinds of literature that influence children's writing, Barrs and Cork (2001: 36) suggest that those with most potential require readers to become active and involved in the world of the text. Their references to 'performance of meaning' (Iser 1978) and the construction of 'virtual text' (Bruner 1986), as part of the process that readers go through to make the text their own, helped me understand that there is something more going on here than miscue. Both her words and insistence suggest that Manisha is engaged in constructing a virtual text which is being acted upon and shaped by the actual text, her own experience and her imagination. Having begun to interpret the images in a more threatening way, it seems that she now conjures up an alternative scenario. As co-author of this text she can increase the tension by waking Rose to a room full of terrifying images. She can even add one of her own: 'There might be a bogey man!'

Her imaginative engagement with Rose's fear continues as Manisha responds to other pictures. She knows that 'He [Jack] don't like his sister' and has an understanding that the waste ground is a threatening site and in some way represents the conflict between them. Her explanation draws on the written text that she has heard for the first time that day: 'She said "It's scary, that place" and the brother said "Why did she[he]come with her"? or "Why did she come with him?" '

Mehmet feels confident that he knows what Jack is up to and this leads Manisha to predict what will happen, knowing Rose as she does:

MEHMET: I know why the brother brings the girl here. The brother wants to scare the girl.

I: And if she's scared what will happen do you think?

MANISHA: She's all scared, she'll scream.

Manisha is so clearly involved in the world of the text and so comfortable in this collaborative exploration that it is easy to forget she is right at the beginning of learning a new language. What is it that has enabled her to see herself as an active meaning-maker, to have a voice and to feel confident to use that voice at a time when she might be most sensitive to making mistakes? My expectation that she will behave like a reader is a crucial factor. Implicit in this is a belief in her as a learner and an acknowledgement that she already has a first language, French, and a history of home literacy experience to bring to the task. Since she is not new to the world (only new to English), she also brings a rich array of personal experience which she will need to make sense of the text. The fact that this experience has been shaped by another place and culture can only be a bonus in a group that is engaged in negotiating meaning.

This brings me to another important factor. If Manisha is to use all her resources, she must have a text that allows her to do so. Meek (1988) describes such texts as 'texts that teach' and recognises the skill of the artists and writers who produce them as being able to 'link what children know, partly know, and are learning about the world, to ways of presenting the world in books'. *The Tunnel* is just such a text and for an inexperienced reader, like Manisha, its rich visual imagery is more accessible (and more inviting) than the written word. There is no doubt that she has been able to decode the images and engage with Rose's loneliness and fear. After all, these emotions are experienced so profoundly by children like herself who arrive in school not knowing anyone, not speaking English and not understanding how school works. What she has to say is important and must be heard but how does she find the words and the confidence to say it?

In my experience this happens naturally when the text and context are right and by 'right' I mean challenging but supportive. These features of the learning environment have already been discussed but one other is essential to Manisha's engagement. Both learning a language and learning to read involve taking risks and making mistakes, a daunting prospect when language and culture are unfamiliar. We have all been in coercive situations and know how paralysing they can be, as well as counterproductive, for all they usually achieve is a further retreat into silence. There is no pressure on Manisha to speak but, importantly, time for her to listen and tune in until she feels comfortable to speak. This happens more quickly if the emphasis is on making and communicating meaning rather than correctness. After a reticent start, she becomes engaged and language arises naturally from the interactions within the group. Her syntax and pronunciation may not always be correct but the meaning is absolutely explicit. Not only is she learning valuable lessons about reading through language, but she is also learning how language works and how to manipulate it. Since language is at the core of reading, what better way to learn about both?

Exploring visual detail

Before we leave this group of 5- and 6-year-olds, I want to turn my attention to Tosin. She was born in this country to Nigerian parents and is growing up in a home and community where she hears English and Yoruba spoken. She was interviewed for the study as well as taking part in the group discussion and it is the expression and development of her ideas in both contexts that I want to explore. Within minutes of meeting Tosin and the interview starting, I was alerted to her sensitivity to visual detail as she notices a host of images on the front cover of *The Tunnel*. Some carry meaning in relation to the story while others encode different kinds of meaning (the Walker Books logo and the strip pattern marking the edge of the picture). The open book at the entrance to the tunnel is the first image she notices and is attracted to because she likes reading. She does not develop this response further but goes on to demonstrate a more insightful reading in the group discussion by linking the characters in the abandoned book with Rose's personality and the unfolding story. These links are not explicit but her words suggest an implicit perception about Browne's intentions: 'I like the cover because the girl's in the tunnel, yeah, and I think, and because she's saying that there's witches and stuff like that and then because there's witches in the book.'

There are other instances when there is an obvious progression in her thinking during the course of the day. Her first response to the end-papers inside the front cover, for example, go straight to the symbolic representation of difference suggested by the two walls covered in contrasting wallpaper:

TOSIN: I think this one [brick] was in the book because the brother went out with his friends and played football.
I: And what does this one [flowers] make you think of?
TOSIN: The girl sitting down because of the book.

In the group discussion she reiterates this interpretation with greater confidence but develops it by drawing on intratextual links to justify her reading of the images. In the interview Tosin's keen eye for visual detail had noticed the flowery wallpaper recurring in the hall outside Rose's bedroom. Her recognition of the wallpaper's significance is particularly insightful as Browne (see chapter 10) has talked of his obsession with wallpapers remembered from his own childhood and their inclusion in the book as a personal expression of early memories. Tosin made an intuitive connection between the pattern and the focal character, a connection which she affirms and consciously recognises through words in the discussion:

> It's meant to be the sister for two reasons. One is that because we're going to see it in the middle of the book and two is that we know it's for the sister because there's a book there.

I am reminded of Watson's (1996b) observations on the changing understanding of 4-year-old Ann during re-readings of *The Tunnel* and how, as time passes, she is able to 'make explicit' what has previously been implicit but 'remained unsaid'. In Tosin's case, time is not days or weeks but a few hours between sessions, long enough it seems for some reflection (conscious or otherwise) to have taken place and for under-standings to shift. These understandings are not fully formed, however, but continue to be acted upon by the pushes and pulls of other children's thinking as they look and talk about the images together.

The representational wallpapers at the beginning of the book are repeated on the final endpapers but with significant differences. Jack's football has appeared in front of the brick wall, lying beside and slightly overlapping Rose's storybook. Tosin is immediately alert to these changes and can tell me the exact position of the book on the opening endpapers but offers no thoughts about meaning. This is explored further in the discussion; and the images are recognised by other members of the group as a pictorial metaphor for reconciliation, but another puzzle opens up. Why has Browne put the ball and book on the brother's page? Mehmet makes a pragmatic suggestion and one which probably reflects the perceived pecking order in the world of the 6-year-old: 'Because the boy is bigger than the girl'.

It is the light and shade in the backgrounds, however, that suggest an alternative explanation to Tosin: 'I think it's because that one [brick wallpaper] has got no hard colours on it and ... it's been painted soft.'

I have to confess to being perplexed at the time as I associated the hardness and coldness of brick with those traits in the brother's character but Tosin taught me to look in a different way. As I pored over the endpapers trying to make sense of her interpretation, I saw that Browne has indeed used predominantly soft, warm, muted colours for the bricks and that they are cemented in place by rather malleable-looking mortar. Although the brick wall is a recurring image in his work, he has described this as his 'first significant brick wall' (2000), drawing attention to the suggestion of wallpaper and the diverse shades and patternings of his handmade bricks. Just as she had perceived the importance of the wallpapers, she now seemed to sense that the execution of such minute detail was for a purpose and demanded attention (far more than I had given it). My eye then travelled to the contrasting wallpaper. The fluid leaf and flower shapes are painted in a spectrum of greens from light to dark and stand out boldly against a cream background. I began to see how hard-edged they could look.

My understanding deepened when I revisited the transcript of Tosin's interview and detected an intratextual connection behind the reading. In the story Rose confronts her fear by following her brother down the dark tunnel. The quest leads through a terrifying forest teeming with surreal images to a barren landscape where Jack stands paralysed in a circle of stones. As she puts her arms around him and hugs him back to life the landscape gradually loses its darkness and the stones turn into daisies. Tosin is immediately alert to the use of light and colour:

I: Why is there a ring of stones around the brother?
TOSIN: I think it is ... because as it gets softer and warmer it gets lighter and lighter.

Her choice of words is interesting. 'Softer' and 'warmer' are words that convey feeling and here she seems to be expressing an implicit understanding that the circle of stones is a metaphor for the transformation of feeling between the brother and sister. Rose's selfless act has quite literally softened Jack up, so why not place the ball and the book together against a brick wallpaper background that she perceives '*has no hard colours on it*' and has been '*painted soft*'. Yet again, Tosin displays an intuitive understanding of Browne's intentions as he has explained his use of wallpaper (i.e. something that is put on) to suggest 'that the boy and girl are similar' and that Jack is not really as tough as he seems.

Cultural identity and linguistic development

During the interview Tosin tells me that she loves computer games and the way 'the pictures are done' makes her 'want to play'. This is an interesting observation as I have a real sense of her playing with this text and the play becoming even more imaginative when she is joined by others. The five others have not been chosen because they read as well as she does or have similar English-language experience; in fact, their profiles are deliberately diverse. In some educational settings the make-up of this group might be thought to inhibit Tosin's learning and prevent Mehmet and Manisha's English-language needs being prioritised. Despite the differences in language, literacy and culture, however, we have seen that this is an effective group and, by effective, I mean that every member has collaborated in making sense of this text and in constructing a shared meaning. This alone would endorse the make-up of this group but there is a further layer of effectiveness, one much subtler, that must be considered.

Robert Siegler (2000) cites identity as one of the key factors affecting learning and describes it as 'a voraciously powerful theory one has about oneself'. Cummins (1996) devotes an entire book to exploring this theory in relation to second-language learners and draws on extensive evidence from educators and researchers across North America to show how schools affirm, ignore or devalue pupils' personal and cultural identities. McCarty's (1993) case study of a Navajo–English bilingual programme captures both the fragility of identity and the awesome power of institutions to act upon and shape the way pupils see themselves:

> In classrooms, curriculum and pedagogy are the mirrors in which children see themselves reflected and through which they

Plate 1: By Yu (4)

Plate 2: From *Zoo* by Anthony Browne

The orang-utan crouched in a corner and didn't move. We tried shouting at it and banging on the glass, but it just ignored us. Miserable thing.

Plate 3: From *Zoo* by Anthony Browne

Plate 4: By Joe (age10)

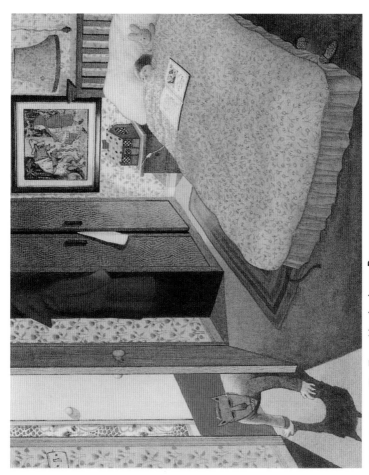

Plate 5: From *The Tunnel* by Anthony Browne

Source: Illustrations from *The Tunnel* copyright 1989 Anthony Browne. Reproduced by permission of Walker Books and Random House Inc.

Plate 6: By Polly (5)

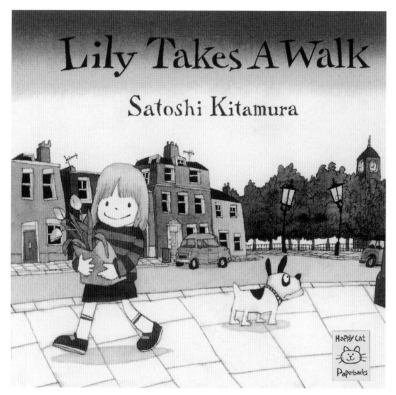

Plate 7: From *Lily Takes a Walk* by Satoshi Kitamura

Plate 8: By Charlie (9)

construct images of themselves as thinkers, learners and users of language. The applied research at Rough Rock suggests the potentials children can exploit when the image they see and develop is one of self-affirmation. By engaging students in relevant, content-rich study that builds on their linguistic and experiential capital, whole language pedagogy opens up these potentials.

(McCarty 1993: 191)

Her words are both uplifting and daunting. If we want pupils to feel confident in their identities as learners, we must pay as much attention to content and context as we do to objectives. This is of course true for all pupils but especially those whose communities are viewed as inferior or deviant in mainstream society. An evaluation of effectiveness must, therefore, include this layer of identity because not to do so would ignore its centrality to learning.

Mehmet and Manisha are potentially the most vulnerable in this group in terms of access to content and context, having had less than six months' experience of spoken and written English. How they are enabled to engage with the reading curriculum is crucial as it will affect how they feel about themselves as learners and influence the kind of readers they become. They may be unable to read the written text of *The Tunnel* at this time but the great leveller in this group is that they can all see. Words may form a barrier but visual image is universal. The brief glimpses we have had of their interactive reading demonstrate an ability to decode symbolism, identify intertextual links, construct a 'virtual text', understand feelings and behaviour and have an emotional engagement with the important human issues in the book. Returning to McCarty's metaphor of curriculum as a mirror through which children construct images of themselves, I feel sure that Mehmet and Manisha left this group with positive images of themselves as 'thinkers, learners and users of language'.

Tosin's visual alertness and sensitivity undoubtedly bring an added dimension to the group's interpretation of this polysemic text. She displays an intuitive understanding of image, detail, light, colour, facial expression and body language as techniques the artist uses to convey ideas, emotions and relationships. But this is no one-way street. Just as she is helping other members of the group to pay attention to these techniques, they are helping her to see unnoticed images and to revisit and reconstruct her original thoughts. Although Tosin has much greater experience of speaking and reading English than Mehmet and Manisha, she too has a need to talk and negotiate meaning. The transcript of the discussion provides rich evidence of the group's capacity to expand learning by scaffolding both her thinking and that of one another through dialogue.

Sam, Mehmet, Manisha and Tosin draw on their experience of life and text to make sense of Browne's images and their experience of language to communicate this sense. Sam and Tosin are more experienced readers. Not only are they at ease being interviewed alone, but I suspect they enjoy having the undivided attention of an adult who is so obviously interested in their responses. From the outset it is clear that they understand and feel comfortable with this kind of literacy event in which the majority of questions are open-ended and the answers not pre-specified in the researcher's head. By contrast, Mehmet and Manisha do not initially display the same level of understanding and assurance but gradually become engaged as they begin to realise what is required in this kind of literacy event and to discover images that have meaning for them. Their levels of perception and interpretation fluctuate with each spread, but both have moments of responding to visual features with insight and empathy.

Cultural practices and learning to read

The same is true for the majority of the twenty-three pupils from different ethnic backgrounds that I interviewed or engaged in group discussions about Browne's books *The Tunnel* and *Zoo*. There are, however, a very small minority of pupils across the age range who were less at ease with this more open kind of questioning and whose responses tended to be predominantly literal. Pupils like Funda (5), who so obviously found 'what' questions more comfortable than 'why' and had effective ways of diverting my questions or signalling to me that there should be no further probing. Here she is responding to a question about *Zoo*. The family visiting Browne's zoo is pictured standing alongside and moving through groups of people who become increasingly surrealist with animal parts and features attached to their human forms. When asked what she notices about the people on these pages, Funda responds appropriately by listing all the strange things she can see but swiftly closes down the conversation when asked to think about why the artist might have drawn these images:

FUNDA: They've got a monster feet ... and a man has got two things [horns]. ... And this is look like a monster [man in kiosk].
I: Look at the other page. Anything different or strange?

FUNDA: Yes. This looks like a pig.

I: Why do you think Anthony Browne drew people with monster feet and horns and a pig's head?

FUNDA: Because he likes it.

On the opposite page stands a lone elephant in a bare enclosure separated from the visitors to the zoo and the reader by a barred fence. Solitude and misery are depicted through the use of positioning and sombre colours. An invitation to 'Tell me about the elephant' elicits the same kind of detailed labelling: 'He's done a wee … and he's eating food … the elephant's got erm, a tail … and he's got ears, big ears … and he's got a trunk … and there's a hole there.'

Whereas open-ended questions such as 'Tell me … ' offered many pupils the freedom and licence to go beyond the surface features and explore the aesthetic and affective dimensions of images, Funda sticks doggedly to the descriptive. She answers my questions by listing only what she can see even when the question calls for a personal response such as her feelings about the family. The reader is positioned as voyeur, following the progress of Mum, Dad and two boys on a typical family outing to the zoo. Whereas the males become increasingly disrespectful, mocking the animals' appearance and behaviour, Mum's body language and facial expressions portray sadness and concern about the animals' plight. Funda responds to the question in this way. She is positive about Mum 'because she's got long hair' and the rest of the family because 'Dad's got straight hair, and the boy's got straight hair too. … And the little boy's got a smiley face and he's got his hair.' She takes few risks. It is not that she is unwilling to answer my questions or unhappy about being interviewed, but I am left with the impression that Funda is simply confused. She does not know what is required in this kind of exchange.

I discover at the end of the day that Funda is in the lowest ability group for reading. She is described as having little confidence and being unwilling to take risks, rarely offering responses during individual and class book-sharing sessions. Nor does she opt to read in free choice time. It would be all too easy to draw a correlation between her ability with written text and her analysis of visual text (and attach a deficit label) but I want to stand back at this point and take a wider view of the context in which she is developing her literacy. Funda was born in Britain and started her school four terms ago speaking Turkish which is the language of her home. Neither parent is literate in English, but she has a sister in her late teens who speaks fluent English and takes responsibility for sharing the books that come home as part of the home/school reading scheme. Although I have no way of knowing how this book-sharing is conducted, Funda's responses to the interview questions suggest to me that she is more familiar or more comfortable with a procedure that requires her to retrieve information from the text with little or no opportunity for personal response or discussion.[1] The literacy practices of the home are beyond the scope of this study so here I want to draw on research to help me understand Funda's interaction with the book and the situation.

Brice Heath's (1983) ethnographic study of three communities in Carolina provides convincing evidence that children do not just acquire literacy, but learn different ways of being a reader and writer through involvement in social practices with adults and children from earliest days. The literacy traditions they are socialised into differ according to cultural context, as Gregory's studies of 5-year-old Tony (Gregory and Biarnès 1994: 18–24), who comes from a Chinese background, and 6-year-old Maruf (1997: 107–16), from a Bangladeshi background, illustrate so well. Like Funda, Maruf shares the books he brings home from school with an older sister. This book-sharing is tightly structured and replicates strategies experienced by his sister in both Bengali community class and school reading sessions. The emphasis is on learning to read in English so there is a focus on the written text first with no interruption for picture clues or discussion. Feedback on miscues is immediate with no time allowed for self-correction. This is followed by explicit questions about meaning; pictures are only used when needed to support questioning as they are thought to be confusing if they do not correspond with the written text. This is in direct contrast to school reading sessions in which Maruf's teacher moves between reading and discussion. She uses pictures to help him interpret the text and encourages him to make personal meaning by identifying with characters in the story and relating what he has read to his own life. Gregory highlights the discontinuity between home and school literacy practices and its effect on Maruf's learning:

> If we refer back to Maruf's reading with his sister, we notice that nowhere in the interaction was he expected to offer preferences or judgements; hence, perhaps, his lack of skill in using exploratory talk as he reads with his teacher. Rather than a lack of understanding as such, it seems most probable that the child is not used to this type of exchange which the teacher implicitly assumes he will share.

Further evidence (1998) suggests that Maruf's home and community literacy experiences are not confined to Bangladeshis but may be typical for many linguistic minority children in Britain. Certainly, Funda's familiarity with labelling what she can see and her unease with more exploratory questions bear strong similarities to Maruf's responses in both home and school reading sessions. The observation that words are privileged above pictures is particularly relevant to this study. Our preoccupation with the visual text may be completely at odds with what Funda understands about reading and how reading sessions are conducted. In Maruf's home reading sessions, a mismatch between picture and text is seen as misleading (and to be avoided); yet we have chosen our focus books precisely because of this mismatch and the potential for moving into the readerly gap. Funda has probably not experienced this kind of complex text at home or been required to engage so closely with pictures in school. Her predominantly literal response to the straightforward story is understandable in one so young who is having to learn what reading means, as well as negotiating the potential difference between home and school literary practices.

Universal themes

But one image does touch her and provokes a deeper response. On one side of the final double-page spread we see the older boy in the family sitting on the floor of a cold, bare room with knees drawn up and head hanging down. Shadows of bars across his body give the impression of a cage. The two lines of written text appear above and below the picture (see figure 4.3):

> That night I had a very strange dream.
> Do you think animals have dreams?

I ask Funda what she thinks this picture is about and she responds in this way: 'He has a dream. ... He's going in a cage ... and not going back to his mum and dad and brother.'

This response is quite different from any other. The list-making of previous exchanges is gone and we see Funda moving into the 'readerly gap' (Iser 1978), imagining what it is like to be inside this child. In Iser's words, 'she sets the work in motion and becomes a kind of co-author'.

Funda is so clearly responding empathetically to the image of the solitary child who has become separated from his family and imprisoned by disturbing dreams. The image triggers reflections of loneliness, powerlessness and fear which find their expression in the most shocking thought of all – 'and not going back to his mum and dad and brother'. Funda is moved by this image because it means something to her. She is able to draw on life experience to see beyond the literal and anticipate another's thoughts and feelings. By contrast, she does not bring the same degree of empathy to the images of solitary animals imprisoned in comfortless surroundings, whose body language and facial expressions signal a deeper message than the straightforward story of a family outing to the zoo suggests. She does not access the moral issue and here I suspect that culture (as well as age) plays a vital role. Domestic animals may not be part of her everyday experience and the plight of animals and the debate about freedom and captivity talked about or prioritised in her home and community. If this is the case, she will have difficulty recognising the message. It may mean nothing to her.

The influence of culture on interpretation has been explored by Mines in her study of three different groups of 6-year-olds reading *The Tunnel*. Her analysis of the response of recent arrivals from Bangladesh, of second-generation Bangladeshi immigrants and of English children living in rural Sussex led her to conclude: 'how they looked at the pictures and what they saw was determined by the mental template that they applied to their reading, this being a largely cultural construction' (2000: 201).

She registers her surprise at how much this particular text enabled all children, including the recent arrivals, to draw upon their own cultural resources to make meaning and how hard they worked to fill in the gaps. This is consistent with my own findings. I am convinced that the universal themes of love, fear, conflict and reconciliation in *The Tunnel* act as reference points in the narrative mapping and, no matter how unfamiliar the territory becomes, readers can use them to get their bearings. The transcripts of *Zoo*, however, suggest that the theme of animal rights is less universal and does not provide the same reference points for those whose cultural experience does not encompass this issue. I am hypothesising that cultural difference may not only mean an absence of talk about animals in captivity but may also mean no domestic pets. It could have an effect on which television programmes are chosen or books bought, borrowed or browsed. Although children's knowledge, understanding and values are culturally saturated, the extent to which this affects literary interpretation will always be mediated by each child's unique personality as well as the influence of peers. Having heeded this caveat, I am suggesting that for Funda at this time the culture gap in *Zoo* is as wide as a chasm and one she simply cannot traverse alone. Greater maturity, life and book experience should narrow the gap and position her more favourably to understand (while not necessarily agreeing with) the author's message. Meanwhile, it is important to bring cultural difference into the picture as well as potential discontinuities in home and school literacy practices when trying to understand her response to the images.

The teller and the told

One other factor nags away at me. I am alerted to it in Funda's transcript but become even more aware of its presence and influence on Eylem. He is 9 years old and, like Funda, second-generation Cypriot. Their profiles are similar in other ways: Turkish is the language spoken in their homes; neither set of parents is literate in English; and both children started school as emergent bilinguals. Meek (1988) reminds us that:

> To learn to read a book, as distinct from simply recognising the words on the page, a young reader has to become both the teller (picking up the author's view and voice) and the told (the recipient of the story, the interpreter).

What is nagging away at me is the recurring evidence of children privileging 'the words on the page' and the effect this has on their capacity to become both 'the teller' and 'the told'. The effect is particularly striking with a complex picturebook such as *Zoo*, in which the words tell a straightforward story while a different kind of narrative is unfolding in the pictures. The transcript of Eylem's interview shows how the written text is the predominant influence in his attempts to make sense of the book and it is one that continues to exert power throughout the group discussion.

These words appear beneath a picture of the family wandering through the zoo. On the page opposite is a picture of a solitary elephant in bleak surroundings:

> We hadn't got a map of the zoo so we just wandered round. Me and my brother wanted to see the gorillas and monkeys, but we had to see all these boring animals first. We went into the elephant house which was really smelly. The elephant just stood in a corner stuffing its face.

I focus Eylem on the pictures and ask him to 'Tell me about the elephant and the people visiting the zoo':

EYLEM: … they didn't like it because it was too … it was boring and it's just standing in the corner … they like the baboons and the gorillas.

I: Why do you think they like those animals?

EYLEM: Because they're first of all saying 'let's go and see the baboons and the gorillas'.

I: So you don't think they like the elephant?

EYLEM: No. 'Cos they thought it was boring.

I: Why do you think they thought it was boring?

EYLEM: Because it just stands in a corner and just erm … standing like ice.

As far as I can see, Eylem does not read the text but has remembered words and phrases from the class reading which he draws on heavily. His teacher later confirms my observation when she comments on his ability to 'quote from stories verbatim'. I encourage him to look at the people visiting the zoo and this prompts a rather minimal inventory of animal features growing out of human forms. He thinks Browne has done this 'so he could make the pictures more lively'. The transcript suggests a familiarity with the traditional, reading- comprehension-type question in which all that is involved is the retrieval of basic information from the written text. He does not move beyond this purely descriptive phase, even when the question is couched in exploratory language, so long as the actual text can provide an answer. The contrast between his facility with this passive kind of exercise and apparent inexperience with a more active, exploratory approach suggests to me that Eylem understands reading as a process of retrieval, one in which the meaning is fixed in words with little or no space for interpretation. Our focus on the visual image and the interplay between words and pictures is completely at odds with this under-standing. He confirms my hunch when he tells me that the words and pictures in *Zoo* tell the same story. Although he recognises the distinct roles of both media, words are accorded greater status because, without them, 'you won't be able to read the book. You'll still get some ideas from the pictures but it won't be that good when you read it.' The pictures seem to play a subsidiary role in terms of meaning ('because if you can't read the words the pictures give you an idea') but a very important one in maintaining interest ('in the end it will be boring because you ain't seen no pictures').

The privileged status of the written text already quoted is important as it surfaces time and again, both to shape further responses and to act as a check on possible interpretations. An important image is the close-up of a rather wise- but sad-looking gorilla staring out from behind the shape of a cross towards the left-hand side of the page, where the family look on with Dad doing his King Kong impersonation (see figure 4.2). Mum's facial expression and observation that zoos are not really for animals but people betray concern for the animals' welfare. I ask Eylem what he finds interesting about the picture of the gorilla and he responds by drawing on the text that appeared several pages back: 'Because they wanted the gorilla from first of all.' It is possible that Eylem may not recognise that this kind of question requires a personal response or that it is giving him permission to offer one so I rephrase and personalise the question: 'What do you think about this picture, Eylem?' He responds again from the family viewpoint 'They might not … ' but this time I interrupt and repeat 'What do *you think?*' with an emphasis on the last two words. He finally expresses a personal view in which he is able to synthesise his reading of the written text with his interpretation of the images. He is not only reading between the lines but reading between the pictures and between the pictures and the text: 'I think that he might not be really happy because the dad's taking the mickey out of him.'

His empathic response demonstrates a significant shift in viewpoint from the family to the animals and one which gives him access to deeper layers of meaning. At this point I am quietly confident that Eylem is beginning to move through a zone of proximal development in which there is an increasing awareness of image, its openness to interpretation ('*I think*') and its relationship to text. I had not reckoned with the power of print. The same piece of written text resurfaces:

I: What do you think Anthony Browne wants us to think about the family?

EYLEM: He wants us to feel they're happy and the family's just … they're going to the zoo. But the family think they're going to see loads and loads of animals and stuff but they don't because they see loads of boring animals except for the baboons and gorillas.

I: But do you think the family are happy at the zoo?

EYLEM: When they see the baboons and the gorilla and they like that one but when they see the boring animals like the elephant when he is just standing in the corner like the orang-utan like he was … they was like it was frozen.

I now need to return to Eylem's understanding of reading and what being a reader means. If we agree with the notion that children learn ways of being a reader and writer from involvement in literacy practices from earliest days, we cannot exclude those they are involved in at school. The books he is given to read and the kind of reading lessons on offer must surely shape this understanding. Eylem is described as a below average reader who enjoys listening to rather than reading books. He has been put on the National Literacy Strategy (NLS) (1999) Additional Literacy Support programme intended to help pupils in Years 3 and 4 'who have fallen behind in literacy'. The materials reflect a preoccupation with phonics. Each of the four modules is linked to a phonics programme with recommended texts to provide opportunities for pupils to learn, practise and apply the skills. While it is indisputable that Eylem must learn how to read the words on the page, the tran-scripts provide powerful evidence that a practice that focusses primarily on one cueing system (and one signifier) is not helping him to become literate in its fullest sense. If anything, it is investing the written word with such authority that it is working against the development of infer-ential reading. Nor do the recommended books have the depth or complexity in either words or pictures to provide what he so clearly needs, which are texts (and contexts) that engage him and make him think about what is said and unsaid. Both Eylem and Funda belong to a community with a long history of low reading attainment and general underachievement, which is the subject of a report from the University of London (1999). Their experiences are significant in that they may help us understand the factors that impact on literacy. This knowledge can help us provide for their needs more effectively.

Final thoughts

Several years ago, long before the National Literacy Strategy, I initi-ated a Key Stage 2 reading project in a number of schools. The aim was quite simple. I wanted to provide a safe, supportive environment, in which pupils who had recently arrived in Britain not speaking English could develop both oracy and literacy while experiencing the sheer pleasure of sharing books. I wanted pupils to read and go on reading so I chose books that would excite and motivate them. They were all picturebooks with themes that would appeal to older readers and images capable of being contemplated and explored. This was impor-tant as I intended to talk about the books with my apprentice readers even before we shared a language. Anthony Browne's books were favourites in this collection. He provided us with extraordinary images that generated a lot of looking and a great deal of conversation which, in the early days, was carried on through gesture, mime and exclamation rather than conventional words. If you had asked me then what these books were doing for my apprentices, I would have talked about relationships, mutual enjoyment and the importance of readerly-like behaviour. This response came from one who was starting out on a journey (although she didn't know it) and was unaware of the territory or the time it would take. The journey continues but this research has led to a significant place along the route where I have been engaged in reassessing and redefining my initial response, which was inadequate in recognising the potential of these complex visual texts.

Ask me now what these books can do for young bilingual learners and I will talk about emotional engagement and refer you back to Sam and Manisha, who use their experience of love and fear to make personal meaning of the text despite alternative cultural traditions. I will talk about intellectual challenge and the capacity of these books both to stimulate and provide ways of demonstrating thinking, especially for recent arrivals like Mehmet and Manisha who are not yet able to read the words. No reductive text could provoke such thought or provide them with the same opportunities for discussion yet all too often the reductive text is their sole reading diet. I will talk of aesthetic analysis and how such detailed visual texts can overcome the barrier of words for those who do not yet speak or read English, providing more equal access to the world of story. And for those who have greater experience of spoken and written English, I will talk about the potential for accessing deeper layers of meaning through the interpretation of both word and image and the space between. Finally, I will talk about language learning and the power of these texts to inspire pupils to talk in a way that pushes their language to the outer limits, with the drive to communicate overcoming their very natural fear of making mistakes. I am certain Sam is aware that his responses are riddled with syntactical errors but this does not prevent him from talking at length about his understanding and I want to leave the last word to him. Asked for his opinion of the book, he responds by saying that 'when you read the story and see the pictures this makes you feel interested at the book' and then delivers his final verdict when he declares that *The Tunnel* is 'a real book'.

Note

1   Funda's approach reflects the distinction that Rosenblatt (1981: 21–2) makes between 'efferent' and 'aesthetic' reading. In the latter, 'the reader's attention is focused on what he will take away from the transaction', while in the former the focus is on 'what he is living through during the reading event' – and this includes personal response.

Chapter 9

Picturebooks and metaliteracy

Children talking about how they read pictures

I think that stained-glass windows in church help you understand pictures too. Sometimes I go to church to look up at the stained glass windows, just look and try and tell the story, that's all I do. Because before you read a book you can understand a stained-glass window, because you just look. You can learn on a stained-glass window and then when it comes to a book you're ready and you can look at the pictures and know what's happening.

(Tamsin 8)

In *A History of Reading*, Manguel (1997: 104) mentions the similarities between the reading of pictures in the Biblia Pauperum (the first books with biblical images) and those in stained-glass windows: both allowed the non-literate to participate more fully and at their own pace in the interpretation of biblical stories – stories they had previously only had access to through someone else's reading. Even today, with so many images around us that the pleasure derived from this freedom is now so commonplace we take it almost for granted, we find that a child refers to these same stained-glass stories in order to describe how she looks at pictures.

Tamsin's explanation of how she 'read' pictures and the comments made by other children about the way in which they interpret image, and also what they say about how the author intends us to look, are clues to understanding how they make sense of pictorial narratives. These clues are usually based on children's previous book knowledge and on their experience with other types of media, from comics to computer games. This type of knowledge comes together with metacognitive skills when children answer questions about their expectations of a picturebook, its implied readership and their understanding of artistic techniques. It also reveals their perceptions of the complex relationship between word and image, one of the defining aspects of picturebooks, but also present in other types of media texts. In this chapter, we will analyse some of the comments children made about reading visual texts in an attempt to understand the thought processes behind these skills. We shall discuss how the children described the artistic processes involved in making a picturebook and how they relate this process to their own creative experiences. Finally, we shall try to pull all these observations together in order to understand how children make sense of their own meaning-making processes and suggest ways that these metacognitive skills can be built on, in order to help young learners become more critical and discerning readers.

'You can also read by pictures': how to read a picturebook

Not all the children were able to answer the question we asked about how they read pictures, perhaps because this was a new idea to them, or because they found it hard to articulate an answer. Generally it was the more experienced readers or children of 9 and upwards who were able to describe the steps by which they approached a picture. This is a metacognitive ability which involves stepping back, an objectivisation of themselves as readers, something which is not easy to do even for adults.

The first distinction to be made is between the words and the illustrations. Greg (6), already a keen reader, was one of the few young children who was able to take this step back when asked what he looked at first in a picture. 'I look at the picture to give me a clue of what's happening. And then I read the story, the words.' Jim (7) looks first at the writing within the illustration: 'I look if they have speech bubbles and then I read the bit that it says, then read the writing and then look at the picture.' Joe's (10) description is perhaps the most accurate in terms of the eye going between the image and the text, not once, but several times: 'First I look at the picture just for a short while, then I read the text, then I take a longer look at the picture and see what's happening in it and see if there's anything going on.'

This distinction reveals the powerful attraction of the image and the fact that it is often easier to understand than the written text. But what happens when children look at a picture? Where do their eyes go first? Karen (7) demonstrated for the interviewer how her eyes rolled around the picture; other children described their eye movements in various ways. When asked how they read a picture, Corinna (10), Jason (9) and Erin (7) explained that they look first at the 'main parts', such as the characters and the 'things that stand out' or the actual objects and then they look at the background. Kevin (10) looks 'at the overall thing and then the detail'. Dave (8) revealed his scientific knowledge about how the eyes work: 'in your head you translate it from upside-down to the right way, 'cause when you see it, it's the other way.' Alice (9) said she first notices the usual things and then the unusual, like the 'normal' picture of Lily feeding the ducks and then the dinosaur on the other side of the canal. This way of looking, at the norm and then the exceptions, was also applied to *The Tunnel* and *Zoo* by other children. Another way of looking was to first follow the movement of the characters as described by Eva (7): 'I think you look at the people that are walking, see where they're going. It tells you where they're leading you to in the book.'

As with the reading of text, the reading of images is not a simple left-to-right movement. The eyes tend to focus either on the largest identifiable object or on an object that has a particular interest for the viewer. When Jess (6) was asked what she looked at first in the spread in *Lily* with the vegetable stall, she said 'the bike, because I can ride a bike'. Looking is also affected by the narrative in terms of expectations: a few pages into *Lily*, the children were ready to find both the central characters, but also to search for the monster. So even if Lily was on the left-hand side of the spread, they would look for the monster first. In *Zoo* they learnt to expect the family on the left-hand side of the gutter and the animals on the right, and they were usually drawn first to the more colourful family side. In *The Tunnel* their eyes followed the sister and brother; as Sean (9) said, 'I look at what is actually happening, like the main characters, and then I look like round the edge to see if there's anything I missed, and then I look at the background.'

Older children are not used to having time to look at a book slowly. Because they read so fast, they sometimes missed details which they only saw when they were pointed out. As Joe (10) admitted: 'Well at first I didn't notice that all the humans didn't look like animals, I just thought they looked like normal people at first. The thing I first noticed was the family because they're the main characters, but then when I looked back I could see all the other people in the background and them looking like animals.' Kiefer (1993: 277) refers to studies of visual perception which found that 'children's eye movements within a pictorial plane are quite different from adults' '. The reason for having 'many more and longer eye fixations' may be a learning function, not a sign of immaturity, and the result of this is that children notice more details than adults do.

'Working out things on the page': deductions

Metacognitive skills were also needed to explain the process by which one tried to make sense of the pictures. Only a few of the older children were able to give detailed descriptions of how they thought they did this. Talking about *Lily*, Carol (10), a struggling reader according to her performance at school, pointed out: 'It seems like you take ages on the book but you're actually looking at the picture and you're trying to know why, working out things on the page.' She goes on to say that what you start looking for in the book is the 'problem. Kind of like you want to know what's wrong with the dog.' Carol has already worked out that a reader forms expectations – about narrative patterns in this case – and looks out for them throughout the book.

Usually, the readers' deductive processes were implied through other comments about the book. For example, when Ruth (8) noticed the fairy-tale book on the cover and endpaper of *The Tunnel*, she thought they 'must tell us that whoever likes the book [is] the main person in the story'. A few pages later, she said she was looking for clues about how this person was feeling. So she is aware that the artist is using symbolic clues, which the viewer must interpret to understand a character and also to signal their importance in the narrative. Later, as she described the pictures of the forest, we can follow her thoughts quite accurately:

> Well one picture is nice and jolly and happy and just trees, and this picture is in darkness, forest, the trees there are very ugly, all swirls and squiggles. And you've got some weird trees at the back and they make you think why is that there, those vines? And someone must have been there, chopping wood. There's a rope. Someone must be climbing.

As she talks about the pictures, Ruth first contrasts their atmosphere, based on colour, light and pattern (figure 9.1). She notices the background (weird trees) and then zooms back into the beanstalk and some of the most noticeable details such as the axe and the rope.

Figure 9.1 From *The Tunnel* by Anthony Browne

Source: Illustrations from 'The Tunnel' copyright 1989 Anthony Browne. Reproduced by permission of Walker Books and Random House Inc.

Many children told us that the process of reading a picture seems to involve first noticing the ordinary and expected; next there's the un-expected and extraordinary (there's always plenty of that with Browne and Kitamura); then asking questions, making deductions, proposing tentative hypotheses and then confirming or denying them as the reader moves on to something else, reads the verbal text or turns the page. Tamsin's (8) account, for example, follows this process closely, though she also considers the main characters' actions, as well as detail and colour, as she tries to find the meaning in the pictures. She empha-sises the effort this requires:

> I just look at it and I think, OK now, this is a picture of a stone boy and a little girl with her arms around him. What can that mean? Then you just think the boy's been turned to stone and the little girl's come to save him. That's what I think it is and then you see the stones turning to little flowers, so I think, OK now, this girl has saved her brother and the stones have turned into daisies and

the background's changed colour too. So you just need to look really hard.

'Getting the words off of the pictures': the relationship between image and text

Valuing the contribution of the two signifying systems in a picturebook, the words and the pictures, also leads to insights into how children look at them, both at each system on its own and in conjunction. When we asked about the relative merits of word and image, pictures were usually declared more interesting because they were, of course, colourful and eye-catching. We followed up by asking the children whether the book would work if it just had pictures or if it just had words. Most children gave greater significance to the pictures and said that the book would not be as good without them, because the pictures help to show 'what's going on' and also 'what the characters look like, because some people can't read'. Several children thought that a good artist would need fewer words because it is all there in the pictures. As Denise (9) put it: 'The words are interesting because you can read instead of just trying to get the words off of the pictures.'

Most of the children expected picturebooks to have both words and pictures and found it no problem to 'make up' one or the other if missing (many had participated in these sort of exercises before: drawing pictures for words or making up words for pictures). However, they thought that getting the pictures 'right' was more important than getting the words right. To find out what's happened with just the pictures 'you have to use your head more' (Jason 9), whereas with just words 'you'd have to picture it all in your head, and you could see it would be a lot fatter book because there has to be more writing, describing and everything' (Dave 8). So images are translated into description and detail in a verbal text and are a more economic way of getting a message through, as Tamsin (8) pointed out: 'It would be really hard if he said [wrote] everything that was in *The Tunnel* so he just put in the pictures everything that was in there.'

Another revealing question was whether the words or the pictures told the same story. This proved difficult for many children who simply said 'yes'. However, many of them revised their answer either in the group discussions or in the re-interviews. Because the word/picture dynamics is different in each of the three picturebooks in this study, the pupils' responses were also different. In *Lily*, there is what

Nikolajeva and Scott (2000) call a 'perspectival counterpoint' where words and pictures employ different perspectives to tell the story and involve both contradiction and ambiguity. Lily's story is told by the written text and Nicky's by the pictures. In *Zoo* the written text gives the narrator's point of view (one of the boys visiting the zoo) and the pictures tell the story of the animals; this could be described as a counterpoint in characterisation (humans /animals). Finally, in *The Tunnel*, the text and images tell a similar story except that the text is fairly bland and the pictures reveal much more.

With some prompting, the children who read *Lily* noticed that the words did not explain what was happening to Nicky and why he was frightened or mention the monsters which were only evident in the pictures. The pictures also provide 'the atmosphere' (Angus 9). Without the pictures, said Kevin (10), 'it would just be a happy book'. One of the children with learning difficulties pointed out that 'the pictures tell his [Nicky's] story and if he tells it the people wouldn't believe him'. On the other hand Lauren (11) thought the words were needed 'to take the story along', to provide the narrative thread.

The responses to *Zoo* were similar because (again, with some prompting) most children realised the words and pictures were not telling the same story. Frank (5) noticed this at an elementary level: the words don't tell the same story as the pictures 'because when he said he had lots of food in the writing it didn't show in the picture. They look at the giraffes and the rhinos but they didn't say in the words.' Cristina (9) knew there was a distinction between the pictorial and verbal discourses even though she found it hard to express it: 'I think the pictures give more description about all the animals and the writing tells you a bit about the zoo, more of the zoo.' Older, more articulate children Lara (10) and Joe (10) really got to the heart of the matter. When asked which she preferred, Lara replied:

> the pictures, because the writing doesn't explain everything what you think. The writing only explains what the book is about and what is happening, but it doesn't explain what you feel and what they feel. So I like the pictures better because then you can think more stuff.

Joe also found the images more interesting because 'the pictures show what it's really like and what's going on with the animals'. He then refers to the perspectival counterpoint described by Nikolajeva and Scott (2001):

I think they do tell the story in different ways, because the text is more like their [people visiting the zoo] point of view, but the pictures are more of the animals' point of view.

These responses contrast with *The Tunnel*, where both words and illustrations were felt necessary to understand the story. However, readers noticed that, although the words helped to 'guide' the reader through the book, the pictures created the sense of unease. This was particularly apparent in the spread in *The Tunnel* without any words, where Rose is running through the menacing forest. It was also one of the favourite images in the book for many children. Shanice (10) had to 'make up the story ... it's making me think why the author put them [the various strange objects and figures] there'. Shanice also pointed out that, by looking at the pictures and making up your own story, 'you can understand more things than the writing'. Tamsin[1] (8) summed up many of her peers' observations about the relationship between the visual and the verbal texts:

> Every book needs a bit of picture to make you understand. I mean if this book didn't really have much pictures except for the one in the front, you'd get lost a bit ... if it was just writing you wouldn't really feel like you were in there because there was nothing to show you what it was really like. OK you could use your imagination, but if you want to know what the girl's point of view or the boy's point of view is you'd have to have pictures to see.

The relationship between the words and the pictures leads to another element involved in the act of reading and viewing: the implied author /artist and his creative process.

'He moved his imagination': the artistic process

The children's observations on the artistic processes involved in composing a picturebook not only indicate how they understand pictorial text, but also how they use metacognitive skills in doing so. In the following quote from 4-year-old Janet, she speculates about the steps Kitamura took to write and illustrate *Lily*:

> Well he first wrote the words and then he drew. He read them and then he drew what he thought might be what he wanted to draw

and he looked at the pages. He had a first sketch there and then he looked at them and then he drew them with colours and put them in the book. I always draw people like that [and] if I can write them, I put words. I can write quite a lot of them.

The sequence, as Janet describes it, involves a lot of looking and thinking at various stages, as well as writing and drawing. The words come first and then an attempt at the drawing and finally colouring. She is also aware of the 'sketch' stage which implies the artist might make changes (there was only one other child who mentioned making a sketch first, 'in case he got it wrong'). In her last sentence Janet reflects on her own attempts at drawing, implying she is some-what aware of the thinking, looking and revising involved in the process. The only difference is that she adds the words later because, at 4 years old, she is more confident about her drawing skills than her writing. This was reflected in her second drawing when, after finishing the pictures, she laboriously began to write a text above the drawing.

Throughout her two interviews, Janet attempted to explain her movements, talking about sequence and comparing the way she drew houses (square with triangle on top) with the way Kitamura draws them. She was also very articulate when describing her drawing of the tree monster with strikingly coloured squares above it, representing the warm colours of the curtains in Lily's room, (Janet had told me she had similar curtains in her room and her favourite colour was purple), then a yellow square and a black square representing the lit and dark windows in the houses on Lily's walk. Although Janet struggled to talk about the pictures in the book, her sensitivity to Kitamura's use of colour (which unfortunately we cannot represent here) and pattern, is evident in the drawing. Her awareness of the steps involved in the process is also a recognition of the sophisticated cognitive skills which bridge writing and drawing when it is a creative act.

However, behind the children's comments one can also sometimes hear the cautionary voices of teachers or parents. Browne and Kitamura will be relieved to hear that 'he's very neat', 'he colours in nicely', 'he stays in the lines', and 'there are no mistakes'! This is Carol (10) (mentioned above as a struggling reader), talking about the way Kitamura has drawn the grass at different angles and the way she has been told to do it at school. Note the choice of vocabulary such as 'texture', which she may have picked up from the interviewer:

I like the texture of the grass. When I was little I got told to never do it all different ways, so like I've already done that because I've been learned to do that … if I was an artist I wouldn't have done that because I've been learned from school when I was really little.

In general, comments on the artistic process can be divided into three groups: those that have to do with the actual techniques that the artist used; those that refer to the way in which he expressed his ideas; and those that show how the children understood his intentions. In the first group we find mention of specific paints and techniques, such as the possibility that Browne used a 'blow-pen' to spray the paint in one of the pictures, or that Browne used watercolours and Kitamura used crayons. It does not matter if these speculations are right or wrong, what really matters is that children are not looking at the illustration merely as a finished object but as the result of a process that begins with using a particular medium. Eisner is making a similar point in relation to drawing in his Foreword to Arnheim's *Thoughts on Art Education*: 'In the course of drawing, for example, the child must not only perceive the structural essence of what he wished to draw, which, Arnheim points out, is at the heart of skilled reasoning: the child must also find a way to represent that essence within the limits and possibilities of a medium' (1989: 4).

Children also regularly commented on the use of shadows, line and, perhaps most frequently, colour, in the pictures. For example, Corinna (10) pointed out the importance of Browne using red for Rose's coat because of its reference to Little Red Riding Hood. Martin (7) said the same thing about Kitamura choosing yellow for Lily's tulips to stand out among the darker colours of the evening. Lara (10), an inexperienced reader commenting on *Zoo*, made many insightful references to Browne's use of colour.

You can tell they [the animals] are upset because there is this dark one, not many colours, not bright beautiful colours, and it makes you think well … when it's people, it is happy, and it makes you feel oh we're happy, so we should be on the happy page. And the animals are really upset and are on the black page.

Other comments revealed what the children thought was going on in the artist's head as he drew. According to some children, first the artist has to 'imagine' the pictures in his head before he can draw them. Luke (5) thought that Browne writes the words for the story first and then thinks of a good picture to 'match' because 'words and pictures match exactly'. Sofia (8) believed that Browne drafts the written text first, makes a few changes and then draws pictures that match the text. Like others, she believed in the 'matching' of words and pictures because 'you wouldn't have a picture that says this, that doesn't match it, that doesn't quite make sense'. This thinking encapsulates the more literal engagement that some children had with Browne's work, in which words and pictures were perceived as telling the same story. Some of the older, more experienced readers like Lauren (11) had a more balanced view of how the artist went about his work: 'As I am reading it, the pictures link very well with the text, so he needed to know what was happening in both, both in the pictures and in the text.'

Pupils reading *Zoo* and *The Tunnel* were very aware that the author had to 'really think about it'. For example, as Erin (7) said, 'in a way the boys behave like monkeys and Browne chooses to draw monkeys rather than another animal'. In the group discussion, she also spoke of how Browne would have planned ahead carefully before doing it. Dan (8), who participated with Erin in the group discussion, agreed that Browne must have taken his camera to the zoo and then 'wanted to do something very very careful with this book' and that even if he did make a mistake he would not 'give up'.

One question that children found hard to answer was what the artist had to know in order to do the illustrations. Many chose not to speculate but Carol's (10) reply condenses those who did. She spoke of the research Kitamura would have had to do before being able to create his story:

> Well he needed to know a dog that looks like that and he needed to know a family that has a dog and how they kind of look after their dog and somebody that likes walking. You needed to interview somebody, to kind of know more about people and ... how they kind of look after their dogs, or do they get scared and what do they do when they are scared and do you have any kids, do they walk the dog ...

In other words, like Erin and Dan, there is a sense of the planning and time the work involves, the need to know your subject and then how you are going to set it down on paper.

This links to a third set of comments that imply an awareness of the artist's intentions behind the writing and drawing. Generally, it was considered that the artist had drawn in a particular style to make a picture 'more lively' or 'interesting' or 'funny' so 'people get excited and want to read on'. In some cases, this was linked to enjoyment, but in others it was linked to a commercial interest – creating a desire for reading would also make people 'buy it'. Sometimes their interpretation of the author's motives were linked to the story itself: one child thought Kitamura wrote *Lily* because he had a dog like Nicky (in fact, Kitamura got the idea for this story when he was living with a family who had a small girl he often took for walks in a pushchair). Others thought Browne wrote *The Tunnel* because he had a sister who was very different from him, or *Zoo* because he wanted people to go and see one.

Perhaps the questions that most revealed this awareness about intentions were those about the inclusion of the 'unusual' and this applied to all three books. Most readers suggested that the artists did it for the atmosphere, to make it look 'scary'. Several agreed that Browne and Kitamura draw in a way that makes you want to look carefully and not just turn over pages quickly. However, there were a few children who could only make literal sense of these features. One pupil kept insisting that Browne's 'brain must be off'! Finally, there were also those who said the artist put the things there 'because he wanted to' and as far as they were concerned, that was that.

Thinking, reading, looking and learning: conclusions

It is important to remember that these comments were made by children from different ages, as well as different socio-economic, cultural and linguistic backgrounds. It was impossible to do any further research into how each of these variables might affect viewing, but it is evident that they were all trying to make sense of the texts in front of them and most were able, to a degree, to express how they were actually doing this.[2]

The children's answers reveal how the eye scans a picture, roaming over it, focussing on what they perceive are the salient features, then looking at background and other details. They also reveal how the eye moves between one part of the picture and another, piecing together the image like a puzzle. The eyes also move back and forth between the words and the images, leaning on each other for understanding, confirming or denying hypotheses about what is happening in the story. These movements correspond to some of the compositional elements described by Kress and van Leeuwen (1996) in their 'grammar of visual design' where, for example, the informational value of the left-hand area of an image is linked to what is already known or expected and the right-hand side is linked to the new or unexpected.

The children were aware of the thinking, looking, and planning required to achieve all this successfully and of the possibility of making and rectifying mistakes. They also revealed an ability to put themselves in the artist's head to imagine how he wanted the reader to react by creating images that inspired humour, fear and other emotions. The children were also able to go inside their own heads to describe what they were thinking and feeling as they read a picture (and also as they drew their own).

Their critical comments and observations suggest how these metacognitive skills can be developed and built on in order to help them become more critical and discerning readers. In the first place, their knowledge needs to be taken into account in the classroom. Once there is a space for them to articulate what they know and to discuss it with the teacher or their peers, they will feel more confident about their own skills and more interested in how the teacher can complement it. This can be done through looking at more picture-books, comparing and contrasting them, as well as through children's own art work. Finally, children can be encouraged to bring their experience with other visual media to the classroom and use it to understand the processes of reception and creation and, in turn, reflect upon it, whether it be the latest computer games or ancient stained-glass windows.

A version of this chapter appears in M. Styles and E. Bearne (eds) (2002) *Art, Narrative and Childhood*, London: Trentham.

Notes

1   At school Tamsin was considered a 'weak' reader, someone who had difficulties reading 'long' books, according to her teacher. However, as we can see here, her awareness of the reading process was far greater than any of her classmates and, indeed, of most children in the study. She had not seen *The Tunnel* before, but was familiar with other picturebooks and especially with fairy tales.

2   During our research, we also analysed observations which showed how the children's knowledge of other media influenced their reading of picturebooks (see chapter 11).

Part IV

Conclusions

Chapter 10

The artist's voice
Browne and Kitamura talking pictures

An interview with Anthony Browne

> Looking? It's the most important thing in the world.

Anthony Browne is not just a prizewinning picturebook artist, recently awarded the prestigious Hans Christian Andersen Award for lifetime achievement in children's literature (the first British author to gain this distinction since Eleanor Farjeon), but one of the most popular artists with children working in Britain today and well known in many parts of the world.

Browne's work is often strange and unsettling, full of surreal images, so that nothing is as it seems, yet very young children, as well as older readers, respond very positively to his picturebooks. So it was the excitement his books generated in a wide range of children, as well as the quality of his art work, that made Browne an immediate choice for this study. In the previous chapters, we have documented how children interpreted *Zoo* and *The Tunnel*. Now there is an opportunity to hear Browne's voice and find out what he has to say about making visual texts for children and what his intentions were in those two particular books.[1]

First of all, we discussed his covers, then the readership of his picturebooks. Browne's serious respect for his young readers is evident and his explicit intention to create books that are rich and multi-layered comes through forcefully. Browne is still a regular visitor to schools and bookshops and his delight in, and knowledge of, children undoubtedly contributes to the success of his books.

I: Are you aware when you create a book of an adult as well as a child readership?

AB: Yes I am to a certain extent. I would hate the idea of trying to appeal to the adults over the children's heads. The readership of my picturebooks is of a wide age range and reading abilities, and visually reading, as well as reading the words. And so I like to put things in which are there to be found, by adults or children who are more aware, or children who have read the book three or four times, or have seen something since the first reading that relates to something I put in the book. And I'm also aware that books are very often shared with adults and a bored adult will convey boredom to a child, if the adult isn't excited or interested in the book as well.

[...]

I:　Your covers are obviously incredibly important to you?

AB:　Yes, another page of the book for one thing, but also a way into the book. But they've got to appeal to the marketing people and attract the readers in the first place.

In most of Browne's picturebooks he has produced his own written text as well as the pictures. We were interested in how children perceived the way word and image interacted in two picturebooks from this study and asked Browne how important the written text was for him, and whether he constructed both parts separately or in tandem.

I:　How important is getting the words right as well as the pictures?

AB:　Very important. And it's the area I find most difficult, I suppose because I laughingly say I trained as an artist (I was a terrible student!), I should be able to do that [the pictures]. But words are something that have always interested me. I've been tentatively learning as I go along what to write really, how to write picturebooks which is very difficult.

I:　Do the words come with the pictures?

AB:　Ideally, yes, at its best they go together. I don't write the story first. Some other illustrators do. But it's more like a film. So it's really working out how to tell the story in twenty-eight scenes.[2] And the two things really do come together. I make a story-board the first time with a few squiggles. Neither of them are in any way formed, what they will look like or what the words will say, but they do come together. Which is why I find it more difficult illustrating someone else's text. As I say, it's a ritual for me. Particularly if it's a poem, there's nothing that can be changed. I can't go and say, 'Well actually, I've already drawn X, I'm going to draw this, so do we need that?'

I: Is that something you consciously feel, that some things you'll say in
    words and some things you'll say in pictures and some things you'll
    say in both?
AB: Yes, and *some things you say in the gap between the words and the
    pictures*. I think some of the worst picturebooks are those where
    the words are just captions to the pictures.

Browne is famous for realism and surrealism in much of his work, his
use of intertextuality and what have come to be known as his trademarks – bananas, gorillas and brick walls! We wanted to find out which
conscious techniques Browne employed to achieve his affects and
what, if anything, those motifs symbolised. He also discusses some of
his artistic influences.

I: References to popular culture, other artists and other texts, is that
    something you are conscious of doing?
AB: I'm doing it [intertextuality] because it's what I do, I think. If
    I'm going to work on a book that takes me two years, it's going
    to be me expressing how I feel about things. And if I use paint-
    ings or film images, it's a way of basically telling the story.
    They're there for other reasons as well. If I use a famous
    painting, it's to help to tell the story in some way, because that's
    what the story needs to tell or something that's going on inside
    the character. I don't deliberately set out to do these images for
    relevance, but of course they add layers. ... Something that
    fascinated me as a child were hidden images within pictures,
    those puzzle pictures. So on one level it's that, a picture within a
    picture, or a reference within a picture, so there's something else
    going on, something you can kind of discover the second time
    you look at it. ... In more recent books, whenever I put
    anything in, it's there for a purpose, it's there to take the story
    somewhere else, to tell something about the story.
    [...]
I: I've noticed kids looking backwards and forwards in your books,
    perhaps more than other authors. Your books always seem to make
    them very interactive?
AB: Makes them concentrate on looking as well.
    [...]
AB: I think I was influenced by Magritte long before I'd ever seen a
    Magritte painting actually. The drawings I did as a child ... a lot
    are surreal. And that was always what fascinated me. And to

discover Magritte at the age of 12 or whatever I was, was like discovering something I felt I already knew about. Like reading *Alice in Wonderland* again. It seems like a world you sort of know.

Browne operates on the 'narrative as a primary act of mind' principle. The story is the thing to which all other matters are subservient in his view. Reading Browne is a highly active process and slow, deep, persistent, intelligent looking is usually evident. It is interesting that Browne was fascinated by hidden images as a child, as that is certainly one of the features of his art work children find so intriguing and satisfying. It's a visual and intellectual puzzle they have to solve and most children rise to the summons. In *The Intelligent Eye*, Perkins writes about the challenge of the invisible in art: 'Multiple interpretations are possible as we dig deeper and share readings with one another. … We need to look persistently and intelligently' so that 'the eye and mind [are] allowed to roam and do their work of discovery' for a fully rich reading of an image (1994: 21). This seems to happen quite spontaneously, given the opportunity, when children encounter Browne's work.

I: Why do you use brick walls so often in your work?

AB: I was once asked that many many years ago and I've no idea. Sometimes they are just brick walls! But I think again maybe they are a recurrent thing, a bit like bars, prison bars, borders, things that just visually interest me. If I were an abstract painter, I think my paintings would be lots of straight lines, grids, verticals and horizontals with something organic relating to them. And that organic shape happens very often to be children or animals. And the cages or the walls are something someone in prison might escape from, I suppose. Although, as I say, sometimes they're just brick walls …

I: And, as Doonan suggests, do you think you're sort of writing about human beings as a metaphor for brick walls and dead ends?

AB: Yeah, yeah, yeah.

[…]

I: Why do you have this obsession with gorillas?

AB: I'm almost sure that *Gorilla* came from a greetings card which I did which came from out of nowhere. It was a huge gorilla holding a teddy bear and I loved the contrast of the big, tough-looking creature holding a teddy bear. And King Kong was being made into a film, so again gorillas, of course. But I hadn't really painted gorillas before. So I really think it came from an image and the idea of a huge, tough creature being actually quite soft and gentle. And I suppose I started thinking, well how could that be a story? ... And gorillas had been something I'd been interested in for a very long time. ... I'm certainly no expert on gorillas, for instance, which people seem to expect me to be. But I think I sometimes (I've got to be wary of sounding pretentious here) use animals to show a side of our nature that we repress. And I think many children haven't learned to suppress that side of their nature. And not just that aspect of it, but the creative aspect of children's minds is very exciting. Every human can do that, but how many adults are able to?

[...]

I: What kind of paints do you use?

AB: Watercolour. Sometimes there might be a bit of gouache to cover up mistakes or to paint over something. With watercolour, you can't really paint over.

[...]

I: Are the colours there for the reader to interpret?

AB: Yeah. When I talk to children in schools, I often use these pictures [two contrasting pages from *Gorilla*]. You know a lot of them didn't realise there were such things as warm colours and cold colours. As soon as we start to look at these pictures, they realise there are.

[...]

I: Doonan says of your work that most of it is about trust relationships to a varying degree.

AB: I suppose so. It's only when I have to give a talk or something like that, I realise that my books fall into particular categories, because to me they're all incredibly different. You know, all my books are very different to me, but when I have to think about them I realise that there are common themes running through them.

I: Another point she makes about your work is the need for resourceful central characters. Are you aware of that?

AB: Yes, yes. But as soon as I start talking about it, I become self-conscious. ... I mean I'm happy for other people to observe these things.

The final sections relate to what Browne had to say specifically about *Zoo* and *The Tunnel*. Browne gives us fascinating insights into his own personal history and how it interconnects with his books.

I: Do you find *The Tunnel* is one of your books that has most impact on readers?

AB: It isn't the one that I get most letters about from children. I would say it's *Willy the Wimp*. But there are quite a lot of them [Willy books], so there's more chance of them being seen. But the questions I get about *The Tunnel* are some of the most interesting. So the children are really thinking about this one, whereas with Willy they might just suggest what the next Willy story might be.

[...]

AB: Yes, the tunnel is one that my brother and I used to go in. ... It was terrifying, looking back, absolutely terrifying.

I: And endpapers are important?

AB: Yes they are. This was my first significant brick wall. But it's not actually a brick wall. If you look carefully, I've suggested that it's wallpaper. You can see the joins ... also suggesting that the boy and girl are similar, the boy's not really as tough as he seems. ... That's the same wallpaper I used in *Hansel and Gretel* actually, and it's how I remember wallpaper as a child.

I   You're into, at least you are in *Gorilla*, wallpaper a lot.

AB: Yes, memory of childhood as much as anything. I mean, that's a bit what my childhood felt like. Lots of dark, heavy furniture, intricate wallpaper, lying awake in the dark, imagining things from shapes I could see ...

I: And fairy tales?

AB: Yes, fairy tales, very much so ...

[...]

I: Victor Watson was reading *The Tunnel* with a little 4-year-old girl for the first time. When he asked her what the book and the ball in the final endpaper meant, she said, 'Because at first they didn't get on, but in the end they are nice.'

AB: That's what pleases me so much to hear, *because children in a way are capable of so much more than most people think they are.* So to believe a brick wall can be a boy and a father can be a gorilla ...

[...]

I: What's going on in that picture? [pointing to the spread of the rubbish dump]

AB: Well, it's partly me having fun painting a sort of rubbish dump, and me also trying not to ... there was a great temptation to put too much in here. ... I wanted it to be possibly just a rubbish dump with suggestions that there were other things going on. I wanted that to be just bits of plaster coming off the wall, and also suggestions of him [Jack]. I wanted that to be a bit of old pipe, but also a way of separating the two children, putting her [Rose] on her own.

I: And just partly, he could be the boy who likes the urban and …

AB: Yeah, and he's out playing football with his mates and rough and tumble and that kind of thing. And she's sitting on a box looking like none of this is going on.

[…]

AB: The trees here [points to forest spread] almost suggested the shapes themselves. … Underneath the detail there's just colours which have run into each other which have suggested shapes to me and then I've homed in on them. … I think I had a definite idea that I wanted to work on that hollow tree. And he's walking along and he meets an old woman who said she would give him a fortune if he'd climb down … then he gets inside, there's some dogs who are guarding something who have eyes as big as saucers. The tinderbox, that's what it is. Ultimately, it's the tinderbox he has to bring out of there. … There's a lot that relates to *Hansel and Gretel*. The beanstalk is a recurring image …

I: And the axe as well, is that …

AB: That again could be many fairy tales. … And that reminds me, talking of *Hansel and Gretel*, it's been a story I remember from my childhood. … The first few years of my life, I grew up in a pub in Yorkshire. Great fields at the back went down into a valley and there was a wooded area at the bottom of the stream and this huge viaduct towering over everything. It was terrifying. And I remember my brother and I used to go down into this valley, down into the woods, and it was great, it was really exciting. I fell for it every time. He'd take me down there (he's a smashing bloke) but then he would run off. And, of course, this place transformed from a lovely, leafy foliage into this terrifying. … It was the power he'd got over me.

[…]

AB: It's also a book about coming to terms with different aspects of your own character. In a way, it's a book about a brother and a sister, but it's also the two aspects of oneself. I mean I think I identify with the boy and the girl and in the end you have them coming together in some kind of balance.

Browne lets us in on the genesis of *Zoo* and discusses issues related to the book, including animal rights and gender. He also tells us about what he actually planned for the book and some of the serendipitous features that are part of the mysterious process of creating a picture-book.

AB: I think it was simply originally a book based on observations of human behaviour in zoos really. That's how it started. I hadn't really got much of an idea beyond that. I talked to my son, Joseph, who at the time would have been about 8. ... We were both interested in observing people at zoos. So I asked him to write a story on the idea of the family. We'd also talked about family days out as well. And he wrote a long story about a family trip to a zoo, taking the mickey out of the father. And that really developed into the book. And once I started I realised there were other issues. ... It also came from the project I did at art college. The only decent project I ever did at art college was a series of paintings and illustrations on the theme of Man as an Animal. And I read lots of animal behaviourist books. ... I loved that project. It didn't go down very well!

I: Isn't *Zoo* a rather bleak account of human nature?

AB: I don't think the book is as bleak as people thought it was. I mean I know it's a harsh view of males. I was only reminding us all that we are animals ourselves and we forget that. Sometimes I think with children's books, if you're a man or write about a man in a story, that becomes your view of men. Children will see that's what men are like or that's what fathers are like. But it's one family, it's one father on one particular occasion.

[...]

I: What about the cover? Were the zebra stripes deliberate?

AB: Zebra stripes, but also cage bars as well, yeah. And the stripes are also there deliberately trying to make the book get noticed. I'd been to Central America to do some book things and I'd noticed how few of the books actually stood out. So I thought at least I'll make it noticeable, so if you saw it in a bookshop, you'd think, 'What's that?' It's the reverse of what I normally do. Normally, I will frame something in some way, in some kind of cage-like, wall-like stretch with organic stuff going on inside. In actual fact, it's very stiff, static stuff imprisoned in here.

I: It's wonderfully designed.

AB: Yes, I was very pleased with the design on that one.

I: And do the endpapers reflect your mixed feeling about the zoo? Was that the idea? Starting a debate?

AB: Yeah, yeah.

[...]

I: Was it deliberately not a tacky zoo, but an architect-designed modern zoo?

AB: Well, I thought that was even more ironic, you know. … It would be too easy to take a bad zoo and then it would seem to be attacking a bad zoo. It's not attacking the zoo, it's just trying to make us think about it. … I based the book on London Zoo. …

The first time I saw an orang-utan I was in Jersey Zoo. It was absolutely stunning. It was almost as though it was praying. It was almost like a religious thing in itself.

[…]

AB: I enjoyed painting those pictures, I really did. Partly because it was a welcome change to paint pictures almost for their own sake and not just to link one part of a story with another. When I came to do *Willy the Dreamer* some time later, that was a great relief to me that I could just paint a series of pictures. It's something I can't get away with forever, but it was very nice after twenty odd years … out of 32-page picturebooks, there may be 5 or 6 pictures you really want to do. The rest have to be there.

[…]

I: We are all observers of the animals in *Zoo* until the penguin page where you move the viewer into the cage. Is that deliberate? Were you aware of making the reader move in?

AB: To be quite honest, no. I love the idea of that. I wish I'd thought of it! But I put the little figure in here deliberately [pointing to the faint and tiny human figure in the corner], because it's an observer. It's a human observer. But no, I hadn't realised I'd been getting rid of the bottom border and putting the reader almost inside there.

I: Maybe it was going on unconsciously?

AB: Well exactly. That's how a painting often works.

[…]

I: I remember talking to you about this years ago. And you said the sort of religious iconography in *Gorilla* was deliberate.

AB: Yeah, as is the cross in *Zoo*.

I: You actually said to me once, 'That's my first crucifixion.'

AB: Yes.

An interview with Satoshi Kitamura

'Looking' is seeing with pencil in hand.

There is something about Satoshi Kitamura's unmistakable style that makes his pictures easily recognisable even by very young children. It is not only his child characters' stripey jumpers or his animals' big round eyes. It also has to do with his dynamic black lines and his strong yet warm colour washes. It has to do with the confident look on the faces of his characters who remain unperturbed in the face of UFOs, tigers, dinosaurs or universequakes and at the same time inspire an affectionate response from readers.

Since winning the Mother Goose Award in 1983 for *Angry Arthur*, Kitamura has illustrated many of his own and others' stories as well as poetry collections. He has also won several awards in his native Japan. We were excited to have the opportunity to talk to him about his work in general and about *Lily* in particular, especially as the interview took place after he had heard what the children said about this picturebook and had looked at their drawings in response to it.[3]

Throughout the interview Kitamura seemed quite surprised, not only by what the children said, but also by critics' commentaries on his work as a whole. His books have been analysed in detail by some of the best critics of children's books, such as Doonan (1991 and 1993) and Nikolajeva and Scott (2000 and 2001). Even a quick glance at one of his books clearly shows that much thought and planning has gone into them – not to mention his skill with the materials themselves. Nevertheless, throughout the interview Kitamura made it all sound so easy and almost a matter of luck, not only in terms of the act of creating itself but also, to begin with, in terms of his successful career as a picturebook artist:

SK: I've never gone to art school. I've never been conscious of taking up art as a professional, I just simply liked it. When I was 19, a friend who was a graphic designer needed an artist and he asked me because he knew I could draw. So I started drawing but I never thought of going to art school.

MS: Perhaps it's an advantage.

SK: I don't know, maybe, yes. I'm not against education at all. I mean it's a good thing to spend four years, anything, studying art or science or whatever. But it didn't happen that way.

MS: So how did you get good at it?

SK: Well since I was maybe 3 or 4, I can't remember when I started, but I always drew, and I simply liked it. So every day I drew one or two pictures. Nothing artistic, it's just like imagination. I mean like cars, I drew lots of cars, like any boy. Or machines or planes. And often I drew something imaginary, like imaginary spaceships. And I did some cartoons, sort of comic cartoons. And also I often made models. I spent lots of time just doodling in school. I often did this in the text book! And I had a lot of books with pictures.

EA: How did you start drawing for children?

SK: I was thinking of doing a book when one of my cousins, who was very small then, 6 or 7, asked me to draw, to make a comic book for her. I bought a sketch book and I just made up a first bit of story with pictures. I wasn't planning anything. I went along, and after 20 pages or so I finished the story. And I thought, it's a sort of fantastic story, sort of fairy tale. I went to see publishers and nothing happened. And then I got busy as a commercial artist for a couple of years, so I forgot about it. Then I became so busy that I wanted to stop. I wanted to learn English, so I came to England. And after a year or so, one day I got an idea, I just sort of stole it from my head. So I drew and wrote down a story and I sent about ten copies of this story to different publishers. And to my surprise, they all replied. And several of them said they were interested.

Klaus Flugge of Andersen Press was one of them and he has since become Kitamura's regular publisher.

MS: And then you won the Mother Goose with your first book, *Angry Arthur?*

SK: Yes. So I was very lucky. I went back to Japan as soon as I finished this book, to my old job of doing advertising. I wasn't quite sure whether I could live on doing books and my work with advertising began to go well, so I couldn't decide what to do. Then a telegram arrived saying you've won the Mother Goose Award. And I didn't know what the Mother Goose Award was! But anyway, I came back to England to attend this presentation. I came back to England, and have been living here since, more or less. So yeah, I was very lucky.

It is perhaps Kitamura's vision as a foreigner that influences his drawing. He notices things other people tend to overlook because they are so familiar. His very particular vision of English towns and country-side, from houses and their interiors to the colours of the landscape, can be observed in all his books. As we accompany Lily and Nicky on their walk we also become observers, forced to see things in a different perspective as well-known objects literally change faces. Kitamura puts it simply:

SK: Walking is a chance to see things. I always enjoy all the journey from A to B because I like just simply looking at things. And I seldom get bored. So maybe this book (*Lily*) is about walking.

MS: So maybe this book is about walking and looking?

SK: It is, it is about seeing and looking. Seeing is something you do all the time and looking is seeing with a pencil in hand. Even if you're not drawing, if you're consciously seeing things it becomes looking. And I suppose I'm fairly good at looking.

An understatement if there ever was one!

One of the interviewed children said that perhaps Kitamura had made the book because he had known a little girl like Lily. Kitamura confirmed this and he told us a bit about how the picturebook was conceived:

> Many years ago I was sharing a house with this family and they had two children, Lily and Toby. I looked after Lily a lot while the parents were busy, often I took her out in the pushchair and it made her sleep. So when I was working on the book, I immediately decided to call the character Lily.

Readers are always interested in how the artist gets the 'idea' for a book. Kitamura believes it may have been on one of these evening walks that the initial concept of the book came to him from a 'visual illusion' he himself had, and from there he developed the idea of the double narrative:

> When I got the idea, I was interested in having a story not describing what's going on in the pictures. If you read the words of the book, it's just describing the walk of the girl. But if you look at the pictures, there's something else going on. So I liked the contrast of this. You have to look at the pictures to understand what's going on. The story itself is a sort of self-contained story perhaps, but it's not all of it. It's just a part of the book. ... I developed all these tricks. Although the tricks are not new – I mean it's been done for ages by lots of artists. I don't know what they're called, some sort of visual illusions.

We asked him whether he was trying to say anything else apart from playing with the narrative perspective and the 'visual illusions':

The other thing I wanted to do in the book was kind of the feel of the evening, you know, like she's walking in the evening and going home, that sort of sense of time, when it's getting dark. It might be related to my walk with the girl, it was often about five, six o'clock, about dinner time.

The 'feel of the evening' – together with the visual illusions – was also something the children tried to convey in their drawings (see chapter 6) where Lily and Nicky are usually set against a background of blues and dark greens. That very young children can recognise the hues and tones used by a particular artist is confirmed in an anecdote Kitamura related about the real Lily's older brother:

> One day Toby, who was I guess about 4 or 5, was just outside the window, it was late, maybe after dinner. He was pointing out the sky and he said: 'It's your kind of sky because it's a sort of dark bluish sky.'

Another aspect which distinguishes Kitamura's style is what the children we interviewed identified as 'cartoon-like'.

EA: A lot of children identified with your style, said it was like a cartoon. Do you see it that way yourself?

SK: Yes, because all children love cartoons. … I guess I was impressed by cartoons that I saw when I was a child. … The reason I use black lines is it's very much like cartoons.

One of the reasons the children thought they looked like cartoons was because of his 'wobbly lines' which made everything look slightly crooked – even 'round' tyres. We asked him if there was any significance in drawing them like this (see the children's explanations for the wobbly steps in chapter 3).

SK: Yes, lots of people point out the way I draw any object with these lines. One of my friends said something, sort of, there's some kind of animism to them. But I'm not really saying anything, it's just the way I want to depict. If I try I suppose I can draw more realistically, but it's not my style. It's like Anthony Browne's got a completely different, sort of very realistic, half-realistic style that creates a strange world. The idea is emphasised by being real.

MS: Anthony Browne creates hyper-real worlds, so the buildings are very concrete. When I look out at your houses, your drawing style makes them seem less substantial, as if that world might, not exactly crumble but, it's a world that isn't sort of set in concrete. And I just wondered if that's deliberate or not?

SK: I guess it is. If I'm interested in say the concreteness of the house, or the house being built by marbles or stones, then I would have drawn differently. But what I'm interested in, like when you are on the train, looking out through the windows, you see all these English houses, back gardens and all the washing and so on. You kind of have some sort of emotional thing about it. I mean, if you live in that environment, you feel all sorts of feelings. Although I wasn't brought up in this country, I do feel very much – I don't know what is the right word for it – sentiment. I suppose I want to draw that impression of feeling of objects or buildings, rather than the correct proportion.

Apart from the colours and style, there were two things the children noticed about the pictures in *Lily*: the presence of rubbish in many of them and the absence of other people – particularly on the street and in the cars. First we asked Kitamura if he was trying to make a point about the environment:

SK: It's more like intuition to put rubbish on the street, just to make it more realistic. It's nothing to do with ecology … you put rubbish because the streets always have rubbish. It just makes it more real.

MS: How do you feel about the environment?

SK: Oh, I probably don't put a message in a book in that way. If I have to deal with environmental issues, then I'd do it more obviously perhaps.

MS: I'm just wondering if unconsciously your own views were coming over without you realising.

SK: Well it could happen. Maybe it's unconsciously, subconsciously, my point of view about those things. But I never thought of this environment issue in this case.

When we asked him about the absence of people, again he seemed to have thought about it for the first time: 'I probably wanted to make a lot of atmosphere, it looks a bit more spooky without people.'

During the interviews with the children there was much speculation about why Kitamura had not drawn the mother's face (it is interesting that Browne also chooses not to show us the mother's face in *The Tunnel*). In *In the Attic* (1984) and *Angry Arthur* (1983) the mothers' faces are not depicted either (and, although we see Arthur's father and grandfather, the grandmother's head is covered by the astronaut's helmet). Kitamura laughingly admitted that maybe it was because he was not very good at drawing women. However, he also pointed out that:

> Maybe the presence of the father or mother is not too important if they don't say much. Then it's probably better to avoid drawing that kind of face. Because it gives you too strong an impression.

In fact, Lily's father's face created such an impression on the readers that some children in the study identified him as being the same man as the 'vampire' coming out of the poster.

It was hard to pin Kitamura down on how much he had thought out beforehand whether there were 'significant details' through which he was trying to say something else. About this, Doonan says: 'many of his objects have specific symbolic as well as narrative functions and thus reward close attention, and often he is concerned to promote a surreal effect by the juxtaposition of unlikely objects, to suggest his characters' inner lives' (1993: 25). Although the children did not express it this way, their determination to make sense of the objects that appeared in the pictures seems to have been far more than Kitamura intended. Here he compares this aspect of his work with Browne:

> Anthony Browne, he also plays with things, but it is more symbolic. When I'm drawing, I just think of something, then I put it in. I don't think much about it. I always have that impression of Anthony's art work, it's more planned.

Yet later in the interview Kitamura admitted that 'doing a story needs consistency, you have to have lots of planning'. The appearance of ladders, bats, tigers, pyramids and striped jumpers are self-quotations from his other works, but it is not necessary to have seen them before to understand the story, although it is satisfying to be able to recognise them. They may be there for fun, but as Doonan also says, the connection between these objects 'is waiting to be made ... according to the "reading" skills and experience of the beholder' (1991: 123). Certainly in *Lily* there are connections to be made in the same way between the ladders, the pyramid in the poster, the seagulls, the monsters and the rubbish, to mention just a few.

Despite the fact that Kitamura does not actually have much contact with children (he has none himself and describes himself as 'very nervous in front of small children'), he has strong views about the enjoyment children should have from both looking and creating their own pictures.

MS: How do you feel about the fact that even children as young as 4 or 5 are noticing every detail from the front cover on?

SK: I remember myself when I was about 4 or 5 looking at the same picture for a long, long time, and if it was detailed, I tried to see everything. And I don't know, whether I collected details, and tried to formulate ideas, I don't know. I just enjoyed, just simply enjoyed.

MS: What we've been excited about is just the sort of passion with which children get into books like yours and Anthony's. And the excitement is intellectual, I'm quite convinced of it.

SK: Yeah, I think it is. I kind of have a feeling that I knew when I was 4 or 5, that I had a better idea but once I started kindergarten I started to forget. Often I see my friends' children draw very well when they are 6, 7, 8. And suddenly they stop drawing. Lots of kids, they enjoy drawing and then they suddenly stop. I don't know why but they do. And it's a shame. Somehow a destructive power, maybe schoolwork, or because you have to be like other people and parents have all sorts of expectations, so they forget.

Perhaps it is because Kitamura does not 'write down' for children, but considers them as equals with whom to share his work, that even the older children in our study were convinced that there was more to see and enjoy in *Lily* than it seemed at first glance. We would therefore echo Doonan's words: 'Encouraging creativity in his readers is arguably Kitamura's greatest gift. He also encourages us to return to his books time and time again' (1991: 111).

EA: So where are children in your thinking when you make books? Or are you not thinking 'I'm doing this for children'?

SK: Well I do think a little bit, but not much. I just like doing pictures and doing stories. I just enjoy making something. But sometimes I get a story and I think it might work and I try to do sketches and show it to my publisher, and they say 'This is good, but it's not for children.' So some stories can be children's, some are not. The other thing is that because I'm conscious that the readers are very young, when I write stories I'm a bit careful not to use certain expressions or words, but that's really all. Some other authors use difficult, strange words if they sound funny. So children either do not understand what this word means, but it strikes them as fun or a joke. I have the impression that it's the teachers who think that everything should be understood. But I can't understand that point of view. Because the world is full of things we don't understand. You read novels and you are puzzled, and ten years later you read the same thing again and probably you understand something you missed.

Notes

1   We spent half a day interviewing Anthony Browne before the project started and have communicated with him since. He has seen the children's drawings and taken an interest in our work and read and approved the particular chapters dealing with his books.

2   Most picturebooks are 32 pages long which gives the artist 28 full pages to tell the story.

3   We interviewed Satoshi Kitamura at the International Symposium *Art, Narrative and Childhood* (Homerton College 2000) after he listened to Evelyn Arizpe's paper, 'On a walk with Lily: children reading and talking about Kitamura's picturebook'.

Chapter 11

Conclusions

Seeing, thinking and knowing

> We can never neatly separate what we see from what we know ... in the hands of a great master the image becomes translucent. In teaching us to see the visible world afresh, he gives us the illusion of looking into the invisible realms of the mind ... if we only knew how to use our eyes.
>
> (Gombrich 1960: 329–31)

> By looking at the drawings of my reception class and analysing their discussions during our study of *Zoo*, I have found that children can see the most incredible things beyond what they might be assumed to know.
>
> (Rabey 2001)

We began our research after many years of combined expertise in teaching reading to pupils and undergraduates and with considerable experience of reading picturebooks with children. We were already well versed in most of the standard theoretical and practical texts published in Britain and the USA about teaching reading, children's literature, reader-response theory and the role and scope of picture-books. We thought we were quite well educated in visual literacy when the project started; now we know we were wrong! Two years on, after much reading of art history, art education and aesthetics, and revisiting and supplementing a fairly basic knowledge of psychology (though we did read comprehensive digests of psychological approaches to visual literacy), as well as dipping into relevant reading within media educa-tion and related disciplines, we realise what an enormous body of literature exists on this topic and how many different disciplines impinge on it. This wide reading has underpinned the analysis of our findings and we have used it to support or challenge our arguments and contentions.

The appeal of pictures

Picturebooks are the primary literature of early childhood and the most challenging examples demand highly interactive reading. As far as we are aware, nobody has ever before collected such intensive data on how children from 4 to 11 actually read pictures. All the evidence in our study pointed to the pleasure and motivation children experienced in reading these texts, and the intellectual, affective and aesthetic responses they engendered in children across the ability range and from different cultural and linguistic backgrounds. Pictures in picture-books provide equality of access to narratives and ideas that would otherwise be denied to young readers. As Perkins points out: 'It is not so often the case that we can learn in the presence of compelling objects that engage our senses, allow for many kinds of cognition, connect to many facets of life and sustain our attention. ... We look and we see meaning upon meaning, all more or less immediately accessible' (1994: 5–8).

Gombrich has argued that the visual image is more effective than spoken or written language in evoking an affective response from the reader. Similarly, in discussing the affective pleasure in pictures, Nodelman asserts: 'my pleasure seems to be emotional rather than intellectual – a sensuous engagement with the colours, shapes and textures' (1996: 115). Kiefer also talks about 'the complex nature of aesthetic response. It involves affective as well as cognitive understandings, and it may change over time' (1995: 12). However, Benson reminds us of the limitations of our study, too (1986: 135).

> Art objects, including pictorial art, are specifically made to favour their being experienced aesthetically. If I speak of my experience of a picture, I am in part reformulating in verbal symbolic terms my visual apprehension of the pictorial sign. If I speak of what it is the picture signifies, then I am translating from a pictorial symbolic system into a verbal symbolic system. Translation always and inevitably involves transformation and distortion. ... The picture, especially the picture as a work of art, is a mediation of an idea. That idea is embodied in the perceptible qualities of that picture, qualities which are so presented by

the artist to the spectator as to guide the experience along particular paths. Talk of the picture is a further mediation.

Reading picturebooks – an intellectual activity

> To read the artist's picture is to mobilise our memories and our
> experience of the visible world and to test his image through tenta-
> tive projections. … It is not the 'innocent eye', however, that can
> achieve this match but only the inquiring mind that knows how to
> probe the ambiguities of vision.
>
> (Gombrich 1960)

It was no surprise to find that children were extremely good at
analysing the visual features of texts; that was our hunch before the
research started and it was supported by our findings. In chapters 3–9,
we have provided much of the evidence for this assertion. Children
noticed, admired, wondered at and puzzled over diverse visual
features produced by Browne and Kitamura in Lily, The Tunnel and
Zoo. Most children took on board with equanimity the challenges of
surrealism, the widespread use of intertextuality, postmodern games of
suggestiveness and inconclusivity, the many layers of meaning
offered up by the texts. They read colours, borders, body language,
framing devices, covers, endpapers, visual metaphors and visual jokes.
They responded with alacrity to the various invitations offered by the
different texts and recognised that hard work and endeavour were
required to get as much out of the books as they could. While there
was an obvious line of development in children's ability to interpret
visual texts, the trajectory by age was not always clear cut.

Most children were deeply engaged by our chosen picturebooks and
keen to discuss the moral, social, spiritual and environmental issues
they raised. Our choice of texts was vindicated by the children's overwhelmingly positive responses to them. They wanted to read them,
talk about them, reflect on them, revisit them, draw in response to
them; and even when they were amused (as in parts of Lily and Zoo),
the overwhelming impression we had was of the children's serious
intellectual delight provoked by these picturebooks. Furthermore,
although the three texts were very different in style, tone, design,
mood, story line, they were all sophisticated, multi-layered picturebooks and they all provoked deep, intelligent responses in young
readers.

Reading picturebooks – the affective dimension

In her seminal work on reader-response theory, Rosenblatt underlines the importance of children making ' personal connections' in their reading in order to engage actively with texts and draw on their own experience. Significant numbers of children in our study had strong emotional reactions to our chosen picturebooks. In some cases, this was highly personal and individual, as in the case of Sam cited in chapter 8, who seemed to take great comfort from *The Tunnel*. Children frequently used personal analogy to try to understand the feelings of characters or animals in the books and their responses were often sympathetic and thoughtful.

Moral issues held the children's attention; this was particularly noticeable in those who read *Zoo*. Such was the seriousness and zeal of the children's interpretations that in *Lily*, which was lighter in tone than Browne's books (though it was also mysterious and slightly menacing) and far removed from ethical matters, many found undertones which spoke of environmental issues. Kitamura had no conscious intention of saying anything about the ever-increasing problem of rubbish in the urban landscape in this book, but many children noticed overflowing dustbins and litter and interpreted these details as references to pollution and the spoiling of the planet. It certainly shows children's active search for meaning and Kitamura may, indeed, unconsciously have revealed his own views.

Drawing in response to picturebooks

The decision to include drawing as part of the data collection was almost an after-thought and we were delighted by the quality of some of the art work and what we could learn from it about the children's knowledge and emotional responses to the picturebooks they were studying. In the case of the younger children, their drawings often showed understandings they were unable to articulate. It also taught us much about how children develop as artists. There is no doubt that the bold, spontaneous compositions of the early years metamorphise into more recognisable, but usually duller representations as children strive for realism as they get older. Benson explains this with reference to Gardner's work: 'the preschooler's freedom to use form independently of specific content soon disappears from the work of most children. Instead, the work of 8 or 9 year olds comes to exhibit an increasing precision, regularity, linearity, concern for detail, neatness and command of geometrical form, but it lacks the liveliness of work completed at an earlier age' (1986: 123). Or as Gardner puts it himself: 'It is the pursuit of the realistic and the literally true which casts its spell on the individual in middle childhood' (1980: 142).

An unexpected finding was the strong correlation between the quality of the children's drawings and the input from their teachers prior to and during the research study. We were lucky enough to have two class teachers (one of whom was Kate Rabey, an art educator) who were specialists; one was a humanities teacher who had worked intensively with the pupils on deconstructing image before our study began.[1] Both teachers had clearly influenced the children in the receptive and productive modes, as artists (as the quality of the drawings in those two classes will testify), but also as skilled observers of visual texts. We also noticed that particularly gifted individuals will always buck the trend. For example, Joe's (10) drawing (see plate 4) was every bit as expressive, emotional and finely drawn as the best of the younger children.

Revisiting picturebooks

As we have documented elsewhere, we decided to revisit one-third of our original sample to see if there were any significant changes in the responses made by the children several months after the initial interviews. Early observations had suggested that the more acquainted children were with a multi-layered picturebook, the deeper and richer their responses. Having selected a mixture of children, from those already making sophisticated analyses of image to those just beginning that journey, and adding a few whom we found interesting along the way, we set about asking questions which were more demanding than the first time round and which focussed on the book as a whole and the artist's likely intentions. For example:

- What goes on in your head as you look at pictures?
- How do you think the artist decides what to write as words and what to draw as pictures?
- Tell me about the way Satoshi Kitamura draws lines.
- How do the endpapers of The Tunnel take you into the story?
- What is Anthony Browne trying to tell us about the differences between humans and animals in Zoo?

We also repeated a few of the original questions which the children had found challenging initially and asked for new drawings in response to the text.

At first we found the re-interviews a little disappointing as few children had made great strides in their understanding. While most children returned to the books eagerly enough and remembered a great deal about their earlier encounters with them, there was little evidence of any major new thinking. However, after we scrutinised the transcripts we became aware of small, subtle developments. Amy (now 5), for example, pounced on *Zoo*, declaring: 'I just noticed a funny difference I never noticed before … the colour helps you to find the differences between the animals and the humans' (Amy had meticulously searched for what she called 'changes' in Browne's work the first time round). Her statement about the mother was more clear cut than before: 'Mum is sad and she thinks the animals should be going free.' She also told us that 'I imagine the pictures. I see them with my brain', while Yu (4) concluded that 'I think of pictures when I go somewhere else.'

Erin's (7) thoughtful interpretation on the first visit was again evident on re-interview. Her summing-up of *Zoo* as a whole showed her usual insight: 'Humans change into animals to learn how it feels; animals look a bit like humans so they know what it's like to be free.' She liked Browne's work because 'it makes you keep thinking about things'. Perhaps most noteworthy was Erin's different style of drawing. Her first picture is spontaneous, attractive and expressive, full of the experimentation she enjoyed in Browne's work; five months later she seems to have entered the phase which Davis (1993) calls 'literal translation' and she is now more concerned with naturalism and a sense of morality, so evident in the drawings of the older pupils.

During the re-interviews, children also spotted details in the pictures that they had not noticed the first time round. Unsurprisingly, the pictures were more memorable than the words. Some pupils produced art work which was more elaborate and detailed than the first time round. In all cases, the children went a little further in their understanding of the picturebooks and some of them came up with new insights. Such was true of Dave (now 9), with regard to the fairytale theme and gender roles in *The Tunnel* (see p. 113) and Carol (now 11), who in the first interview had been very observant of visual features such as colour and line, but now focussed on the word/image dynamics in *Lily*.

> I like this bit because Nicky's just a little creature in amongst these other big ones and she (Lily) hasn't worked out any of those bits and he's still got them in his mind which is really good and she's just eating dinner and telling her mum a completely different story. [Without pictures] you wouldn't know what he saw, you wouldn't have his side of the story.

The revisits may have yielded less evidence than we had hoped for because the experience was less intense for the pupils than the first time round and because there was no opportunity for discussion with their peers. Furthermore, apart from being a richer learning context, the discussions were the only part of the data collection where the researchers were free to behave more as teachers and intervene to move the children's learning on. Kate Rabey, who was in the unique position of being class teacher as well as researcher, found that revisiting *Zoo* with the whole class led to extraordinary developments in the children's thinking, mostly manifested in their drawing.

Oracy, language and learning

Language is inextricably linked to our study, not least because we were dealing with children's oral responses most of the time. The pupils' use and understanding of language is what divides them into different ability groups in the English classroom and determines the way they are taught. Knowledge of the English language was evidently important, particularly in the case of bilingual learners, but also in terms of cultural beliefs about language itself (such as value and use). Gender differences were also made manifest through language, as girls tended to be more articulate and forthcoming than boys. Finally, the language children hear and read in the various visual media that surround them – comics, television, films, computer games – filters into their response to picturebooks as well as providing them with a tool to understand and discuss the pictures.

Helen Bromley and Kathy Coulthard have written about the importance of discussion and how talk was operating to promote the children's learning. The sort of questions we asked the children are highlighted in the Introduction (see also Appendix). Discussing the pictures with others gave children opportunities to operate at a higher cognitive level and demonstrated the capacity to turn around their own schemata and construct them afresh – a sort of *visible thinking*. In chapter 9 we also demonstrated young learners using metacognitive ability to step back, and observe themselves as readers going through a series of deductions almost like scientific reasoning, confirming whether their hypotheses were right.

Although we did not set out to conduct a detailed linguistic analysis, the various careful readings of the transcripts resulted in two main observations: one was the way the children struggled to find the words that would communicate their understanding, excitement or doubts to others (both researchers and peers), so that even readers who were shy and/or unsure about their English made an attempt to express their thoughts; the second was how the pupils' choice of words reflected the internal thought processes that occurred as they looked.

Related to the first finding is the way some pupils' language changed as they became more confident in talking about the pictures. This can be seen most clearly in chapter 8 where Kathy Coulthard describes bilingual readers like Sam, Mehmet and Manisha, whose lack of English was positively challenged by Browne's text. But it was also observed among native English speakers and in the children's attempts to find and use technical terms to describe aspects of the pictures, such as pattern, shape, line or perspective.

Mines' doctoral thesis is based on an analysis of how children from different ethnic minority groups read *The Tunnel*. She noticed that certain words appeared more frequently in her transcripts once the children became more involved and 'their reading became more tentative and exploratory and, as it did so, their language became less certain' (2000: 204). She refers to the repetition of words like 'think', 'because', 'might' and 'probably', which indicate an awareness of different possibilities of interpretation. Although we did not quantify systematically the appearance of this type of language throughout our interviews, we did note the frequent use of these same terms, alongside other words and phrases expressing deductions ('so that's why … ', now that means … ', ' 'cos you can see that', 'because the Mum said … ') and opening up hypotheses ('maybe the artist thinks … ', 'he might not be … ', 'by the looks of him a vampire … ', 'so perhaps Nicky knows … ').

As we have mentioned before, Kiefer classified the oral responses from her subjects according to four of Halliday's functions of language: informative, heuristic, imaginative and personal. We found examples of all of these functions in our transcripts, some of them very similar to those mentioned by Kiefer. This is evidence not only of the way children use language functions to make meaning, but also of the range of different expressions children choose to convey this understanding. We found examples of other types of language usage, including:

- questioning the text ('It makes you think why is that there?')
- explaining ('I can show you a scary bit.')
- wondering ('It makes you think someone must have been there ... ')
- analogising ('If I rescued my brother, I would feel happy as well.')
- asking questions ('Where's the woman who is knitting then?')
- exclamations ('Look! Oh, there's something there.')
- personal involvement ('I'd be surprised if ... ')
- awareness of metacognitive implications ('It makes me think ... ')
- explanations (' It's saying that ... ')
- speculation about the plot ('I wonder what's going to happen ... ')
- speculation about the characters ('What she could do is ... ')
- contesting ('I don't agree with ... ')
- awareness of the author ('Maybe the artist thinks ... ')
- agreeing with others ('I think the same as X.')
- justifying opinions ('Because he said ... ')
- comparison ('How would you like to be locked up in a cage?')

Cultural factors

Given that our study was concerned with children who were situated in a particular cultural and educational context, it is important to mention some of the social factors that may have influenced their responses. The discussion of these issues raises a host of questions that are beyond the scope of this study and we can only point to some of the directions which further research could take. The most influential factors, all linked together by their relationship to language, were the following: ethnicity, gender and popular visual media culture. With the exception of Mines's research on children's 'cultural literacies' (see below), none of the studies on children's response to visual texts have covered these issues.

Ethnicity

After repeated analysis of the transcripts, we have come to the conclusion that there were no serious differences between children for whom

English was an additional language (some of whom are multilingual or emergent bilingual, but we will call bilingual in this chapter) and native English speakers in terms of their appreciation and interpretation of visual texts. The former category includes a diverse range of children, several of whom had recently arrived in Britain and others who were third generation, say, Turkish-British, and fluent in English. In fact, Kathy Coulthard's chapter movingly documents the insightful comments made by several bilingual children with little experience of the English language or culture. What happened was that an inviting, multi-layered picturebook allowed them to show just how capable they were at making meaning from a text.

Perhaps most central of all is the notion of teacher expectation. All the children in our sample, however inexperienced at reading and/or speaking English, were invited to make sense of a high-quality picturebook. It so happened that none of our chosen books made any concessions to different cultural traditions; nor were there any images of black or Asian children in them.[2] The books were not chosen to teach English; they were chosen because they were worthwhile texts. Of course, as with any valuable reading experience, the study was also bound to have a positive impact on the learning of English. The researchers believed that the children would get a lot out of the books and treated them all as intelligent readers. As Kathy Coulthard put it, 'when the primary focus was no longer the words, the children were able to fly'.

Unlike Mines, we were not exclusively looking at the relationship between children's ethnic backgrounds and their response to the texts; however, some issues came through, given that about a third of the interviewees turned out to be bilingual and/or from a cultural background that was not mainstream English.[3] Approximately 35 per cent of the interviewed pupils came from varied ethnic backgrounds. The sample included pupils from Asian, African and Caribbean backgrounds, as well as Kosovo Albanians, Italians, Chinese, Greeks and Turks.

In her doctoral study, Mines used *The Tunnel* with three groups of 5- and 6-year-olds with distinct cultural backgrounds: Bangladeshi newcomers, second-generation Bangladeshi immigrants and English children from rural Sussex. As well as detailing her own analysis of the picturebook, Mines studied the transcripts with codes based mainly on Barthes' semiotics. Barthes' cultural code, in particular, links the text to the real world and builds on readers' social and intertextual knowledge. This is particularly relevant to a text like *The Tunnel* where the limits of the 'real world' are blurred and knowledge of other texts is required to make sense of the story.

Mines contends that the reader approaches the text as a cultural being, bringing to the transaction with the text their own experiences of life and the world in order to make the new culture less strange. Thus, for example, the recent immigrants to Britain saw snakes and dragons in the forest, while the Sussex children recognised the references to familiar fairy stories. Mines found cultural differences in each group's reading, particularly with respect to their response to (a) the everyday objects in the book, (b) intertextual references, (c) the ideology of the text, and (d) the secondary world within the text.

Some of the children in our study were the same age and from similar backgrounds as those described by Mines. In chapter 8, Kathy Coulthard analysed the responses of recent immigrants from Tanzania, Turkey, Mauritius and Nigeria, and her findings in this area are not dissimilar to those of Mines. In terms of the everyday objects in the book, these children showed interest in them but, like Mines' first group, were less likely to try to place them within the narrative unless prompted to do so. As to intertextual references, we have seen how Sam was able to connect *The Tunnel* to traditional narratives from his own culture. Mines speaks of the ideology of the text in terms of the sibling relationship and the criticism or acceptance of Jack's attitude to his sister. We did not find such a marked acceptance or criticism of this behaviour, although most children commented on it. Finally, talking about the secondary world within the text, we also found that it was older and native English speakers who were more aware of the fairy-tale alternative, as opposed to the ones who wanted to make more literal sense of the events in the story.

Our findings and observations about cultural influences also coincide with those of Mines, in that we also found this particular picturebook (but also the other two) had the ability to transcend cultural differences precisely because it allowed children of all backgrounds to bring in their personal and cultural experiences in order to make sense of the story for themselves. Mines emphasises the importance of providing these students with an opportunity to speak, of taking into account their previous experience, both personal and genre-related, and their ability to talk about emotions and values such as fear, love, hate, boredom and freedom.

Gender

None of the previous studies on response to visual texts mention the issue of gender[4] even though gender analysis has been carried out in various studies on children's response to literature (Sarland 1991; Davies 1993; Arizpe 2001a).[5] We have shown in the Introduction that the questionnaire on reading choices did not reveal great differences between the preferences of boys and girls in the early years. Their responses began to differ more significantly with age. In the first years of primary, both boys and girls said they enjoyed picturebooks and stories. Later, although picturebook-reading declines, more girls mentioned picturebooks and more boys preferred 'stories'. In the later years of primary both began to read more magazines and comics. Also, girls at all stages preferred books and television over computer games, but boys begin to prefer computer games from about age 7 although they watched as much television as the girls. 'Action'-type books, films and programmes were more frequently mentioned as boys grew older and, although many girls also included them, they also showed more interest in narratives dealing with emotions and relationships. These differences become even more marked at secondary school (Millard 1997).

In terms of the response to the picturebooks in the study, the gender issue can be approached from different angles. In the first place, there are the picturebooks themselves. An immediate analysis reveals that the female characters in all three books appear as emotionally stronger than the male characters, a factor not consciously considered when selecting the books for the study. Lily never shows any fear, while her (male) dog is terrified by real or imaginary monsters; Rose conquers her terror to rescue her brother; it is the mother in *Zoo* who makes the most insightful comment on the day's events. Browne's male characters come over as rather insensitive, even bullying (Dad in *Zoo*).[6] (See interview with Anthony Browne, chapter 10.)

As we have seen in chapter 5, one of the main issues in *The Tunnel* is gender differences and this was reflected in the immediate association made by many of the children to the wallpapers and backgrounds: flowers for girls and bricks for boys. Other stereotypical comments were common: girls are quiet, they like reading; boys are noisy, they like active games. The children's own gendered experience seemed to be the basis of these responses: boys tended to identify with Jack's excitement at finding a tunnel and his impatience with Rose's fears, but then found their expectations literally 'frozen' as Jack is imprisoned in stone and depends on his sister to be freed, while girls could relate to Rose's terror and immersion in a fairy-tale fantasy world. In *Zoo*, the boys seemed to relate easily to the brothers (eating, wrestling, feeling bored), yet at the same time also became aware of the contrast with the animals' situation. In the end, the readers' expectations of stereotypical gender roles were subverted in *The Tunnel* and in *Lily*, while *Zoo* might have led them to question so-called masculine, insensitive attitudes.

This links with another aspect of gender which is the identification of readers with the characters. The confidence and bravery of Lily and Rose made it much easier for the girls to put themselves 'in their shoes'. More girls than boys commented on the feeling that they were 'there', in the story, particularly in the case of Rose. Both boys and girls talked about the family in *Zoo* as being a bit like their own family. To the question of 'How does it make you feel when she rescues her brother?' apropos *The Tunnel*, more boys answered 'don't know', while the girls tended to immediately say 'happy'. It is hard to know whether this was because the boys had not really thought about it or whether they were reluctant to reveal their feelings. The latter explanation is perhaps closer to the truth, given the next two observations on gender differences.

Boys were, perhaps, slightly less willing than girls to keep on looking and thinking, particularly when faced with difficulties in the visual text. This was observed by all the researchers in all the schools. Boys generally became more impatient with the questions and were more likely to say 'I don't know' when faced with anything perplexing. However, boys took as long as the girls – if not longer – when drawing, an observation that suggests that boys may find it easier to express themselves through this type of activity rather than through words. This is linked to the final way in which gender differences were manifest, which was in the girls' willingness to talk and in their generally being more articulate. Both girls and boys tended to make comments comparing situations in the books with their personal experiences. However, the boys tended to be objective while the girls expressed their feelings more openly. Although this may have had something to do with all the interviewers being female, the fact that some of the more experienced male readers were more forthcoming than those who were struggling with print, suggests that this particular observation may have more to do with confidence than anything else.

This leads us to a tentative conclusion regarding gender and response to visual texts, which is that differences are more apparent in inexperienced readers who are less confident, not only about their ability to understand, but also to express their thoughts in front of others. Using a medium which boys usually enjoy – drawing – is one way to build up their confidence. It is also important to find pictorial texts that reflect images of masculinity with which boys can identify – images that incorporate the positive side of masculinity, but also bring out qualities more associated with caring and sensitivity. Browne's recent *My Dad* is a good example. Could it also be the case that the differing qualities of boys and girls' engagement with the texts was indicative of a different 'voice' even among such young respondents (see Gilligan 1982)?

Popular culture

As we mentioned in the Introduction (see Appendix for more detail), the questionnaire results reveal that children's lists of favourite television programmes, films, videos and computer games were much longer than those of picturebooks. In all age groups computer games were preferred over books and television, although the lists of games were not as long as the lists of programmes and films and there were 43 out of 486 children (8 boys and 35 girls) who said they did not play computer games, while only a small handful did not watch television or videos. Pupils engaged with a wide range of media texts, from those designed for children to those intended for adults – many mentioning extreme examples of both types in the same list. (One 9-year-old girl, who included *Winnie the Pooh* and *Dirty Dancing* in the same list was the most extreme example!) The lists grew much longer in the later years of primary school, with many children running out of space on the questionnaire form. In this multi-media world, is it possible to find out how exposure to these different types of visual texts affects the reading of picturebooks?

During the interview, with the aim of finding out the relationship between other visual media and picturebooks, we asked children whether other types of images helped them to read pictures in books. In most cases, children answered that it did not help or that they couldn't think how it might help, but some of those who answered 'yes' came up with responses that revealed interesting aspects of how they 'look', not only at television, computer games and comics, but also how this influences looking at picturebooks. As they compared and contrasted different media, several points emerged.

The movement of the narrative was one of the points of comparison. Children spoke of moving through the narratives in a comic book or on the computer screen, guided by the pictures which help keep the reader 'on track'. Other points of comparison were the visual conventions used in comic books and on screen which are also used in picturebooks, such as speech bubbles or speed marks. Not a single child failed to recognise that Rose is running in the forest, that the snail in *Zoo* is moving fast, and that Nicky is shaking in *Lily*. This knowledge may be reinforced in school, but it has clearly been acquired at an early age. Oliver at the age of 5 explained to the interviewer how speech and thought bubbles work in books like *Asterix* and *Tin Tin*. Many children were also familiar with terms like 'slow motion', '3D', 'pause', and used them regularly in their responses.

Some children emphasised the differences between the viewing processes required by each medium, usually referring to the common-place, but (we would argue) mistaken, assumption, that media texts automatically encourage passive viewing while books require active engagement. According to the children, television and video involve watching and listening, while reading a picturebook involves 'thinking', 'concentrating' or 'imagining'. However, this did not apply to computer games because as Sofia (8) said: 'Sometimes on the computer games you have to think really carefully what to do before a go.' Also, as Lauren (11) suggested, playing computer games was like reading picturebooks because 'you can make up your own imagination and make a story in your mind'.

Another point of contrast, linked to the previous one, is that media texts were perceived to be dynamic while pictures in books are static. Dan (7) compared the transformations in *Zoo* with the way they would have appeared on television, pointing out that because there was no movement in books:

> [in the picturebook] you can't see the whole body changing into animals. In cartoons, they are moving and change at the same time, so you can see different parts of the body changing into different parts at different moments.

Yet description as well as colour was thought to help make a reader understand when there is movement in picturebooks. According to Natasha (10), films or videos show what's happening through move-ment, so it was easier to tell a character was angry on the screen because they use gestures like stamping their feet, while in a picture it is neces-sary to take in details such as facial expressions. Gemma (9) explained that the use of colour in a picturebook could be an expression of move-ment, for example where the colours get lighter in the four-picture sequence in *The Tunnel* when Jack returns to his human form.

Another difference with film was pointed out by Ron (10) who said that 'in film you don't see words come up on the bottom of the screen telling you what happened'. So written text is considered one of the determining characteristics of picturebooks, while 'noise and voices' are the sound elements of television and video which you can't 'hear' in a book. Some children also mentioned that, with videos, films and computer games, the images were going very fast compared to the images in a book which one can look at more slowly. However, it is also possible to stop a video or film in order to have a closer look, as Mark (7) pointed out: 'When you are playing the game you can always pause it and look at the details and textures of the picture.'

Children were aware of the way visual media can influence someone's thinking, even a dog! According to John (7), Nicky sees the monsters because he's been watching 'TV about all this stuff – he's thinking of all this stuff and when he looks he sees them there, when they are not really there'. Jessica (4) unconsciously revealed the media's influence when she mistakenly called Mrs Hall (a character who is named but not depicted in *Lily*) by the name of Mrs Goggins, the old woman in Postman Pat who also knits. Christina (9) talked about the way a viewer's emotions were influenced by the type of media and, according to how realistic it was: 'even though it's not real it makes me feel that it is a real story and that it really happened and that it's so sad and stuff'. Cartoons, on the other hand, were not real and Christina said they just made her laugh.

The extent to which popular forms of visual culture influence the children's descriptions of their metacognitive abilities is perhaps not so surprising. Polly (6) actually described her thinking processes like 'a computer inside my head' which she can 'switch' on and off. 'I do loads of things in my head', she boasted to the interviewer, even mentally 'watching television' as she did her schoolwork!

At the end of her study, Mines (2000: 201) concludes that: 'The transcripts show how hard the children worked to fill the gaps, and the fact that how they looked at the pictures and what they saw was determined by the mental template they applied to their reading, this being a largely cultural construction.' We agree with these conclusions and, like Mines, feel that much more research is needed on how these cultural constructions influence the meanings children make of the visual. We need to learn more about what role all these factors play in visual literacy. It is also important that these constructions are recognised by teachers and are brought into the classroom. Language and pictures are invaluable tools for taking advantage of the potentially enriching aspects of the children's experiences and at the same time helping overturn stereotypes and prejudices.

Our findings and the National Literacy Strategy

In *Reading Images*, Kress talks about 'the staggering inability on all our parts to talk and think in any way seriously about what is actually communicated by means of images and visual design'. He goes on to celebrate how 'children seem to develop with little help a surprising ability to use elements of visual grammar' (Kress and van Leeuwen 1996). Despite the expanding visual base of contemporary culture, low status is still accorded to image in education. Pictorial cueing systems do not figure in the skills required for reading in the National Curriculum and the National Literacy Strategy makes scarcely any reference to visual texts.

Analysing visual text, and the relationship between word and image, makes demands on what are often called 'higher order reading skills' (inference, viewpoint, style and so on) and involves deep thinking. Some of the key skills highlighted in the National Literacy Strategy at text level for 10–11 year olds are as follows.

- reading and interpreting texts in which meanings are implied or multi-layered;
- analysing how messages, moods, feelings and attitudes are conveyed;
- articulating a personal response to literature;
- identifying why and how a text affects a reader;
- explaining preferences in terms of authors, styles and themes;
- taking account of viewpoint;
- analysing the success of texts and authors in evoking particular responses in the reader;
- being familiar with the work of established authors and knowing what is special about their work;
- describing and evaluating the style of an individual author;
- identifying the key features of a text etc.

All these categories were covered using our texts over the course of a day with readers of 7 and above; quite a few were explored with children under 6. Although lip-service is paid to such notions in both the National Curriculum for English and the National Literacy Strategy, their content and pedagogy lead to very different practices, where texts are often shared in bite-sized chunks for short amounts of time, with an emphasis on filleting them for phonic or punctuation potential. Fortunately, the most recent emphasis in the National Literacy Strategy has been on creative ways with text, and the glaring hole of oracy is beginning to be incorporated into their materials. There has been encouragement for local initiatives and flexible adaptations have been welcomed in schools which are clearly doing a good job with literacy. There is enough freedom for teachers with confidence and vision to develop literacy in more imaginative ways, including the use of visual texts.

Working on the principles and practices detailed in our research, Kathy Coulthard has, indeed, developed a series of Literacy Hours, helped by teachers and a Literacy Consultant in north London. In particular, ten imaginative Literacy Hours based round *Zoo* and *The Tunnel* have been successfully trialled in Enfield primary schools, using some of the questioning techniques adopted during our interviews and discussions and drawing on the data generated during the project. (In addition, some drama techniques have also been employed and the scope of our research has been extended to include work at word and sentence level.) The outcomes look very promising, as pupils and teachers alike have been overwhelmingly enthusiastic about this work. Some of the most pleasing anecdotal evidence points to the following:

- analysing multimodal texts appears to extend the most academic pupils as much as the least experienced learners;
- pupils were able to transfer the skills they employed in analysing visual text to wholly written texts;
- this type of work proved particularly successful with English as an Additional Language learners.

Memory, creativity and thinking

> Imagination and thought appear in their development as the two sides of opposition ... this zigzag character of the development of fantasy and thought ... reveals itself in the 'flight' of imagination on the one hand, and its deeper reflection upon real life on the other.
>
> (Vygotsky 1986)

Hubbard, an American educationalist, has produced an inspiring longitudinal study based on systematic observations of 6- to 9-year-olds, as she tried to learn more about how children used art in their thinking processes. The teachers tackle literacy in as structured a way as the Literacy Hour in Britain and there are many overlaps between the two approaches. However, the priorities of the American study have to do with memory, creativity and imagination, as well as teaching literacy, and that is what makes the difference. They also include activities like visual response logs where pupils draw and write their personal responses to their reading. As well as teaching reading and writing as enjoyable and worthwhile activities in themselves, with plenty of opportunities for personal choice in subject matter, the American teachers do not neglect the necessary skills of spelling, punctuation, grammar, phonics etc.[7] But crucially, they understand that:

> As we share literature with children and adolescents, we want to foster their genuine reactions and responses – and we want to find ways to link up their own experiences to the ones in the books they read. ... By including visual responses to literature (and responses to visual literature), we can tap into areas that we might not otherwise reach through talk and writing alone. ... In both classrooms, the key role of memory images in the meaning-making processes of the children was a finding that leapt out at us.
>
> (Hubbard 1996: 309–23)

Sinatra, however, speaking of education in the United States, says something different. He points out that non-verbal modes are rarely taken into account in the curriculum, especially art, and that visual literacy is an unfamiliar concept to educators. His description of what happens to those who do not show a strong verbal development is similar to what happens in the UK:

> We may praise and reward artists, inventors, and technological geniuses when they achieve their feats but we do not reward them during their schooling years if their non-verbal strengths interfere with written literacy attainment. For those youngsters who don't attain written literacy early or rapidly enough, we may label these youngsters disabled and subject them to analytical, parts-specific verbal remediation. By doing so we curtail the power of holistic,

analogic thinking for those youngsters and minimise the opportunity to cultivate the non-verbal, creative mode in which they may excel.

(1986: 42)

Perkins (1994: 89) offers the same sort of message, talking about the need to create classroom environments where serious thinking can take place, and outlining the role of art to bring diverse strands of thinking together:

a culture that honours giving thinking time, establishes it as legitimate, avoids the rush to hasty resolutions, musters time for thinking things through, and allows time for the revisiting and rethinking of things ... [since] well mastered skills are more likely to stand up in new contexts. And diverse practice prepares the mind for a variety of future applications. Unfortunately, in most school settings, skills and knowledge are underpractised or practised only in a narrow range of circumstances. ... Art connects because artists make it connect, because artists strive to express not just the anatomy of bodies but the anatomy of the human condition and of the universe that impinges upon it. If most disciplines build moats, art builds bridges.

There is still much more work to be done in understanding visual literacy, but our results are heartening. When children are given the time they need to look at visual texts and talk, listen, draw, reflect and think about them, the results can be outstanding. When opportunities are provided to privilege visual and verbal skills, instead of concentrating on reading and writing, many children can *fly* intellectually, especially those who are inexperienced with written text or learning in an unfamiliar language. Engaging in exploratory activities with beautiful, challenging visual texts is a worthwhile way to spend time in the primary classroom. The picturebooks amused, provoked, sustained and inspired the children we worked with. In turn, the children's responses have surprised, moved and thrilled us. We hope that this book conveys something of our excitement in the enterprise and the deep respect we owe to the young readers whose ways of interpreting visual texts we have struggled to understand, analyse and celebrate.

Notes

1 This was good luck not design.
2 Initially, we had intended to use at least one picturebook which focussed on cultural issues, but in the end the advisors for ethnic minority achievement discarded all such books as insufficiently inviting and extending for 4–11 year olds.
3 While we consciously sought children from different ethnic minorities within our study, and chose the north London schools with that factor in mind, we didn't realise that significant numbers of the children selected by teachers in the Cambridge schools would also be from ethnic minorities. It was only in the Essex school where all the interviewed pupils were of white British origin.
4 As far as we know, although the response of women readers has been studied, there are no major studies of women as viewers of art.
5 Sarland (1991) does mention some of these aspects in his concluding chapter although he was working with adolescents and their response to popular literature.
6 This puts into question Spitz's reading of Browne's *Willy the Wimp* as sexist and racist (we totally disagree; see Spitz 1999), a reading also criticised by Nodelman (2000) in his review of her book.
7 Of course, confident, gifted teachers in Britain also tackle literacy imaginatively as well as rigorously, but the NLS requirements makes it harder to do so and many less experienced teachers fulfil the coverage of large numbers of specific skills at the expense of deep engagement with whole texts.

Chapter 12

Post-script

Pedagogical interventions in the development of visual literacy

> In terms of this new visual literacy, education produces illiterates.
>
> (Kress and van Leeuwen 1996: 14)

> So why is it that the education system does not seem to acknowledge the importance of being visually literate? One of the principal reasons for this situation is the mistaken belief that children do not need to be taught the skills of visual literacy since it is self evident that the process is learned from direct experience. To some extent this is true of the lower order skills but the superficiality of pupils' comprehension of much of what they view, suggest that higher order visual literacy skills do not develop unless they are identified and 'taught'.
>
> (Avgerinou and Ericson 1997: 280)

Researching or teaching?

In this post-script, we examine the unintentional pedagogical interventions we made in the course of our research which probably influenced some of our outcomes. Our interactions with children may have shaped their responses in ways which were not planned and which are now, after the event, impossible to identify with precision. (It is, however, hard to conceive of an exploratory research strategy in an area of this sort which could have avoided such interventions and effects.)

One of our biggest surprises was that as well as finding out what children already knew about picturebooks and how they read them, our research procedures themselves became inseparable from a complex teaching/learning process through which the pupils became more accomplished at looking, talking and thinking about pictures. The children came to us with varying degrees of prior knowledge, experience and aptitude at reading visual texts; in most cases we moved their understanding on during less than a day spent working with us. This pedagogical influence was largely unconscious and unintended on our part – we did not fully appreciate how much our interventions had influenced the children until we came to analyse the transcripts systematically.

This may be a good moment to remind the reader that our methodology included open-ended discussion and drawing in response to picturebooks, as well as individual interviews. This meant that the children in our sample had several different opportunities, spaced out over the day, to experience the same text in a variety of ways. First of all, the children listened to the story told by their teachers who also made an effort to show the pictures. (As there are no Big Book versions of our chosen texts available, the children would at this stage only have had a cursory look at the illustrations.) The point of this exercise was to familiarise the children with the text in their accustomed setting, to give the researchers a chance to observe the initial responses of the children we were about to interview, and to get a quick 'snapshot' of a typical story-time in each classroom. At worst, therefore, the children arrived at the interview with a superficial impression of the story; at best, they were reasonably familiar with the pictorial and written text and eager to study it more closely.

This initial reading was followed by an intensive interview where each page of the book was examined; although the interviewer had set questions, the children were constantly invited to make any comments they wished about any picture they encountered. Most children preferred to stick to our questions, but there was flexibility for those who wanted to take things further in a chosen direction. Also, by asking the children to draw in response to the text, they were forced to keep thinking about it, and to explore its meaning in a different way, even when they returned to the classroom and no longer had the book open in front of them. Finally, the book was examined one last time in the group discussion.

Various implications can be drawn. The children had three chances to look at one text and a fourth requirement to think about that text while they were drawing, so there was the time and opportunity for leisurely perusal. If, as Perkins and others suggest, the response to a work of art requires time (and many viewers in contexts like art galleries do not take that time), it was precisely this extended period of guided viewing that was provided for in our research. In one instance (Kate Rabey's class of 4- and 5-year-olds) the children continued working on the picturebook in question for a further week, then returned to it later in the year. We believe that the remarkably mature visual and oral interpretations reached by these children could partly be accounted for by the sheer length of exposure to an aesthetically appealing, emotionally rewarding, intellectually stimulating book, and the opportunities this provided for thinking, discussion, unconscious processes of 'gestation' and response in a range of modes.

Our activities included individual and group work, (three out of four activities were collaborative) ranging from a one-to-one interview where the children were often tentative and uncertain, to a group discussion at the end of the day, by which time most pupils were relaxed, confident and involved in the text. They had enough time to become immersed in the book; they had some private time and space; they had a researcher's total attention for nearly an hour; and they had a chance to work things out with their peers. Vygotsky's teachings about the value of communal learning were borne out by our study.

Bob Dylan once famously wrote in a song that you can't please all of the people all of the time. Too true! What our research did was hopefully please almost all of the little people *some* of the time. For Yu (4), who was reluctant to speak, probably because she was very young, shy and could not articulate her emotional response to *Zoo*, the research situation and the sensitivity of her class teacher to her needs, allowed her numerous opportunities to express her powerful reactions to the text. Mehmet (6) was unwilling to speak during the interview, even with an interpreter present who was well known to him, perhaps because as someone recently arrived in England and new to the language, he did not yet feel confident enough to express his ideas. The group discussion a few hours later gave him a second opportunity, which he was willing to take, expressing this time round his thoughtful reactions to *The Tunnel*. The group discussion was also a catalyst for Dave (8) and Charlie (9), who showed the intelligent and perceptive responses of which children with special needs are capable in their comments and drawings about *The Tunnel* and *Lily*.

Teachers *do* make a difference

One important issue that our research threw up was that of teacher expectation. We had asked teachers to select pupils with a cross-section of reading ability, but not to tell us in advance who were confident and fluent and who were struggling with reading print. In fact, the children's responses often confounded teacher expectation. This reinforces all the research evidence that positive teacher expectation (and its corollary) can have a beneficial effect on pupil learning. We believe that the high expectations of the researchers that all children are capable of insightful analysis of visual text, combined with time and talk factors discussed already, encouraged the less experienced readers to 'go for it' and break new ground.

We have to admit that subtle variations in the approaches of individual researchers do seem to have made a considerable difference. We all had our own styles of working and, although we asked the same original questions in interview, we responded differently to the pupils' contributions; our follow-up questions were idiosyncratic; and we brought different strengths and weaknesses to the interview and discussion situation. However, what all of us engaged on the research shared were educational and ideological beliefs which included belief in children as sophisticated readers of visual texts; belief in the texts we chose as likely to inspire serious interest and commitment from the children; and belief that younger children, inexperienced readers, readers with learning difficulties, and learners with English as an Additional Language could be successful at reading image. These commitments, despite our individual differences, were probably central to the diverse ways in which the 'reading' capacities of the children were revealed and developed. The fact that we were all in tune philosophically was not deliberately planned, and it was only something we realised might have had a bearing on our results towards the end of the data analysis.

Although we all strove to be neutral in conducting the interviews, every word we spoke, every look exchanged with the children, our body language, our enthusiasm for the task, the purposeful way we looked at the books gave the children strong messages about themselves, the activity we were engaged in and the texts we were examining. They could not be in much doubt that we regarded reading these texts as worthwhile and high status activities, so the children were naturally encouraged to join in this interesting intellectual game and please the researchers. ('Giving the researcher what she wants' may, at least in certain senses, be intrinsic to methodologies of the kind we were employing.) We expected the children to be fascinated by the books and their responses not merely met but surpassed our expectations. In other words, the children in our study found reading picturebooks an intellectual activity partly because we did. We do, however, believe that most of the children would have become engaged with the texts, had we not been present, faced with authors of the distinction of Browne and Kitamura. This included a few older children who thought the books babyish at first glance (because they were picturebooks), but gradually found themselves caught up in the spell of communal creative endeavour.

With the benefit of hindsight, it was probably inevitable that this group of highly motivated, experienced teacher/researchers would do more than find out what children already knew and did in relation to pictorial texts. Without realising it, we were teaching them how to look, by example, by our questioning, by approaching the text from different angles and by our evident fascination with what they had to say – an apprenticeship model of learning, of course. But by definition, the capacity to develop their visual literacy in these diverse ways was already latent in each of the children.

There were many similarities between the responses of the children in schools with completely different catchment areas. There was also, however, one variation which needs commenting on. In one school which served a conspicuously socially and economically deprived area and an ethnically diverse group of pupils, the children were not only more reluctant to take part in the study and to give picturebooks their thoughtful attention, but they were also those least influenced by our study. There are several possible reasons for this divergence from the rest of the sample: it could have related to an unfortunate choice of day for the visit (but this would be unlikely to equally affect three classes of different age groups); or it might have been the choice of book, but *The Tunnel* was used very successfully in two other schools, one of which served a rather similar catchment area. The role of the researcher was slightly different here as the person concerned (owing to circumstances beyond her control) was the least involved in the project as a whole and, interestingly, stayed closest to the interview brief. In other words, the researcher who was most meticulous in asking *only* the questions we had agreed on, avoiding supplementary questions and keeping a tight rein on the discussion, did not evoke to the same extent the exciting range of responses elicited by the other interviewers, who followed where the children led.

Kiefer (1993: 271) talks about the difference teachers can make to the way pupils repond to visual texts. 'When teachers gave children encouragement, opportunity and time to respond to picture books beyond the group read-aloud or individual reading sessions, children often chose a variety of ways to extend their initial reactions to books.' We have already suggested that having a teacher who was trained in art made a huge difference both to the quality of the children's own drawings and their ability to interpret visual text. It was also noticeable that the pupils taught by a gifted humanities teacher, who had shown them how to look for meaning in photographs and deconstruct images, brought that knowledge to their own drawings. The project they had just completed on refugees and outsiders probably made them more emotionally engaged with, and receptive to, the contrasting themes of captivity and freedom in *Zoo* than they might otherwise have been (see also chapter 6).

The invisible teachers who made a difference were, of course, the artists who constructed these rich, deep, thought-provoking picture-books in the first place. Or, as Meek puts it, describing untaught reading lessons offered by good books, 'What texts teach is a process of discovery for readers' and this includes life-to-text lessons, lessons in how narrative works, cultural features that have to be understood, and lessons in 'the nature and variety of written discourse' (1988: 21).

Listening to children

A most effective recent advertisement showed a child behaving extremely badly. Instead of the expected commentary on the need for firm discipline or the appalling rise of youth crime, the caption read, 'This child needs a good listening to.' In our study, more by chance than design, not only did we give the children time to look and talk, flexible approaches to the books, a belief in their ability to analyse visual texts and good models to follow, but *we listened intently to what they had to say*. We realise that careful listening is very difficult for a class teacher faced with a large group of pupils, but if it results in much more effective teaching and learning, surely it should be incorporated more prominently into our pedagogical practices. But the current emphasis on literacy instruction in Britain tends to be dominated by teacher talk and the teacher's own agenda to impart particular pre-selected skills. Careful listening can lead to genuine intervention at the point of learning, something the National Literacy Strategy cares about, but sometimes fails to 'deliver'.

The children in our study learned effectively for all the reasons we have already outlined and *because they found the activity they engaged in to be worthwhile*. We have emphasised throughout this book our delight in the children's intellectual excitement at analysing visual texts and how it deepened over time and exposure to the picturebooks which they were engaged with emotionally and aesthetically. This brings us back to what we consider to be the 'basics' – the power of literature (visual and verbal) to move, enthral and enrich our lives. Our focus was on the whole text explored for pleasure, thoughtful rumination and engaged discussion within a community of fellow readers leading, eventually, to increased knowledge and understanding of issues raised by the book, qualities inherent in the book, authorial intentions, artistic styles and conventions, moral ideas and much much more.

The children in our sample were anything but visually illiterate; they could make sense of many features of visual texts without any input from us, most of it probably picked up by osmosis from watching television and videos and playing computer games. But Avgerinou and Ericson are probably right in suggesting that children mostly operate in terms of visual literacy at a superficial level. Our research certainly confirms that children can become more visually literate and operate at a much higher level if they are taught how to look.

> Good picture books, then, offer us what all good art offers us: greater consciousness – the opportunity, in other words, to be more human.
>
> (Nodelman 1988: 285)

Afterword

Anthony Browne

When I first read *Children Reading Pictures* I found it intensely moving. I was deeply touched by the children's response to *Zoo* and *The Tunnel*, and equally impressed by the gentle and subtle questions of the interviewers.

The children's sophisticated reactions didn't surprise me as I've known for some time how we often undervalue the abilities of children to see and understand. I was particularly struck by how below-average readers of print were often excellent readers of pictures. They were able to pick up on themes and ideas that I hadn't expressed in the text, only in the pictures. Children are wonderful readers of visual metaphors and it was particularly pleasing for me to see even the youngest fascinated with the connection between the gorilla and the cross in *Zoo*. This book, I think, proves beyond doubt children's innate ability to derive true meaning from pictures.

Appendices

Questionnaire

Questions to be asked orally by teacher:

1 I like to read picturebooks now.
2 I used to like to read picturebooks.
3 I like to look at books on my own.
4 I like to talk about books with my friends and family.
5 Where do you do most of your reading (home/school)?
6 What types of books do you read most at home?

- finding out books
- stories
- magazines
- poetry
- comics
- picturebooks
- computer manuals
- other

7 Do you prefer books, television and video, or computer games?
8 What videos do you watch?
9 What programmes do you watch on television?
10 What computer games do you play?
11 Have you read books by (chosen author: Anthony Browne/ Satoshi Kitamura, other)?
12 My favourite picturebooks are:

PUPIL RESPONSE SHEET:

NAME: _____ AGE: _____

1. 🙂 😐 ☹️

2. 🙂 😐 ☹️

3. 🙂 😐 ☹️

4. 🙂 😐 ☹️

5. HOME   SCHOOL

6.
FINDING OUT BOOKS   COMICS

STORIES   PICTUREBOOKS

MAGAZINES   COMPUTER MANUALS

POETRY   OTHER

7. BOOKS   T.V. AND VIDEO   COMPUTER GAMES

8.

9.

10.

11. YES   NO   NOT SURE

12.

APPENDIX 2

Interview questions for **Lily Takes a Walk**

1 Does the cover make you want to read the book? Why? What does the cover make you think the book is going to be about and why?

2 What does the title page suggest to you?

3 [*first picture*] What are the expressions on Nicky's and Lily's faces? Why do you think they are different?

4 [*snake*] What's happening here? What are they looking at? Who's thinking that [*written text*]?

5 [*tree*] How do you think Nicky is feeling? Why?

6 [*shopping*] Tell me about this picture.

7 [*lamp posts*] Would you like to be on this street on your own? Why/why not? Why doesn't Nicky look at the Dog Star like Lily? Why are the steps wobbly-looking? How does Satoshi Kitamura use colour in this picture?

8 [*Mrs Hall*] Who is Lily looking at? Where is Mrs Hall? What is Nicky barking at? Why do you think Lily and Nicky always seem to be looking in different directions?

9 [*bats*] Tell me about this picture. Where did that man come from? What else do you notice?

10 [*canal monster*] Tell me about this picture. What is Nicky doing? How do you know he is shaking? Do you notice anything that has appeared in the other pictures? Have you seen these in other books by Satoshi Kitamura?

11 [*dustbin monsters*] What sort of expression do you think Lily has on her face now? Where do you think she lives? Why? What sort of monsters are these?

12 [*supper*] What do you think Lily tells her Mum and Dad? Do you think Lily noticed any of the monsters? What do you think Nicky would like to tell Mum and Dad? How do you know? Tell me about these [*speech bubbles*]? What did Satoshi Kitamura need to know in order to draw this picture?

13 [*bedroom*] Tell me about this picture before and after lifting the flap. What's in Nicky's head now? Did Nicky imagine the monsters? Did Nicky imagine the mice? What do the mice want the ladder for?

14 [*bedroom*] Did you notice any other ladders in the other pictures/other Satoshi Kitamura books? Why do you think they are there? How does this picture of Lily's bedroom make you feel? What else do you notice?

15 Does *Lily* remind you of any other picturebooks? If so, which? Have you seen any other books by Satoshi Kitamura? Have you seen *Lily* before or is it new to you? Did you see any other things or patterns in the pictures that remind you of other books by Satoshi Kitamura?

16 What is your favourite picture? Could you show me how you read it?

17 Do you think the pictures are well done? Is Satoshi Kitamura a good artist? Why? Do you think the cover was good for what was going to happen?

18 Did you notice anything special about how Satoshi Kitamura used colour, body language, perspective? What do you notice about the way he draws? How does Satoshi Kitamura make ordinary things look like monsters?

19 Do you find the words or the pictures more interesting? Do they tell the same story in different ways? Would the words still be good without the pictures? Would the pictures still be good without the words?

20 Would you describe *Lily Takes a Walk* as a good book? Why?

21 Which do you like best: cartoons/films/videos/comics/computer games/other? Do any of those things help you with reading pictures in a picturebook?

22 Is there anything else you would like to tell me about the book?

APPENDIX 3

Interview questions for Zoo

1 Does the cover make you want to read the book? Why? What do the black and white wavy lines suggest to you?

2 Why do you think Anthony Browne chose black and white end-papers?

3 Why do you think Anthony Browne showed a hamster before the story begins when it's a book about going to the zoo?

4 What do you think the snail is doing in the first picture?

5 What do you notice about the people in the queue and on the next page? Why do you think Anthony Browne did that?

6 Tell me about the elephant and the people visiting the zoo?

7 Why do you think we are not shown the orang-utan's face? How do you think it is feeling?

8 What do you find interesting about the gorilla picture? Why? What do you think Anthony Browne wanted readers to feel about these animals in the zoo?

9 What do you think the last two pictures are about? What do you think Anthony Browne wants us to feel about zoos?

10 What do you think Anthony Browne wants us to feel about the family visiting the zoo?

11 What is your favourite picture? Could you show me how you read it?

12 Would you describe *Zoo* as a good book? Why?

13 Do you think the pictures are well done? Is Anthony Browne a good artist? Why?

14 Do you like programmes on TV/cartoons/film/video/comics/computer games? Which do you like best?

15 Do any of those things help you with reading pictures?

16 Did you notice anything special about how Anthony Browne used colour, body language, perspective?

17 Do you find the words or the pictures more interesting? Do they tell the same story in different ways? Would the words still be good without the pictures? Would the pictures still be good without the words?

18 Is there anything else you would like to tell me about the book? Does *Zoo* remind you of any other picturebooks? If so, which? Have you seen this book before or is it new to you?

APPENDIX 4

Interview questions for The Tunnel

1 Does the cover make you want to read the book? Why?

2 Tell me about the endpapers.

3 [*spread with sister in bed*] Tell me about this picture.

4 [*spread in junkyard*] Tell me about the differences between the brother and sister. What does this picture tell us about both of them? Why?

5 [*spreads where brother and sister go into tunnel*] Is there anything you want to tell me about these pictures?

6 [*2 spreads of forest*] Is there anything strange about these pictures? What do they make you think of? Can you see any animals in the forest? Why is there an axe? Who do you think has nailed the strips of wood to that tree/lit that fire/lives in that cottage?

7 How does it make you feel when the sister rescues the brother? Why is there a ring of stones around the boy? Why does it disappear and reappear as a ring of daisies?

8 Why are the children smiling at each other on the final page?

9   Tell me more about the football and book on the final endpapers. Is this the same as the front endpaper? Why not?

10 Does *The Tunnel* remind you of any other picturebooks? If so, which? Have you seen any other books by Anthony Browne? Have you seen *The Tunnel* before or is it new to you?

11 What is your favourite picture? Could you show me how you read it?

12 Would you describe *The Tunnel* as a good book? Why?

13 Do you think the pictures are well done? Is Anthony Browne a good artist? Why?

14 Which do you like best: cartoons/films/videos/comics/computer games/other? Do any of those things help you with reading pictures in a picturebook?

15 Did you notice anything special about how Anthony Browne used colour, body language, perspective?

16 Do you find the words or the pictures more interesting? Do they tell the same story in different ways? Would the words still be good without the pictures? Would the pictures still be good without the words?

17 Is there anything else you would like to tell me about the book?

APPENDIX 5

Follow-up interview questions

1   Have you seen this book since we read it last time? Have you seen any other Anthony Browne/Satoshi Kitamura picturebooks? What about any other interesting picturebooks you've seen recently?

2   Do you remember the book or would you like to read it again? Tell me what you remember most about this book.

3   What do you remember most about the way things look?

4   What does Anthony Browne/Satoshi Kitamura want to make the people who read this picturebook think about?

5   Why do you think Anthony Browne/ Satoshi Kitamura make us look at things this way in this picture [*Zoo*: gorilla, *The Tunnel*: junkyard, *Lily*: alley with skip]? Does it make you read the book in a different way?

6   What goes on in your head as you look at the pictures? Is it the same as when you watch a programme on TV, a film, or play a computer game? What about a book without pictures?

7   How do you think each artist decides what to write as words and what to draw in the pictures?

Questions for each book

Lily Takes a Walk

1 Tell me about the way Satoshi Kitamura draws lines.
2 Do you remember that Lily and Nicky are always looking in different directions? Now that you've looked at it again, what does that tell us about them?
3 Quite a few people noticed that Satoshi Kitamura drew rubbish in some of the pictures. What do you think he's trying to tell us?

The Tunnel

1 How do the endpapers take you into the story?
2 Why do you think Anthony Browne chose to draw things that remind us of fairy tales?
3 Why does Rose look so happy at the end?

Zoo

1 Partly this book is about an ordinary family's day out. What is Anthony Browne saying about families?
2 What do you think Anthony Browne thinks of cages and prisons?
3 After thinking about this, why do you think he made the cover this way and the endpapers black and white?
4 Everyone mentioned that the humans are turning into animals. What is happening to the animals? What is he trying to tell us about the differences between humans and animals?

APPENDIX 6

Codes for data analysis

Levels of interpretation

- no explanation given
- mis-readings (wrong)
- literal explanation
- implausible/imaginative explanation but not supported by either text or illustrations
- plausible/based on information from narrative
- critical understanding, awareness of significance in relation to whole, including ethical and moral issues
- engaged description
- interrogation: superficial/engaged, anticipation
- imaginative deduction

Categories of perception

- significant details: including artist's games or 'tricks' and apparent incompleteness/incoherence
- intratextual references
- visual features: appreciation of craft/colours, patterns etc.
- relationship between text and picture
- empathy: elementary, complex, expectations
- analogy: personal, drawing on own experience
- intertextual references
- artist's intentions
- implied audience
- awareness of own reading/viewing process
- characters: 'inner-standing', motives, relationships, expectations
- atmosphere/mood
- genre awareness
- book/story knowledge, including bibliographic aspects
- world knowledge

Some of these codes were adapted from Thomson (1987).

Bibliography

Alderson, B. (1973) *Looking at Picture Books*, London: The National Book League and Bocardo Press.

Allen, D. (1994) 'Teaching visual literacy – some reflections on the term', *Journal of Art and Design Education*, 13: 133–43.

Anstey, M. and Bull, G. (2000) *Reading the Visual*, Sydney: Harcourt.

Arizpe, E. (2001a) 'Responding to a *Conquistadora*: readers talk about gender in Mexican secondary schools', *Gender and Education*, 13: 25–37.

—— (2001b) ' "*Letting the story out*": visual encounters with Anthony Browne's *The Tunnel*', *Reading*, 35: 115–19.

—— (2002) 'On a walk with Lily: children's responses to Satoshi Kitamura's words and pictures', in G. Bull and M. Anstey (eds) *Crossing the Boundaries*, Sydney: Pearson.

Arnheim, R. (1966) *Towards a Psychology of Art*, University of California Press: Berkeley.

—— (1970) *Visual Thinking*, London: Faber.

—— (1986) 'The images of pictures and words', *Word and Image*, 2: 306–10.

—— (1989) *Thoughts on Art Education*, Santa Monica, CA: Getty Center for Education in the Arts.

Avgerinou, M. and Ericson, J. (1997) 'A review of the concept of visual literacy', *British Journal of Educational Technology*, 28: 280–91.

Baddeley, P. and Eddershaw, C. (1994) *Not So Simple Picture Books: Developing Responses to Literature with 4–12 Year Olds*, Stoke-on-Trent: Trentham Books.

Bader, B. (1976) *American Picture Books: From Noah's Ark to the Beast Within*, New York: Macmillan.

Bang, M. (1991) *Picture This: Perception and Composition*, Boston, MA: Little Brown.

Barrs, M. and Cork, V. (2001) *The Reader in the Writer*, London: Centre for Language in Primary Education.

Barthes, R. (1975) *S/Z*, translated by R. Miller, New York: Hill and Wang.

—— (1977) *Image-Music-Text*, translated by S. Heath, London: Fontana.

Bartlett, F.C. (1932) *Remembering: A Study in Experimental and Social Psychology*, Cambridge: Cambridge University Press.

Benson, C. (1986) 'Art and language in middle childhood: a question of translation', *Word and Image*, 2: 123–40.

Benton, M. (2000) *Studies in the Spectator Role*, London: RoutledgeFalmer.

Berger, J. (1972) *Ways of Seeing*, London: British Broadcasting Corporation and Penguin.

Best, D. (1992) *The Rationality of Feeling: Understanding the Arts in Education*, London: Falmer Press.

Boughton, D. (1986) 'Visual literacy: implications for cultural understanding through art education', *Journal of Art and Design Education*, 5: 125–42.

Bradford, C. (1993) 'The picture book: some postmodern tensions', *Papers: Explorations in Children's Literature*, 4: 10–14.

Bromley, H. (1996) 'Spying on picture books: exploring intertextuality with young children', in V. Watson and M. Styles (eds) *Talking Pictures*, London: Hodder and Stoughton.

—— (2001) 'A question of talk: young children reading pictures', *Reading*, 35: 62–6.

Browne, A. (1979) *Bear Hunt*, London: H. Hamilton.

—— (1983) *Gorilla*, London: Julia MacRae.

—— (1987) *Piggybook*, London: Magnet.

—— (1989) *The Tunnel*, London: Julia MacRae Books.

—— (1992) *Changes*, London: Walker.

—— (1994) *Zoo*, London: Red Fox (first published by Julia MacRae Books, 1992).

—— (1999) *Voices in the Park*, Picture Corgi: London.

—— (2001) *My Dad*, Picture Corgi: London.

Browne, A. with Evans, J. (1998) 'The role of the author/artist: an interview with Anthony Browne', in J. Evans (ed.) *What's in the Picture. Responding to Illustrations in Picture Books*, London: Paul Chapman.

Bruner, J. S. (1962) *On Knowing: Essays for the Left Hand*, Cambridge, MA: Harvard University Press.

—— (1983) *Child's Talk: Learning to Use Language*, Oxford: Oxford University Press.

—— (1986) *Actual Minds, Possible Worlds*, London: Harvard University Press.

Chambers, A. (1993) *Tell Me: Children, Reading and Talk*, Exeter: Thimble Press.

Clark, K. (1960) *Looking at Pictures*, London: John Murray.

Considine, D. (1986) 'Visual literacy and children's books: an integrated approach', *School Library Journal*, September: 38–42.

Cox, M. (1992) *Children's Drawings*, London: Penguin.

Cummins, J. (1996) *Negotiating Identities: Education for Empowerment in a Diverse Society*, Ontario: California Association for Bilingual Education.

Davies, B. (1993) *Shards of Glass. Children Reading and Writing Beyond Gendered Identities*, Sydney: Allen & Unwin.

Davies, J. and Brember, I. (1993) 'Comics or stories? Differences in the reading attitudes and habits of girls and boys in Years 2, 4 and 6', *Gender and Education*, 5: 305–20.

Davis, J. (1993) 'Why Sally can draw. An aesthetic perspective', *Educational Horizons*, 71: 86–93.

Day, K. (1996) 'The challenge of style in reading picture books', *Children's Literature in Education*, 27: 153–65.

Debes, J. (1968) 'Some foundations for visual literacy', *Audiovisual Instruction*, 13, 961–4.

Dewey, J. (1978) *Art as Experience*, New York: Doubleday.

Dondis, D. A. (1973) *A Primer of Visual Literacy*, Cambridge, MA: MIT Press.

Doonan, J. (1986) 'The object lesson: picturebooks of Anthony Browne', *Word and Image*, 2: 159–72.

—— (1991) 'Satoshi Kitamura: aesthetic dimensions', *Children's Literature*, 19: 107–37.

—— (1993) *Looking at Pictures in Picture Books*, Exeter: Thimble Press.

—— (1998) manuscript, 'Drawing out ideas: a second decade of Anthony Browne' (printed in *The Lion and the Unicorn*, 1998, 23: 30–56).

Edwards D. and Mercer, N. (1987) *Common Knowledge*, London: Routledge.

Evans, J. (ed) (1998) *What's in the Picture? Responding to Illustrations in Picture Books*, London: Paul Chapman.

Fisher, R. (1998) *Teaching Thinking: Philosophical Enquiry in the Classroom*, London: Cassell.

Gardner, H. (1973) *The Arts and Human Development*, New York: John Wiley & Sons.

—— (1980) *Artful Scribbles*, London: Jill Norman Limited.

—— (1982) *Developmental Psychology*, Boston, MA: Little Brown and Co.

Gilligan, C. (1982) *In a Different Voice*, Cambridge, MA: Harvard University Press.

Glaser, B. and Strauss, A. (1967) *The Discovery of Grounded Theory*, Chicago, IL: Aldine Publishing Co.

Goldsmith, E. (1984) *Research into Illustration: An Approach and a Review*, Cambridge: Cambridge University Press.

—— (1986) 'Learning from illustrations: factors in the design of illustrated educational books for middle school children', *Word and Image*, 2: 111–22.

Gombrich, E. H. (1960) *Art and Illusion*, London: Phaidon Press.

—— (1982) *The Image and the Eye*, Oxford: Phaidon Press.

Goodman, N. (1976) *Languages of Art: An Approach to a Theory of Symbols*, Indianapolis, IN: Hacket Publishing Co.

Graham, J. (1990) *Pictures on the Page*, Sheffield: NATE.

Gregory, E. (1996) *Making Sense of a New World: Learning to Read in a Second Language*, London: Paul Chapman.

—— (1997) *One Child, Many Worlds*, London: David Fulton.

Gregory, E. and Biarnès, J. (1994) 'Tony and Jean-François looking for sense in the strangeness of school' in H. Dombey and M. Meek, (eds) *First Steps Together*, Stoke-on-Trent: Trentham Books.

Halliday, M. (1975) *Learning How to Mean: Explorations in the Development of Language*, London: Longman.

Heath, S. B. (1983) *Ways with Words*, Cambridge: Cambridge University Press.

—— (2000) 'Seeing our way into learning', *Cambridge Journal of Education*, 30: 121–32.

Heathcote, D. (1983) *Learning, Knowing and Language in Drama*, Milton Keynes: Open University Press.

Hilton, M. (2001) 'Are the KS2 Reading Tests becoming easier each year?' in *Reading*, 35: 4–12.

Hollindale, P. (1997) *Signs of Childness in Children's Books*, Stroud: Thimble Press.

Hubbard, R. (1996) 'Visual response to literature: imagination through images', *The New Advocate*, 9: 309–23.

Hunt, P. (ed.) (1995) *Children's Literature: An Illustrated History*, Oxford: Oxford University Press.

—— (ed.) (1996) *International Companion Encyclopedia of Children's Literature*, London: Routledge.

Hurlimann, B. (1968) *Picture-Book World*, Oxford: Oxford University Press.

Hutchins, P. (1970) *Rosie's Walk*, London: Bodley Head.

Iser, W. (1980) *The Act of Reading*, London: Johns Hopkins University Press.

Kellog, R. (1979) *Children's Drawings, Children's Minds*, New York: Avon.

Kiefer, B. (1993) 'Children's responses to picture books: a developmental perspective' in K. Holland (ed.) *Journeying. Children Responding to Literature*, London: Heinemann.

—— (1995) *The Potential of Picture Books: From Visual Literacy to Aesthetic Understanding*, Englewood Cliffs, NJ: Merrill.

Kitamura, S. (1983) (with H. Oram) *Angry Arthur*, London: Andersen Press.

—— (1989) *UFO Diary*, London: Andersen Press.

—— (1992) (with H. Oram) *A Boy Wants a Dinosaur*, London: Red Fox.

—— (1994) *In the Attic*, London: Andersen Press.

—— (1997) *Lily Takes a Walk*, London: Happy Cat Books.

Kress, G. (1997) *Before Writing: Rethinking Paths to Literacy*, London: Routledge.

Kress, G. and van Leeuwen, T. (1996) *Reading Images: The Grammar of Visual Design*, London: Routledge.

Kümmerling-Meibauer, B. (1999) 'Metalinguistic awareness and the child's developing concept of irony', *The Lion and the Unicorn*, 23: 168–76.

Langer, S. (1953) *Feeling and Form: A Theory of Art Developed from Philosophy in a New Key*, London: Routledge and Kegan Paul.

Lewis, D. (1990) 'The constructedness of picture books: picture books and the metafictive', *Signal*, 62: 131–46.

—— (1992) 'Looking for Julius: two children and a picture book', in K. Kimberley *et al.* (eds) *New Readings*, London: A & C Black.

—— (1996) 'Going along with Mr Gumpy: polysystemy and play in the modern picture book', *Signal*, 80: 105–19.

—— (2001) *Reading Contemporary Picturebooks*, London: RoutledgeFalmer.

Lewis, D. and Greene, J. (1983) *Your Children's Drawings – Their Hidden Meanings*, London: Hutchinson.

MacCann, D. and Richard, O. (1973) *The Child's First Books. A Critical Study of Pictures and Texts*, New York: H. W. Wilson.

Madura, S. (1998) 'An artistic element: four transitional readers and writers respond to the picture books of Patricia Polacco and Gerald McDermott', *National Reading Conference Yearbook*, 47: 366–76.

Manguel, A. (1997) *A History of Reading*, London: Flamingo.

Mannoni, M. (1999) *Separation and Creativity: Refinding the Lost Language of Childhood*, New York: Other Press.

Marriott, S. (1998) 'Picture books and the moral imperative', in J. Evans (ed.) *What's in the Picture? Responding to Illustrations in Picture Books*, London: Paul Chapman.

Martin, T. and Leather, B. (1994) *Readers and Texts in the Primary Years*, Buckingham: Open University Press.

McCarty, T. (1993) 'Language, literacy and the image of the child in American Indian classrooms', *Language Arts*, 70: 182–92.

Meek, M. (1988) *How Texts Teach What Readers Learn*, Exeter: Thimble Press.

Messaris, P. (1994) *Visual Literacy: Image, Mind and Reality*, Oxford: Westview Press.

Michaels, W. and Walsh, M. (1990) *Up and Away. Using Picture Books*, Melbourne: Oxford University Press.

Millard, E. (1997) *Differently Literate: Boys, Girls and the Schooling of Literacy*, London: Falmer Press.

Mines, H. (2000) 'The relationship between children's cultural literacies and their readings of literary texts', Ph.D. thesis, University of Brighton.

Mitchell, W. J. T. (1986) *Iconology: Image, Text and Ideology*, Chicago, IL: University of Chicago Press.

—— (1994) *Picture Theory. Essays on Verbal and Visual Representation*, Chicago, IL: University of Chicago Press.

Moebius, W. (1986) 'Introduction to picturebook codes', *Word and Image*, 2: 141–58.

Mroz, M., Smith, F. and Hardman, F. (2000) 'The discourse of the literacy hour', *Cambridge Journal of Education*, 30: 379–90.

Nikolajeva, M. and Scott, C. (2000) 'The dynamics of picturebook communication', *Children's Literature in Education*, 31: 225–39.

—— (2001) *How Picturebooks Work*, London: Garland.

Nodelman, P. (1988) *Words about Pictures. The Narrative Art of Children's Picture Books*, London: University of Georgia Press.

—— (1996) 'Illustration and picture books', in P. Hunt (ed.) *International Companion Encyclopedia of Children's Literature*, London: Routledge.

—— (2000) 'Book review of *Inside Picturebooks*', *The Lion and the Unicorn*, 24: 150–6.

Ormerod, J. (1985) *The Story of Chicken Licken*, London: Walker Books.

Parsons, M. J. (1987) *How We Understand Art*, Cambridge: Cambridge University Press.

Perkins, D. (1994) *The Intelligent Eye: Learning to Think by Looking at Art*, Cambridge, MA: Harvard Graduate School of Education.

Piaget, J. (1997) *The Origin of Intelligence in the Child*, London: Routledge.

Protheroe, P. (1992) *Vexed Texts: How Children's Picture Books Promote Illiteracy*, Sussex: The Book Guild Ltd.

Pullman, P. (1989) 'Invisible pictures', *Signal*, 60: 160–86.

Raney, K. (1997) *Visual Literacy: Issues and Debates*, London: Middlesex University, School of Education.

—— (1998) 'A matter of survival. On being visually literate', *The English and Media Magazine*, 39: 37–42.

Rosen, B. (1989) *And None of It Was Nonsense*, London: Mary Glasgow Publications.

Rosenblatt, L. M. (1978) *The Reader, the Text and the Poem: The Transactional Theory of the Literary Work*, Carbondale, IL: Southern University Press.

—— (1981) 'On the aesthetic as the basic model of the reading process', *Bucknell Review*, 26: 17–32.

Roxburgh, S. (1983) 'A picture equals how many words? Narrative theory and picture books for children', *The Lion and the Unicorn*, 7–8, 20–33.

Sarland, C. (1991) *Young People Reading: Culture and Response*, Milton Keynes: Open University Press.

Schiller, M. (1995) 'The importance of conversations about art with young children', *Visual Arts Research*, 21: 25–34.

Schwarcz, J. H. (1982) *Ways of the Illustrator. Visual Communication in Children's Literature*, Chicago, IL: American Library Association.

Schwarcz, J. H. and Schwarcz, C. (1991) *The Picture Book Comes of Age*, Chicago, IL: American Library Association.

Sedgwick, D. and Sedgwick, F. (1993) *Drawing to Learn*, London: Hodder & Stoughton.

Siegler, R. S. (2000) 'The rebirth of children's learning', *Child Development Journal*, 71: 26–35.

Sinatra, R. (1986) *Visual Literacy Connections to Thinking, Reading and Writing*, Springfield, IL: Ch. C. Thomas.

Sipe, L.R. (1998) 'How picture books work: a semiotically framed theory of text–picture relationships', *Children's Literature in Education*, 29: 97–108.

—— (2000) 'Those 2 gingerbread boys could be brothers: How children use intertextual connections during storybook reading', *Children's Literature in Education*, 31: 73–88.

Smith, V. (2000) 'Developing critical reading: How interactions between children, teachers and text support the process of becoming a reader', Ph.D. thesis, University College, Worcester.

Spitz, E. H. (1999) *Inside Picture Books*, London: Yale University Press.

Stephens, J. (1992) *Language and Ideology in Children's Fiction*, Harlow: Longman.

Stewig, J. W. (1995) *Looking at Picture Books*, Fort Atkinson, WI: Highsmith.

Strauss, A. J. (1987) *Qualitative Analysis for Social Scientists*, Cambridge: Cambridge University Press.

Street, B. (1984) *Literacy in Theory and Practice*, Cambridge: Cambridge University Press.

Styles, M. (1996) 'Inside the tunnel: a radical kind of reading – picture books, pupils and post-modernism', in V. Watson and M. Styles (eds) *Talking Pictures*, London: Hodder & Stoughton.

Styles, M. and Arizpe, E. (2001) 'A gorilla with "grandpa's eyes": how children interpret visual texts – a case study of Anthony Browne's *Zoo*', *Children's Literature in Education*, 32: 261–81.

Styles, M. and Drummond, M.J. (eds) (1993) *The Politics of Reading*, Cambridge: Cambridge Institute of Education and Homerton College.

Suhor, C. and Little, D. (1988) 'Visual literacy and print literacy – theoretical considerations and points of contact', *Reading Psychology*, 9, 469–81.

Thomson, J. (1987) *Understanding Teenagers' Reading*, Melbourne: Methuen.

University of London (1999) *Turkish Cypriot Children in London Schools*, Institute of Education.

Vygotsky, L. (1986) *Thought and Language*, A. Kozulin (ed.) Cambridge, MA: MIT Press.

—— (1978) *Mind in Society*, M. Cole, V. John-Steiner, S. Scribner and E. Suberman (eds) Cambridge, MA: Harvard University Press.

Watson, V. (1993) 'Multi-layered texts and multi-layered readers', *Cambridge Journal of Education*, 23: 15–24.

—— (1996a) 'Her family's voices: one young reader tuning into reading', in V. Watson and M. Styles (eds) *Talking Pictures*, London: Hodder & Stoughton.

—— (1996b) 'The left-handed reader: linear sentences and unmapped pictures', in V. Watson and M. Styles (eds) *Talking Pictures*, London: Hodder & Stoughton.

—— (ed.) (2001) *The Cambridge Guide to Children's Books in English*, Cambridge: Cambridge University Press.

Watson, V. and Styles, M. (eds) (1996) *Talking Pictures*, London: Hodder & Stoughton.

Wells, G. (1986) *The Meaning Makers*, London: Hodder & Stoughton.

Wood, D. (1998) *How Children Think and Learn*, London: Blackwell.

Yenawine, P. (1991) *How to Look at Modern Art*, New York: Harry N. Abrams.

Index